EXONERATED

Exonerated

A History of the Innocence Movement

Robert J. Norris

NEW YORK UNIVERSITY PRESS

New York

NEW YORK UNIVERSITY PRESS
New York
www.nyupress.org

References to Internet websites (URLs) were accurate at the time of writing. Neither the author nor New York University Press is responsible for URLs that may have expired or changed since the manuscript was prepared.

Library of Congress Cataloging-in-Publication Data
Names: Norris, Robert J., author.
Title: Exonerated : a history of the innocence movement / Robert J. Norris.
Description: New York : New York University Press, [2017] | Also available as an ebook. | Includes bibliographical references and index.
Identifiers: LCCN 2016045489| ISBN 9781479886272 (cl ; alk. paper)
Subjects: LCSH: Judicial error—United States—History. | False imprisonment—Law and legislation—United States—History. | Post-conviction remedies—United States—History. | Criminal justice, Administration of—United States—History.
Classification: LCC KF9756 .N67 2017 | DDC 345.73/0122—dc23
LC record available at https://lccn.loc.gov/2016045489

New York University Press books are printed on acid-free paper, and their binding materials are chosen for strength and durability. We strive to use environmentally responsible suppliers and materials to the greatest extent possible in publishing our books.

Manufactured in the United States of America

10 9 8 7 6 5 4 3 2 1

Also available as an ebook

In memory of Jane Raley and all that she stood for

CONTENTS

ACKNOWLEDGMENTS

First and foremost, I wish to thank Caitlyn O'Donnell, my best friend, who continues to keep me grounded and make all that I do worthwhile. And I thank my family for making this possible through their unwavering support.

This research would not have happened without the kind and passionate people who opened up to me about their work and their lives. To all of those at Centurion Ministries, the Innocence Project, the Northwestern Center on Wrongful Convictions, and elsewhere who were willing to spend time with me and share their perspectives, I thank you and continue to admire the work you do.

This project benefited greatly from the insight of the many incredible scholars, teachers, and mentors with whom I have had the pleasure of working over the past few years. Whether through informal advice, random conversations, or feedback on the manuscript, this book is undoubtedly better due to their input. I am particularly thankful to James Acker, Alissa Worden, Allison Redlich, Frankie Bailey, and Richard Leo for their invaluable guidance and comments on earlier versions of this manuscript. I also wish to thank, in no particular order, Catherine and Vin Bonventre, Saundra Westervelt, Jon Gould, Marvin Zalman, Daniel Medwed, Christopher Dum, Jamie Fader, Kelly Socia, Andrew Davies, Giza Lopes, and Justin Pickett, all of whom, in various ways and whether they realize it or not, had an important impact on this work. I am also grateful to my research assistant, Carmen Lowe, who helped me get this manuscript across the finish line.

In the midst of this project, I moved to North Carolina to begin a new job at Appalachian State University. While the stress of moving and starting a new phase of my life seemed overwhelming at times, I was helped immensely by my wonderful new colleagues and friends. In addition to helping Caitlyn and me adjust to mountain life, they never failed to help me negotiate my professional transition and offer support x | ACKNOWLEDGMENTS

for this research endeavor. In particular, I am indebted to my department chair, Phillip Ardoin, Cathy Marcum, Jeff Holcomb, Marian Williams, Derrick Lail, Will Hicks, Kevin Mullinix, Mark Bradbury, Adam Newmark, and Katy Dewhirst.

The development of this work from proposal to book has been possible thanks to Ilene Kalish, my editor at NYU Press, who was willing to take a chance on a first-time book author. She has been wonderful to work with, offering encouragement and constructive criticism throughout the process and helping make this book the best product it can be. I also owe great thanks to Caelyn Cobb, who has been immensely helpful in answering questions and keeping me on track, and Andrew Katz, who found and fixed my many errors and oddities.

Finally, I must acknowledge those about whom I write. It is one thing to read about wrongful convictions, but getting to know exonerees and their families, who withstand unimaginable suffering but manage to endure, as well as the advocates who work tirelessly on their behalf, has truly been inspiring. The struggles they face and the injustice they fight provide a daily reminder of why I do what I do.

Introduction

Innocence and the Criminal Justice System

In September 1986, a drug deal in Springfield, Massachusetts, went awry. As many as six people were involved, but after shots were fired, an innocent bystander, 25-year-old Victoria Seymour, lay dead on the ground. Weeks later, in Connecticut, police arrested Mark Schand, a 21-year-old who had been identified in a photo lineup. He was charged with murder, robbery, and assault. At trial more than a year later, six witnesses claimed to know Mark was involved in the crime; seven others testified that Mark was in Hartford, Connecticut, on the night of the crime. Still, he was convicted and sentenced to life without parole.

Mark maintained his innocence while he sat in prison for nearly three decades, during which time his wife visited him weekly. In 2010, Centurion Ministries, a nonprofit organization, began investigating his case. Following a series of witness recantations and the discovery of additional evidence, Mark's attorneys and Centurion filed a motion for a new trial, unopposed by the district attorney. On October 4, 2013, Mark walked out of prison, and on October 16, after 27 years, the charges were dropped. Mark was a free man.

"It's Sad That There's So Many of Us"

I met Mark in January 2014 at an event with Centurion Ministries, a remarkable celebration for the 100th birthday of one of the organization's most generous donors, William Scheide. I was with a handful of Centurion workers and about 15 exonerees. Mark was the rookie of the group, or "rook." Having only been freed months earlier, he was still adjusting to life on the outside. Looking around at the others in the room, he summarized his thoughts in one simple sentence: "It's sad that there's so many of us."

Mark had never attended an event like this before, surrounded by others who understood what he had been through. And these 15 were just a subset of the more than 50 individuals freed by Centurion Ministries, who themselves are just a fraction of the more than 1,800 who have been exonerated in the past 30 years.[1] The sentiment Mark expressed is not surprising among this group, who share a similar story. Having endured the hardships of a failed system, they share the belief that wrongful convictions happen all too often and that the criminal justice system is in need of serious reform. What is more surprising is how this notion has spread. The idea that there are, as Mark put it, "so many" wrongful convictions—enough to warrant attention and systemic change—has become a prominent one in criminal justice circles.

The belief that errors occur often enough to warrant system-wide reform is a fairly new development. Not long ago, the common belief was in the near-infallibility of the justice system. Throughout history, of course, there were those who were concerned about the conviction of innocent defendants,[2] but a prevailing notion among prominent legal actors was that such cases did not happen or were too rare to demand concern. As early as 1923, Judge Learned Hand described the conviction of the innocent as "an unreal dream";[3] in the mid-1980s, U.S. Attorney General Edwin Meese suggested the same: "But the thing is, you don't have many suspects who are innocent of a crime. That's contradictory. If a person is innocent of a crime, then he is not a suspect."[4]

That such miscarriages of justice can occur and should be avoided is fundamental to the United States' system of criminal justice, but historically, to insist that they were more than rare aberrations would be met with skepticism. At the very least, wrongful convictions were far from the forefront of the collective criminal justice consciousness. Yet the past three decades have seen a remarkable shift in perception. The growing number of exonerations—when, after being convicted, it is discovered that someone is actually innocent and is freed—along with the development of organizations dedicated to innocence advocacy and a reform agenda at all levels of criminal justice policy and practice suggest that a new era is upon us.

This historical development, the birth and growth of this "innocence movement," is the focus of this book. How did it begin? What is the current movement, and what are its future prospects? And what does it mean to those whose careers are dedicated to the cause?

An Era of Reform

U.S. history is scattered with cases of wrongful conviction. As professor Marvin Zalman notes, nearly 100 years ago, "wrongful convictions were not unknown" and, in fact, "were newsworthy."[5] Yet innocence was never more than a fleeting issue for most criminal justice practitioners, policy makers, the media, and the public. That is not so any longer.

Over the past three decades, innocence has become a prominent issue, so much so that law professor Keith Findley described it as "the most dramatic development in the criminal justice world since the Warren Court's due process revolution of the 1960s."[6] The most visible aspect of this development is the exonerations themselves. According to the National Registry of Exonerations—the largest collection of known exoneration cases—since 1989, more than 1,800 wrongful convictions have been discovered and overturned; in recent years, exonerations have occurred at a rate of more than two per week.[7] Nearly 400 of these errors have been overturned, at least in part, because of DNA evidence, and more than 100 of them have been cases where an innocent person was sentenced to death.[8]

The actual number of wrongful conviction cases is impossible to know, but estimates suggest that 1%–5% of all felonies may be wrongful convictions.[9] Although these rates may seem fairly low, in practice, this means that more than 100,000 innocent people may currently sit in U.S. prisons and jails and more than 235,000 innocents may be on probation and parole.[10] Thus, the National Registry's exoneration list is far from a complete collection of *all* wrongful convictions—these are just the relative few that were discovered and overturned—but from these cases, we have learned a significant amount about how the U.S. justice system can and does make mistakes. We know that errors happen both at trial and through plea bargains and that they occur in a variety of cases. According to a National Registry report based on the first 1,600 exonerations, the leading factors that contribute to wrongful convictions include perjury or false accusations, misconduct by police and prosecutors, eyewitness errors, misleading forensic evidence, and false confessions.[11]

These wrongful convictions are powerful, gripping stories that provide valuable lessons about our criminal justice system, but these cases have become more than just compelling reports on the evening news.

Innocence reform is now an organized effort. An Innocence Network, made up of nearly 70 organizations, including more than 50 in the United States, works on wrongful conviction–related issues. Nearly all of these organizations work on freeing innocent clients, but many also pursue policy reform through legislation, litigation, and collaboration with agencies.

At all levels, the innocence policy agenda has had some success. At the federal level, the 2004 Innocence Protection Act provided standards and funding for postconviction DNA testing, standards for defense in capital cases, and increased federal compensation for those who were exonerated. More recently, Congress passed the 2015 Wrongful Convictions Tax Relief Act, which stipulates that compensation awards and civil suits won by exonerees are exempt from taxes. In addition, at least 40 states have enacted some type of preventive reform or established commissions to study wrongful convictions and propose potential improvements in the system.[12] Nearly all states provide inmates some access to DNA testing, and many require the preservation of certain types of evidence and allow appeals based on DNA evidence from prisoners who have exhausted other appellate remedies.[13] Furthermore, over half of the states have compensation laws to provide assistance to exonerees as they reintegrate into society.[14]

Even without state initiatives, many agencies have adopted reforms. More than 1,000 police agencies now have policies in place for recording interrogations, including many in states where it is not required by law.[15] Eyewitness identification procedures have been altered to better conform to scientific recommendations in some major jurisdictions, including Boston, Massachusetts, and Santa Clara County, California. Prosecutors have also taken note: two dozen district attorneys' offices, including those in Manhattan, New York, and Dallas, Texas, have established "Conviction Integrity Units" to review questionable convictions, and several of these groups have been involved in recent exonerations.[16]

Innocence has also made its way into the popular consciousness as compelling case narratives have been covered in mainstream media and cultural outlets. Wrongful convictions have been the topic of plays and movies. After a successful off-Broadway production, *The Exonerated* was translated into a film starring Susan Sarandon and Danny Glover. Hilary Swank also starred in *Conviction*, a popular film about the wrongful conviction of Kenny Waters and the work of his sister, Betty Anne, to free him. Cases have been the subject of popular books, both true and fictional, most notably those authored by John Grisham.[17] Sarandon and Grisham are among the many writers, directors, actors, musicians, and other celebrities who have worked to raise awareness and funds to help support innocence advocacy. Wrongful convictions have also been a regular topic in popular documentaries such as PBS *Frontline* and A&E's *American Justice*, and two recent hits have exposed potential flaws in the justice system to the general public on a scale never before seen: *Serial*, a 2014 podcast that covered the questionable murder conviction of Adnan Syed in Maryland, was downloaded more than 100 million times, reaching the top spot on the iTunes charts,[18] and *Making a Murderer*, a 2015 Netflix documentary series on the case of Steven Avery, may have been watched nearly 20 million times within 35 days of its release.[19]

The world is now more aware of wrongful convictions than ever, and it may have an impact on public opinion, particularly regarding the death penalty. As early as 1993, polls showed that innocence was a leading concern that raised doubts about capital punishment among voters,[20] and although many Americans still favor the death penalty, the prospect of errors is a key factor in eroding confidence in the practice. Surveys have shown that a majority of the public cite exonerations as a reason for their weakening support or increasing opposition to the death penalty, and many (as high as 87%) believe that innocent prisoners have been executed in recent years.[21] A study by political scientist Frank Baumgartner and colleagues found that not only has innocence become the most common theme in death penalty discourse, but it also has been influential in reducing the number of death sentences handed out and in capital punishment policy making.[22] In Illinois, for instance, innocence was a major factor when the legislature voted to abolish the practice in 2011.[23] Even Supreme Court justices have recently cited the risk of error—the death penalty's "serious unreliability"—as a main argument against its constitutionality and, ultimately, for its abolition.[24]

Beyond these clearly tangible effects, innocence has important implications for legal education. Dozens of law schools now have clinics in which students work on potential innocence cases, and they are among the most popular programs. Participation can have immense benefits for law students, including important lessons about investigation, skepticism, and evaluation of facts.[25]

In the criminal justice world, innocence is in vogue. Together, the developments just outlined make up what is now commonly referred to as the "innocence movement." A conglomeration of advocacy organizations, lawyers and legal activists, exonerees and their families, journalists, students, and legal practitioners who believe that wrongful convictions are common and deserve attention on a large scale, this movement has become a force in the legal and criminal justice community. In fact, advocates have referred to the innocence movement as a "new civil rights movement," a sentiment echoed by law professor Daniel Medwed, who proclaimed this "transformation" the "civil rights movement of the twenty-first century."[26] Others have described the "innocence revolution" as "an exciting new period of American criminal justice."[27]

Despite this powerful and transformative rhetoric, few have written about innocence as a movement. While a number of legal scholars have written about innocence projects and their impact on legal education, they generally have not analyzed innocence broadly as a social movement.[28] Others have written *around* the movement, discussing it indirectly or implicitly. It is mentioned in passing as many articles acknowledge the growing interest in innocence, but few have actually focused on the movement itself.

There is a common thread running through previous writings on wrongful convictions: the movement is generally dated to 1989, when DNA was first used to clear an innocent prisoner. There is much truth to this statement; as will be discussed in detail later, the development of DNA technology had an incredible impact that allowed innocence advocates to make headway in entering the criminal justice reform arena. It is, however, a limited explanation. We are missing a real story of the innocence movement that includes some of the subtle, important, and interesting nuances of the movement's development: the people, organizations, decisions, and events involved. As Zalman has said, we are lacking "a true history of the innocence movement, which has yet to be written."[29]

With this in mind, I have two objectives in this book. The first is historical—to provide a descriptive account of the innocence movement's development. The movement is full of interesting stories, of people, organizations, and events. Many of these are known; others may not be. My hope is to put them together to tell the most complete story of the innocence movement yet written. Still, it is far from a complete history. My goal is to highlight how and why the movement emerged, so I focus here on individuals who were involved at the earliest stages, before there actually was an innocence movement. Thus, the emphasis is largely on the early leaders, the first innocence organizations (Centurion Ministries, the Innocence Project, and the Northwestern Center on Wrongful Convictions), and the innocence developments related to the anti–death penalty movement. In terms of the modern innocence movement, I focus on key legal and investigative organizations, mostly members of the Innocence Network that are involved in the movement today. I largely do not explore the advocacy of exonerees themselves, their families, or others (such as victims), though this most certainly is an important element of the innocence movement. However, I focus on how the movement developed broadly, which mostly revolves around lawyers, investigators, and others involved with formal organizations and key events.

In addition to providing a narrative of the innocence movement, this book is designed to be analytic as well. I aim not only to describe the movement but also to provide some understanding of how and why it developed when and as it did. To this end, the latter portion of the book draws from analyses of social movements, and a brief, cursory introduction to the key theoretical concepts is provided here.

A Theoretical View of the Innocence Movement

Historically, studies of social movements came from three perspectives: political opportunities, mobilizing structures, and framing. The political opportunities perspective suggests that in order to understand a movement, one must understand the major changes that made the target system—that is, whatever system activists seek to change—more vulnerable or receptive to reform efforts.[30] A mobilization perspective, on the other hand, focuses less on broad opportunities and more on the ways in which people actually engage in activism. In other words, to understand collective *action*, one must examine the people, organizations, networks, and resources that make up a movement.[31] Finally, framing refers to the ways in which meanings and understandings are developed that make collective action legitimate or worthwhile.[32] Cultural images and social constructions shape social movements, and it is here where a framing perspective focuses.

These three perspectives are integrated in the *political process* model of social movements. This model acknowledges the importance of opportunities in making a system receptive to reform but suggests that without organizational strength, such opportunities may pass without action. Together, opportunities and organization provide the "structural potential" for a movement, and meaning must then be attached to a situation to facilitate action. Sociologist Doug McAdam calls this third element "cognitive liberation."[33] This perspective also encourages us to consider the importance of the broader sociopolitical context in which a movement occurs.

In applying the political process model to the innocence movement,[34] I argue that all three elements have been important. The powerful narratives of wrongful conviction, particularly those exposed through DNA technology, and the state of the anti–death penalty movement, which was in need of a boost in the 1990s, provided the opportunity for innocence to get its foot in the criminal justice door. Key leaders joined the movement early with a vision for reform, and a network of dedicated organizations and individuals, with strong emotional connections to their work, ensured that the movement had the organizational infrastructure necessary to grow. Finally, the ability for innocence to be framed in a way that has broad moral appeal and crosses ideological lines expanded the understanding and acceptance of innocence as a problem worthy of reform. I also suggest that the period during which innocence reform began to take hold—the era of mass criminalization and mass imprisonment that has been called the "punitive turn,"[35] during which crime rates consistently declined—may have played a subtle but interesting role in the development of the innocence movement.

Organization of the Book

Part 1 provides a descriptive, chronological narrative of the innocence movement. Chapter 1 includes a brief history of wrongful convictions in the United States beginning with the first one in 1812. It then covers, in detail, the development of the first modern innocence organization,

Centurion Ministries; the beginning of the modern era of innocence scholarship; and the popular coverage of wrongful convictions in the media that became more common in the 1980s. Chapter 2 describes the development of DNA technology and its introduction into the U.S. legal system. It then covers the first DNA exonerations in the United States, the founding of the Innocence Project, and the attention garnered by the growing number of wrongful convictions exposed through DNA testing, including an important report by the National Institute of Justice. Chapter 3 may be the most important part of the narrative history, covering the period when innocence began to resemble a *movement*. It covers the intersection of wrongful convictions and the death penalty from the mid-1990s through the early 2000s, with a focus on several key events in Illinois. It also discusses the publication of an important book, *Actual Innocence*, and a national policy, the Innocence Protection Act. It concludes the narrative history by describing the development of the Innocence Network and providing an overview of the current scope of the movement.

Part 2 analyzes innocence as a social movement. Chapter 4 begins by providing an analysis of the innocence movement's foundations, with a focus on the framing of DNA. I argue that the organizational foundation of the movement, the introduction of movement leaders, and the identification of wrongful convictions as a systemic problem that occurred during this era allowed DNA to be reframed as a tool not only to secure accurate convictions but also to seek justice through exonerations. Chapter 5 analyzes innocence as a social movement from a political process perspective as described earlier, arguing that the opportunity structures in place, strong organizational infrastructure, and widely appealing message allowed innocence to coalesce into the movement we now recognize. Chapter 6 then discusses social movements more abstractly, considers whether innocence is truly a social movement, and considers whether it can or should be characterized as a civil rights movement. I argue that while innocence may rightly be called a social movement, its current scope is too narrow to lay claim to being a "new civil rights movement."

The conclusion discusses several critiques of the innocence movement, both from within and without. It also describes some of the key challenges facing the innocence movement in the years ahead and concludes with a discussion of the future of innocence in the United States.

PART I

The History of the Innocence Movement

1

"Voices in the Wilderness"

The Beginning of Innocence

As long as there have been systems of criminal justice, there has been a chance for innocent persons to be wrongly accused, convicted, and punished. Though the widespread recognition of errors has only recently coalesced into an organized reform movement, such cases have a long history in the United States.

The U.S. story begins in Manchester, a small town in the midst of the Green Mountains in southwestern Vermont. Chartered in 1761 and named for Robert Montagu, the Third Duke of Manchester, the town is steeped in revolutionary history. It is also known as the location of the first known wrongful conviction in the United States.

A Brief History of Innocence

In 1812, farmhand Russell Colvin disappeared unexpectedly from Manchester, Vermont. Suspicion quickly fell upon his brothers-in-law, Stephen and Jesse Boorn. Seven years later, following an intricate set of circumstances involving ghostly visitations, a child born out of wedlock in need of support, and a dog digging up supposedly human bones, the Boorn brothers were convicted. The factors that led to the convictions will look familiar to anyone acquainted with wrongful convictions: a jailhouse informant who provided the state with information in exchange for his release from jail, false confessions made under threat of a death sentence, and shaky eyewitness testimony.

The sequence of events leading to the Boorns' exonerations unfolded the same year as their convictions and was truly a stroke of luck. While in a hotel in New York, a random traveler heard the reading of a newspaper article celebrating the convictions. He knew a man named Russell Colvin who worked on a farm in New Jersey, and he wrote a letter explaining this to both the *New York Post* and the Manchester postmaster. When the *Post* published the letter, a Manchester native who lived in New York found Colvin—the same Russell Colvin who had been "murdered"[1]—at the New Jersey farm. The supposed murder victim returned to Manchester in December 1819, and the Boorns were ultimately exonerated. The case, considered the first wrongful conviction in the United States, generated interest around the world and later served as inspiration for Wilkie Collins's 1873 novel *The Dead Alive*.[2]

Though records make it difficult to determine with any certainty, the Boorn brothers were certainly not alone as victims of wrongful conviction in the 1800s. In a case of mistaken identification, Thomas Berdue was convicted in 1851 for severely beating and robbing a store owner in San Francisco. William Woods and Henry Miller were both convicted and sentenced to death for the murder of John Hantz, Jr., in Kansas in 1889. And in 1891, Ameer Ben Ali was convicted in Manhattan for a particularly interesting murder; the victim's body bore a mark of Jack the Ripper, the notorious serial killer who murdered at least five women in London between 1888 and 1891.[3] The small cross on the victim's thigh prompted several New York newspapers to proclaim the arrival of the notorious serial killer in the United States. Ali was convicted for the murder and sentenced to life in Sing Sing prison.[4]

The turn of the 20th century brought with it dozens more wrongful convictions—more than 25 in the first decade[5]—and the birth of innocence as the focus of academic study. Edwin Borchard, the law librarian of Congress, published a critical article in 1913 about compensation for the wrongly convicted, specifically the United States' lack of support for those who had been exonerated. Borchard found it strange that in the United States, where individual rights are so vital and where the government must compensate citizens for the taking of property, "society . . . utterly disregards the plight of the innocent victim of unjust conviction or detention in criminal cases."[6]

Borchard's article called attention to the issue of compensation for exonerees, but his 1932 book *Convicting the Innocent* is his more famous and arguably more important work. Borchard, by then a law professor at Yale University, described 65 cases of what he believed to be erroneous convictions (including the Boorn case), described the reasons for the convictions, and proposed preventive reforms. The reforms for which

Borchard advocated were mostly changes in criminal procedure including, among others, that the defendant's prior convictions be introduced only after conviction at sentencing, that indigent defendants be provided with a public defender, that appellate courts review the facts of a case in addition to the law under which the conviction occurred, and that no defendant be given a death sentence solely on the basis of circumstantial evidence.

Although the reforms proposed by Borchard may not have actually prevented many wrongful convictions,[7] the book, now an oft-cited classic, was "at the time a bold and courageous utterance"[8] that "argu[ed] against the then prevailing idea that innocent people were never wrongfully convicted."[9] Borchard himself has been described as "a one-man policy juggernaut";[10] his work was motivated by the desire to enact exoneree compensation statutes, and he was heavily involved in the passage of the federal compensation law in 1938, which allowed exonerees to sue the federal government for damages up to $5,000.[11] Compensation remained an important issue for Borchard; even after the federal law was passed, and nearly a decade after his groundbreaking book was published, he was still advocating for states to pass their own compensation bills.[12]

Borchard's work is among the first, if not the first, real attempts at policy advocacy focused specifically on innocence, and he consciously made his work accessible to policy makers. His progressive ideology drove his passion for reform, but in terms of wrongful convictions, his focus was mainly on compensation rather than broader criminal justice reform.

Convicting the Innocent was also important in that it helped shift the question from whether wrongful convictions occur to why they happen, and in its wake, several "diagnostic and reform-minded books" followed over the next several decades.[13] In 1957, the well-known judge and legal philosopher Jerome Frank and his daughter, Barbara, published *Not Guilty*, which narratively described a number of erroneous convictions. Similarly, author Edward Radin, known more for his portrayal of the Lizzie Borden murders, published *The Innocents* in 1964.

These books and others like them were written for the layperson. They often used sharp, vivid language to capture the attention and emotions of the reader; *Not Guilty*, for example, proclaims, "If the conviction of an innocent man were as rare as a death from the bubonic plague in the United States, we could afford to mourn the tragedy briefly and turn back to everyday affairs. Unfortunately such convictions are by no means rare."[14] They made several suggestions designed to prevent wrongful convictions, and while they mention some of the same contributors to errors that are so well-known today—eyewitness misidentification, perjury, and false confessions—their suggestions were often extremely broad. For instance, Frank and Frank suggested that the standards to become a "full-fledged prosecutor" be increased,[15] and Radin argued that where the main source of evidence is an identification, "police should investigate the prisoner's story thoroughly before starting the legal machinery against him."[16] While such statements lay out general ideals, they are far from clear-cut policy recommendations.

In addition to the seemingly once-a-decade chronicles, several other high-profile incidents throughout the 20th century raised awareness about the possibility of wrongful convictions and sparked public discussion. The questionable convictions of Sacco and Vanzetti for murder in 1921, and their executions in 1927, sparked worldwide outcry about discrimination in the criminal justice system leading to unjust outcomes.[17] Several prominent individuals, including Albert Einstein, George Bernard Shaw, and H. G. Wells, advocated on behalf of Sacco and Vanzetti. Their guilt or innocence was widely debated for decades after their executions, and their case remains something of a mystery. Although the Sacco and Vanzetti case is not typically counted among the known wrongful convictions, reinvestigations into their case have led to relatively widespread belief in their innocence, and in 1977, Massachusetts governor Michael Dukakis exonerated them.[18] At the very least, the Sacco and Vanzetti case sparked some debate about the possibility of erroneous convictions in the public sphere, though broadly, hearts and minds were not changed.

Other happenings throughout the century are more directly related to wrongful convictions as currently conceived. The 1940s brought the first organized attempt to uncover miscarriages of justice when lawyer and famed mystery writer Erle Stanley Gardner, the creator of the fictional detective Perry Mason, founded the Court of Last Resort, a panel of legal and investigative experts who reviewed cases of potential wrongful conviction and worked to reverse them if possible. The group is credited with exonerating at least 18 individuals and was popularized in a 1952 book, which earned Gardner an Edgar Award from the Mystery Writers of America in the category of Best Fact Crime and was portrayed in a television show that aired in the late 1950s.[19]

Another high-profile case in 1967 brought public attention to a questionable conviction, when rising professional boxer Rubin "Hurricane" Carter and his friend John Artis were convicted of a triple murder in New Jersey. In the mid-1970s, Carter's case became a cause for public and celebrity action. Muhammad Ali led a public demonstration in 1975 to advocate on Carter's behalf; the demonstration was also attended by actress Ellen Burstyn. That same year, famed singer-songwriter Bob Dylan recorded the well-known protest song "Hurricane" and visited Carter in prison. After being freed in 1976 pending a new trial, Carter was again convicted and sent back to prison. It was not until his case was discovered by teenager Lesra Martin and a group from Canada, who worked with Carter's legal team, that his release was secured in 1985 and exoneration in 1988. Hurricane's case attracted much media attention and sparked an outcry heard the world over.[20]

Carter's case is among the most famous wrongful convictions and attracted significant attention, but it was not the only one during the 1970s. While Carter's case was in the spotlight, and while the U.S. Supreme Court was effectively abolishing and reinstating the death penalty, 14 individuals were exonerated from death row between 1973 and 1979.[21]

Despite the spate of exonerations throughout the 20th century, innocence never caught on as a major reform issue in the United States. Although the specific number of wrongful convictions is unknown, particularly during this era, it is clear that such errors can and did occur, that people knew about them, and that some of those people cared. But as an issue for activism and reform, innocence lacked organization and was never sustained until the 1980s.

The Birth of an Industry

In 1978, Jim McCloskey decided to make a change in his life that surprised his friends and family. He had graduated from Bucknell University in 1964 with a degree in economics and joined the United States Navy. After being stationed in Tokyo and serving in the Vietnam

War, McCloskey returned to the States and earned a master's degree in international business. He returned to Japan for corporate work but eventually settled into a Wall Street job and later tried his hand as a management consultant in Philadelphia.[22] By his mid-30s, McCloskey was financially successful yet unsatisfied: "My life was like a rainbow," he once remarked. "It might have looked pretty, but it was vapor."[23] Single and childless, McCloskey was missing something in his life.

Feeling "shallow, selfish, unfulfilled,"[24] McCloskey "wanted to lead . . . an authentic life . . . to get to the real stuff of the world."[25] He began attending church again and found inspiration in the sermons and in Scripture, the lessons from which "compelled one to serve others."[26] McCloskey decided to leave his successful job and, in 1979 at age 37, entered Princeton Theological Seminary. For the field work component of his program, he worked as a student chaplain at Trenton State Prison.[27]

McCloskey was not long into his student chaplain service when he met Jorge de los Santos. Known as "Chiefie," de los Santos had served six years of his life sentence for a murder in Newark, New Jersey, during which he continually proclaimed his innocence. McCloskey described de los Santos to one journalist as "an engaging person, very compelling, and obsessed with talking about his innocence."[28] McCloskey, of course, did not know if de los Santos was innocent, but he was intrigued: "I was moved by his persistent claims of innocence, and it challenged me to do something other than return to the safety of seminary."[29] He tracked down the 1,500 pages of trial transcripts and spent the holidays of 1980 reading them. Chiefie's conviction had rested largely on a jailhouse informant who testified that de los Santos had confessed to him. Reading through the transcript, McCloskey was "enthralled and excited," thinking, "my God, could this guy really be innocent?"[30]

Before this, McCloskey had never really thought about wrongful convictions: "[It] wasn't even on my radar, about innocent people being convicted in America. . . . [I] almost thought the criminal justice system was flawless" and that "police and prosecutors were just doing their noble duty."[31] But he found Chiefie's trial transcript persuasive. The case was an opportunity to find the higher purpose he had been seeking, and he made another drastic decision: McCloskey "felt so moved by [Chiefie's] plight" that he took a year off from school to work on the case. "For the first time in my life," McCloskey once remarked, "I was being given the opportunity to do something meaningful for somebody else. It gave me a sense of purpose and authenticity, and it was exciting and adventurous."[32]

The decision surprised McCloskey's friends, but for him, it was the only thing to do. "How can I, believing in innocence, just turn my back and go about my life?" he told them. "I can't just throw up words of prayer to God to somehow help out and then move on without doing anything."[33] McCloskey took his leave of absence, raised $25,000 (including a $7,500 gift from the legal defense fund of the national Presbyterian Church), and found a lawyer to work with in Paul Casteleiro.[34]

Casteleiro had first been exposed to the issue of wrongful conviction as a law student when he worked with Morton Stavis, cofounder of the Center for Constitutional Rights. After graduating, Casteleiro became a public defender and eventually moved on to private practice. He found wrongful conviction cases interesting and gravitated toward them early in his career. When McCloskey needed a lawyer to help him in Chiefie's case, he first talked to Stavis, who did not have time to handle the case. Stavis then asked Casteleiro if he wanted to take over. Casteleiro agreed, and they dug in.[35]

McCloskey located the jailhouse informant, Richard Delli Santi, in a Bronx jail. Delli Santi admitted to lying about Chiefie's confession. This was enough to secure a subpoena for the prosecution's complete file, and McCloskey found that prosecutors knew Delli Santi had testified in previous cases even though he had said that Chiefie's was his first.[36] McCloskey eventually persuaded Delli Santi to come clean, and Delli Santi admitted that he had lied in numerous cases, including Chiefie's. This evidence was presented to federal judge Frederick Lacey, who said that Delli Santi's original testimony "reeked of perjury" and threw out the conviction.[37]

By the time de los Santos was released in 1983, McCloskey had completed his master of divinity degree. He had also come to believe in the innocence of two other prisoners serving life sentences, Nate Walker and Rene Santana. McCloskey had found his life's calling, saying, "I felt this is what God has ordained for me to do."[38] Rather than be ordained and become a pastor, he decided to work full-time on behalf of the wrongly convicted. With a $10,000 gift from his parents, he founded Centurion Ministries, named after the Roman Centurion who stood at the foot of the cross on which Christ was crucified and said, "Surely, this one is innocent."[39]

Unlike innocence organizations founded in recent years, there was no model for McCloskey to follow. "There was no book on this," he told me. "There's no college course on this. There was nothing, because it was really a pioneering effort."[40] So McCloskey, with no clear plan for the development of his organization, began working as a one-man operation out of his bedroom in the mansion of a wealthy Princeton widow.[41] As he tells it, "My bedroom was Centurion's office for eight years."[42]

Despite the lack of a clear plan, one thing was clear from the start: McCloskey was interested solely in actual innocence, not legal technicalities. "Innocence came to me," he said. "I didn't go seeking it. And being a lay person, not a lawyer, that's all I was interested in."[43] Taking it "one step at a time, one case at a time,"[44] McCloskey immediately went to work on his next cases. Working with attorney David Ruhnke, he was able to secure the release of Rene Santana in February 1986. He and Paul Casteleiro managed to exonerate Nate Walker in November of that same year. The Walker case generated some national publicity, garnering coverage on *The Today Show*. Centurion soon began to receive requests from prisoners around the country, and McCloskey began to develop a sense of how big the issue of wrongful conviction might actually be.[45] "Is it this widespread?" he asked himself. "Is it systemic?"[46]

The issue had fully entered McCloskey's consciousness, but many of the letters necessarily remained unopened. Fortunately for McCloskey, these successful cases attracted assistance from Kate Germond, who had recently moved to New York City from California with her husband: "I opened up the *New York Times* in November '86, which is the first time Jim had gotten national attention for his work, literally national attention. There was an article in the *New York Times* and papers all over the country, and he had been on a couple of the morning TV shows like *The Today Show* . . . . I read this article, and I thought, 'Well, he could use my help.' And so I called him up, we met, thought we could get along, and I started working with him in January of '87."[47] Although Germond had no experience in the criminal justice system, she was drawn to Centurion's social justice work, though she is not entirely sure of the reason for her attraction to justice and activism. She describes her life as having always been "bifurcated"—that is, having a working life to pay bills but also always having "a social work end of it, either starting soup kitchens or stopping logging or marching." Without a particular reason or motive behind her attraction to social justice issues, she told me simply, "I'm hard-wired to worry about wrongs. I've been this way my entire life."[48]

McCloskey was glad to have Germond's help, and together they took Centurion's work national. The organization was able to take its first non–New Jersey cases and its first death row cases: Clarence Brandley in Texas and Jimmy Wingo in Louisiana. They also eventually took their efforts to Canada, working on the case of David Milgaard.[49] At Germond's suggestion, McCloskey found a small office for Centurion Ministries.[50]

The organization gained further assistance in 1988 when Paul Henderson, who had won a Pulitzer Prize in 1982 for a series of investigative articles in the *Seattle Times* that helped lead to the exoneration of Steve Titus, began working on cases with them. He later joined Centurion as a full-time investigator.[51] And, just like that, McCloskey "developed an organization. Case by case, year by year, it evolved." He had not anticipated the growth: "I had no idea I was going to go national [or] into death penalty cases" and had "no thought" of taking the work into Canada.[52]

By the late 1980s, McCloskey was willing to declare that a convicted innocent "was as rare as a pigeon in a park."[53] Centurion was working on a number of cases, freed four individuals, and was gaining attention. Two particular cases provided widespread publicity. In 1987, the popular television show *60 Minutes* broadcast the story of Clarence Brandley, an African American janitor who had been wrongly convicted and sentenced to death for the 1980 rape and murder of a 16-year-old white girl at Conroe High School in Texas. The episode was part of an attention wave that ended with Brandley's exoneration in January 1990.[54]

The second case, that of Joyce Ann Brown, who had been convicted and sentenced to life in prison in 1980 for the robbery and murder of a fur-store owner in Dallas, Texas, was shown on *60 Minutes* in October 1989. With the help of Centurion's investigation, Brown was freed just weeks after the episode aired, on November 3, 1989, making her one of the first female exonerees.[55]

These cases were not the only wrongful convictions to gain attention but rather are indicative of a broader trend that was important to the early development of the innocence movement: media coverage of wrongful convictions.

Early Popular Attention

Although sensational media coverage of crime can contribute to wrong-ful convictions, the media can also be important in drawing attention to new issues.[56] According to journalist Maurice Possley, early exoneration cases were something of a "novelty": "You had these people with really compelling stories. . . . [They] were fascinating."[57] McCloskey echoed these sentiments, suggesting that when an exoneration occurred, "it was a huge story because they were so rare."[58]

Much of the early media attention came from Chicago, spearheaded by crusading journalist Rob Warden. After working as a foreign corre-spondent for a Chicago paper, during which he survived "a rather dra-matic escape from a hotel in Beirut at the height of the internal strife in Lebanon,"[59] he turned his attention toward the legal system. Police in Chicago had a reputation for misconduct; the ACLU in Chicago had investigated the use of electric shocks by the Chicago Police Department to extract confessions from suspects in the 1950s, and Warden worked on "a big investigation of police spying" in the 1970s. After the *Chicago Daily News* closed in 1978, Warden had a brief stint with the *Washington Post*. While there, Warden covered a deportation case involving an al-leged Nazi, Frank Walus, that turned out to be a case of mistaken iden-tity, and although it was a civil matter, "it was perceived as a wrongful conviction": "I suddenly heard from people in prison, . . . and I started looking at some of these cases."[60]

Warden soon returned to Chicago, where he started a publication called *Chicago Lawyer* with the Chicago Council of Lawyers, "which was a liberal bar association, basically comprised of people who thought the Chicago Bar Association was too in bed with . . . the political es-tablishment." He served as editor for ten years, during which *Chicago Lawyer* took a critical look at the criminal justice system. As Warden said, "It had occurred to me, investigative reporting to that time had focused very heavily on the executive and legislative branches, but there had been virtually none of the judicial branch. And in many ways, even though almost everything that the judiciary does is really a matter of public record, and often much more accessible than the other kinds of stuff that you'd get in investigating other branches of government, there's so much paper that you just drown in it."[61] Although others had written about cases of wrongful conviction, *Chicago Lawyer* was among the first to start covering it as a major problem. "Others merely wrote it off as something that was just sort of an anomaly of a well-functioning system," Warden said. "However, these first few flaws affected thousands, maybe as many as 100,000 people in America who are imprisoned at any given time for crimes that they didn't commit. No one had ever approached it in that manner before."[62]

One important case for Warden occurred in October 1986, when La-Vale Burt, a 20-year-old who falsely confessed to shooting a young boy in September 1985, was convicted at a bench trial. The next day, evidence surfaced suggesting that Burt was innocent. The judge reopened the case and acquitted Burt on retrial. Warden interviewed Burt and wrote a story about the case in *Chicago Lawyer*,[63] and Warden was off on a career path dedicated to examining the legal system and fighting injustice.

Although Chicago was the hotbed of early media attention for wrongful convictions, the national media covered them as well. As noted earlier, two Centurion Ministries cases—Clarence Brandley and Joyce Ann Brown—received coverage on *60 Minutes* in the late 1980s. A few other cases received coverage on that show and on *Good Morning America*.[64] Centurion was also featured in the *New York Times Magazine* and *Newsweek* for the cases of Clarence Chance and Benny Powell.

Despite this early coverage, the media was not always friendly to investigative journalists who covered wrongful convictions or took a critical view of the criminal justice system. Warden described the early media environment as "hostile": "Of course, for years, people sometimes would look at me just like I was crazy, and I would find that, when I talked about it, I sort of pulled my punches, because I knew if I told it the way it really was, people . . . would think I was just absolutely crazy. I would have no credibility whatsoever. So I had to basically keep my rhetoric pretty toned down over the years."[65] But the early reporters were persistent, and their coverage of wrongful convictions began to provide the public with a glimpse of the flaws in the criminal justice system.

The public gained another glimpse into the justice system's flaws in 1988, when filmmaker Errol Morris released *The Thin Blue Line*. Morris was interviewing Texas inmates for a documentary about James Grigson, a Dallas psychiatrist whose testimony about the sociopathic nature and future dangerousness of killers had contributed to countless death sentences and earned him the moniker "Dr. Death." While doing this, he met an inmate named Randall Dale Adams who was serving a life sentence for the murder of a police officer but who claimed to be innocent. Morris, formerly a private detective, investigated the case and made it the focus of his film.

The Thin Blue Line was released in 1988 at a time when documentaries were remarkably popular among general audiences,[66] and it soon became a major hit with fans and critics alike. Morris, who referred to himself as a "detective-director,"[67] created a "trance-like, almost lyrical rendering of a small, messy murder case" that had an "urgent, compulsive quality."[68] It was seen as exploring not just the Adams case but the nature of truth itself.[69] The Thin Blue Line was described as "a powerful and thrillingly strange movie" that "evoke[d a] kind of existential unease in its audience."[70] In a Washington Post survey of film critics, it was voted the best film of 1988, and Premiere magazine described it as one of the most influential films of the 1980s.[71] In 2001, it was inducted into the National Film Registry, a list of films considered to be "culturally, historically, or aesthetically significant that are earmarked for preservation by the Library of Congress,"[72] and in 2006 was described in Variety as "the most political work of cinema in the last twenty years."[73] The film, and Morris's reinvestigation of Adams's case, ultimately led to Adams's exoneration in March 1989.[74]

Morris views his work as similar to investigative journalism,[75] but it appears to have been much more. The Thin Blue Line was a popular, public critique of the criminal justice system, portraying in a way "more vivid than any judicial decision or fictional account . . . the vulnerability of the adversarial process . . . and the ease with which an innocent man could be put to death."[76] Professor Ron Huff described the film as "a turning point" for the level of national attention it received.[77]

Increased attention to the fallibility of criminal justice was not restricted to the media, however. For the first time since the 1930s, academic researchers—both social scientists and legal scholars—began to systematically examine wrongful convictions, laying the groundwork for innocence scholarship in the years since.

Modern Innocence Scholarship

The modern era of wrongful conviction research began, oddly enough, "over a Reuben sandwich." C. Ronald Huff and Ed Sagarin, two professors at Ohio State University, were trying to help Arye Rattner come up with a topic for his doctoral dissertation, and "like a lot of good ideas, it started at a Jewish deli." Sagarin, a professor and activist committed to issues of social justice, initially made the suggestion, pointing out that although Borchard had conducted some early work on the subject, little had been done recently, leaving a large gap in our knowledge about wrongful convictions.[78] The idea caught their imaginations.

In 1986, Huff and colleagues published their first article, drawing on their own database of nearly 500 wrongful convictions. They described the potential scope of the problem, some of the factors that led to wrongful convictions, and some possible preventive measures. Their sympathetic language harks back to older innocence writings; the abstract begins with the declaration, "Few problems can pose a greater threat to free, democratic societies than that of wrongful conviction."[79] Their work was developed into a book that was published a decade later.[80]

Another scholar who became a leader in the field of wrongful convictions, Samuel Gross, published his first article on the topic in 1987, though at the time he "didn't think of it as innocence work."[81] He was an acting associate professor at Stanford Law School at the time, teaching a clinical course on the use of expert witnesses in litigation. Gross was interested in eyewitness identification and had become familiar with the work of Elizabeth Loftus, a leading psychologist whose research pointed to the fallibility of human memory. He was curious why, given the known unreliability of eyewitness evidence yet its importance in so many cases, there were *so few* erroneous convictions based on eyewitness misidentifications,[82] so he collected eyewitness misidentification cases throughout the 20th century. His strongest conclusion was that in "a surprisingly high proportion of cases of misidentification . . . the defendant was originally suspected because of his appearance, rather than other information or evidence. They looked like a sketch or something." The simple answer to the question of why there were relatively few false convictions based on eyewitness error, as Gross put it, is because "the system has a lot of redundancy in it."[83]

Unlike earlier scholarship, Gross avoided value-laden language and did not begin with a model declaration about how the system *should* work. Rather, his language might best be described as cautiously suspicious, pointing out that while wrongful convictions are relatively rare, likely occurring at a lower rate than we might expect based on what we know about unreliable eyewitness evidence, they are still important, horrible occurrences that warrant protecting against. He likened them to airplane crashes, which "are exceedingly rare," yet "we go to great lengths to maintain that fact and to make them even less likely."[84]

While both Huff and Gross went on to become leading innocence scholars, the work that made the most waves was written by philosopher Hugo Adam Bedau and sociologist Michael Radelet. Bedau had assisted Sara Ehrmann, a death penalty abolitionist whose husband, Herbert, was associate counsel for Sacco and Vanzetti, with a 1962 article, "For Whom the Chair Waits," that was designed to present the "human" side of capital punishment by describing the individuals convicted of capital crimes. In the paper, Ehrmann cited a number of cases of men who were believed to be wrongly convicted and sent to death row.[85] Two years after Ehrmann's article was published, the first edition of Bedau's classic volume *The Death Penalty in America* was released, in which he wrote briefly about miscarriages of justice. In later editions, he expanded this discussion and by the early 1980s wanted to develop a larger project on the topic.

Radelet had been working with a death row inmate in Florida who had maintained his innocence and was encouraged to look into the issue of miscarriages of justice. He wrote to Bedau, and the pair came up with a collaborative project that began in 1982. Using historical records, they collected and described cases in which it appeared that innocent individuals had been convicted in capital cases. They presented their work in 1985 at the American Society of Criminology meeting and released their paper. The project got "a huge amount of press," including coverage in the *New York Times*. The authors also appeared on several national television shows, including "the big talk show of the time," *The Phil Donahue Show*. They began to receive letters from families of inmates saying their loved ones were innocent. That was "when the counterattack began."[86]

One of their early critics was Ernest van den Haag, a Fordham University professor and well-known death penalty supporter, who briefly discussed the Bedau-Radelet project in an article published in the *Harvard Law Review*. He asserted that errors were bound to happen on occasion in capital cases, but that was not reason for significant concern; "nearly all human activities, such as trucking, lighting, or construction, cost the lives of some innocent bystanders," van den Haag wrote. "We do not give up these activities, because the advantages, moral or material, outweigh the unintended losses."[87]

Bedau and Radelet's study was published in the prestigious *Stanford Law Review* in 1987. With 350 cases of what they believed to be erroneous convictions in capital and potentially capital cases—23 of which they believed to be cases in which an innocent person was actually executed—they described the types of errors that led to the convictions and the ways in which the errors were uncovered. The authors were very clear in making an anti–death penalty argument. They did not shy away from using sharp, critical rhetoric to appeal to those who had a similar ideological bent, and the article opens with a quotation from Marquis de Lafayette, which reads, "Till the infallibility of human judgments shall have been proved to me, I shall demand the abolition of the penalty of death."[88] They later dedicate an entire section to a discussion of innocence and the abolition of capital punishment.

Bedau and Radelet's article created quite a stir in the death penalty debate. Edwin Meese III, attorney general under President Ronald Reagan, recognized the potential damage the study might do to the institution of capital punishment and recruited two Justice Department attorneys, Stephen Markman and Paul Cassell, to respond. Markman and Cassell took a strong pro–capital punishment stance in their critique, published in the same journal one year later, and suggested that the Bedau-Radelet study was not only methodologically flawed but that "it wholly fail[ed] to demonstrate an unacceptable risk of executing the innocent." They even went so far as to say that the study "confirms . . . the view that the risk is too small to be a significant factor in the debate over the death penalty."[89] They described the Bedau-Radelet study as misleading and subjective, accused the original authors of misrepresenting and excluding important evidence, and suggested that all 23 of those who had supposedly been wrongly executed were actually guilty.

The fiery exchange continued when Bedau and Radelet published a rejoinder, pointing out that while Markman and Cassell critiqued their allegedly subjective methods, they did the exact same thing to support opposing conclusions. Furthermore, they suggested that the critiques rested solely on politics and ideology: "The Department of Justice under the Reagan Administration has made quite clear its support for the death penalty, and the critique of our research by Markman and Cassell is but one more indication of that support." They went on, saying the critiques "appear to spring largely from unacknowledged political roots" and are "an effort to protect the myth of systemic infallibility."[90]

This situation may not have had a major impact on public and political opinion at the time, but such an exchange among well-known scholars and prominent attorneys, in such a prestigious and widely read law journal, was certainly noticed in the legal community and brought the issue of miscarriages of justice to a wider scholarly audience.[91] Radelet and Bedau continued this line of research and collaborated with Bedau's wife, Constance Putnam, on a book. They expanded their analysis to include more than 400 cases. As Radelet said, they had a perfect working group: "Hugo was the thinker, I did the research, and Constance was the writer."[92]

It is worth noting that, in the 1980s, wrongful conviction was a somewhat controversial research topic. This is evident in the reaction to the Bedau-Radelet study; they "knew from the start how controversial this would be" and thus were careful about including and not including cases.[93] Huff also discussed the controversial nature of the topic. He had difficulty securing a National Institute of Justice fellowship for his student, suggesting that the government might have been hesitant to touch the issue. "Just because they don't want to hear it, that doesn't mean it isn't important or worth knowing," he told me. "This is important."[94] One particular passage from their article highlights the controversial nature of innocence research at the time. The authors sent surveys to attorneys and judges from around the United States, with an emphasis on their state of Ohio. One particular respondent, an alumnus of Ohio State University, offered these comments to describe how he felt about the study: "I am deeply disappointed that my old university is even remotely involved in this type of venture. Aren't there more pressing topics in this world that your efforts can be funneled to?"[95] Despite tackling a controversial topic, these researchers did not necessarily have a sense of how vast the issue was or that it would become a major focus for criminal justice reformers. When Bedau and Radelet began their research, they "thought it was just a summer project." As they dug into it, however, they "just kept finding more and more": "We found many, many more cases than we ever imagined."[96] When asked if he had a sense of what this might turn into, Huff replied simply, "No. We thought we were voices in the wilderness."[97]

*   *   *

The period described in this chapter marks an important time for innocence in the United States, albeit one that is seldom discussed by scholars in any detail. The 1980s marked the first time that a nonprofit organization dedicated itself to innocence work and was sustained, as Centurion Ministries was founded and worked to secure the release of several wrongly convicted prisoners; on several occasions, I heard Jim McCloskey referred to as "the godfather" of the industry, though he does not necessarily embrace the nickname.[98] Several of their cases managed to reach the national mainstream media. These cases, along with journalistic efforts spearheaded by Rob Warden in Chicago and the popular documentary *The Thin Blue Line*, brought at least some popular attention to the issue of wrongful convictions. The mid-1980s also marked the beginning of the modern era of innocence research, in which social scientists and legal scholars engaged in systematic research and published academic studies on the topic. The journalistic exposure of flaws in the criminal justice system and the broad scholarly studies began, for the first time, to shift the focus from the travesty of individual cases of error to the question of whether there was a more systematic problem of wrongful conviction.

This time period is sometimes overlooked in discussions of the innocence movement, but the importance of these events should not go unnoticed. They provide the first sustained clues that *something* was there, that wrongful convictions may be more than mere aberrations, and that they deserve attention. In short, this period marks the first time in the United States that there was a real sense of something brewing on the innocence front that could grow beyond a few isolated cases. And while these events were unfolding, a scientific revolution was beginning— based on a discovery across the Atlantic that, initially, had little to do with criminal justice—that would dramatically alter the criminal justice system and, in turn, the issue of wrongful conviction.

2

"A Eureka Moment"

DNA, the Legal System, and the Meaning of Innocence

Early exonerations of innocent prisoners, including those secured by Centurion Ministries, relied on traditional forms of evidence: confessions from true perpetrators, discoveries of perjury, and the like. But the notion of "actual innocence" sometimes remained shaky; after all, short of a murder victim turning up alive, how can one ever know if a prisoner is *truly innocent*?

Sir Alec Jeffreys had no intention of answering this question. When he entered his lab at the University of Leicester in England on the morning of September 10, 1984, he thought it was going to be a Monday like any other. Little did he know what awaited him. "My life changed on Monday morning at 9:05 am," he once said. "In science, it is unusual to have such a 'eureka' moment."[1] What happened that morning, a discovery he and his team made in the science of deoxyribonucleic acid (DNA), would turn criminal justice on its head.

Discovering the DNA Fingerprint

The first genetic fingerprint was discovered "purely by accident," according to Sir Alec Jeffreys.[2] A professor at the University of Leicester, Jeffreys and his team were studying the evolution of mammalian globin genes when they discovered variable patterns of DNA in almost all of the species tested. Further examination showed that they were present in most mammals and that the patterns appeared to be different in each animal. Thinking that these might act as markers that would help pinpoint the genes responsible for particular traits, they set up an experiment to look for them in humans.[3]

In September 1984, the experiment revealed several markers in the human genome, which appeared to be passed down through families and unique to each individual. At first, Jeffreys thought the results were too complicated. But "then the penny dropped," and he realized they "had genetic fingerprinting."[4] The team first published its findings in 1985 and in a second article that same year concluded that the probability of two individuals having the same DNA fingerprint was less than one in 33 billion.[5]

Two implications of the discovery were immediately clear to the research team: criminal investigations and paternity cases. Jeffreys's wife added immigration to the list, opening up his eyes to the "political dimension" of the discovery.[6]

The first immigration case came in March 1985 at the request of the family and attorney of 15-year-old Andrew Sarbah. Born in London, Sarbah had gone to live with his father in Ghana when he was only four. Returning to London 11 years later, with a passport showing he was born there, Sarbah was denied entry as a British citizen. He was granted temporary admission, but suspicion abounded that someone had tampered with the passport. The family's attorney, Sheona York, collected evidence (including serological testing) to show that Sarbah was indeed the biological son of his mother, Christine. Still, the tampered-passport theory remained. As options were running out, a colleague of York's showed her a newspaper article about Jeffreys's discovery of genetic fingerprinting. York contacted Jeffreys, who agreed to run the tests. When the results showed that Andrew was Christine's son, the Home Office reluctantly conceded the case.[7]

The case generated publicity for the newly discovered DNA technology, which was praised as a "new way to depoliticize controversial immigration decisions."[8] According to Jeffreys, the positive reception may have been partly due to the fact that the case "was to save a young boy and it captured the public's sympathy and imagination. It was science helping an individual challenge authority." The first paternity case soon followed, and then "the flood gates opened."[9]

At this time, the forensic implications of genetic fingerprinting— that is, its application to law and criminal justice—were becoming clear, but the process originally developed by Jeffreys and his team was inadequate. Starting in 1985, they developed a variation of the technique, which they called "DNA profiling," to be used for forensic applications.[10] Like the first use of genetic fingerprinting in an immigration case, the first forensic application of genetic profiling captured public attention.

The Blooding

In November 1983, the body of 15-year-old Lydia Mann was found in the village of Narborough, England. She had been raped and strangled. The crime drew the attention of the community and sparked a major investigation but went unsolved. Three years later, in July 1986, a similar crime occurred in the neighboring village of Enderby, where another 15-year old, Dawn Ashworth, was found beaten, raped, and strangled. This time, however, investigators had a suspect: Richard Buckland, a 17-year old who worked in the kitchen of a local mental hospital. Buckland had a very low IQ and upon questioning confessed to Ashworth's murder but not to Mann's. Investigators asked Jeffreys to compare Buckland's DNA with a sample taken from the Mann crime scene, which he did in September 1986. The results showed that the samples did not match. Surprised and unsure how to proceed, police asked Jeffreys to test Buckland's sample against material from the Ashworth investigation, the crime to which he had confessed. The tests showed that the two crime-scene samples matched, but neither one matched Buckland, shocking not only the police but also Jeffreys, who found the result "blood-chilling."[11] After the Home Office's Forensic Science Services confirmed the results, all charges were dropped against Buckland. Thus, "the first time DNA profiling was used in criminology, it was to prove innocence."[12]

Police were unsure how to proceed. They knew they were dealing with a multiple-murderer, but their only suspect had been cleared. With no additional suspects, no leads, and increasing pressure from the community to solve the crimes, the police took a "revolutionary step": they requested that all men between the ages of 17 and 34 who lived in the vicinity of the crime scenes submit voluntary blood and saliva samples. Their goal was to eliminate suspects using traditional blood tests. Those who could not be eliminated would have their DNA samples tested by Jeffreys.[13]

More than 4,500 men submitted blood and saliva samples. Of those, more than 500 could not be eliminated through basic blood testing, and the DNA tests began. None, however, matched the samples from the Mann and Ashworth investigations. The police yet again thought they had reached a dead end, until a woman who worked at a bakery in

Leicester called the police and informed them that one of her coworkers, Ian Kelly, had said he fooled police by submitting a sample on behalf of someone else. When police questioned Kelly, he spoke of the plan he had concocted with a coworker: Kelly had agreed to submit a sample on behalf of Colin Pitchfork, who said he had already submitted a sample for another friend. Pitchfork was soon arrested and confessed to both murders. It was confirmed when DNA tests revealed that his profile matched both murder-investigation samples. Pitchfork pleaded guilty in January 1988 and was given two life sentences.

The Mann-Ashworth case "was hailed as the first significant success for the use of DNA typing in forensic investigation"[14] and was later popularized by Joseph Wambaugh in a book titled *The Blooding*. Pitchfork's positive test results and conviction were a relief for Jeffreys: "I felt relief because he was serial murderer and would kill again, and because if the operation had failed then the public's perception of forensic DNA would have been shattered."[15] As it was, the technology was praised, and DNA fingerprinting spread quickly through the forensic community in the United Kingdom. The case also "triggered the application of molecular genetics to criminal investigations worldwide,"[16] particularly in the United States.

DNA in the United States

After Jeffreys and his team handled the immigration dispute in the Sarbah case, they were inundated with requests for assistance. Jeffreys described this time as "simply insane."[17] In response to the incredible demand, Imperial Chemical Industries (ICI), the largest chemical company in the United Kingdom, opened its first DNA-testing laboratory in the summer of 1987. The company wanted to expand its market overseas, particularly in the United States, and did so after the Pitchfork case. ICI Americas started offering DNA tests in the United States in October 1987 through Cellmark Diagnostics USA. Although the company initially planned to focus on paternity testing, it soon began accepting forensic casework. Concerned about the stricter admissibility standards in U.S. courtrooms, Cellmark hired the former chief of the United States Bureau of Alcohol, Tobacco, and Firearms' forensic laboratory Daniel Garner. Garner immediately began preparing the company to introduce its tests into court, hiring scientists and building a network of expert advisers to shore up the scientific and technical side of things.[18]

Cellmark also began to connect with criminal justice professionals through direct mail campaigns, advertisements in legal publications, and presentations at professional meetings. It presented its DNA fingerprinting technology as a definitive way to link offenders to a crime scene. In one 1988 advertisement, for instance, the company claimed that "criminals leave more conclusive evidence than ever before" and that DNA fingerprinting "may be the difference between conviction and acquittal." The advertisement went on to say that the company could obtain "conclusive results in only one test," even "from samples that are months or even years old."[19]

Cellmark was not alone in the commercial DNA-testing business; another company, called Lifecodes, was in the picture. Whereas Jeffreys had stumbled on the DNA fingerprint, Lifecodes had been purposefully developing its technology for the purpose of commercializing it and applying it to forensic analysis under the direction of scientist Michael Baird.[20] The Lifecodes team published two research articles in 1986 concluding that its technology could successfully identify individuals from dried bloodstains and biological fluids recovered after the fact.[21] Like Cellmark, Lifecodes began to advertise its new test to criminal justice professionals, citing it as "exquisitely accurate."[22] It presented its test as not only valid and reliable but also relatively simple and ready to be presented in the courtroom, touting the number of Ph.D.-level scientists on its staff but failing to mention that the test had not yet been the subject of an admissibility hearing. That step came soon enough.

The Andrews Case

In the spring of 1986, a string of rapes and assaults struck the south side of Orlando, Florida. The attacks were similar: they occurred in the victims' homes after midnight, and the man carried a knife, covered the victims' heads with a sheet or blanket, and tended to flip the lights on and off during the attacks. The first victim, 27-year-old Nancy Hodge, had gotten a look at the attacker. It was not until the following year, in March 1987, that Tommie Lee Andrews—by then suspected of more than 20 incidents of prowling, breaking and entering, attempted assault, and rape—was arrested. Hodge identified Andrews in a photo lineup, and Andrews was charged with the sexual battery and armed burglary of Hodge, as well as a similar rape that occurred only a week prior to his arrest.[23]

The case was prosecuted by assistant state attorney Tim Berry. While Berry was building his case, he was talking to his colleague Jeffrey Ashton, who suggested that he consider a new type of genetic test, DNA typing. Ashton had heard of the new technology from a news report about the Pitchfork case in 1986 and had recently seen a Lifecodes advertisement in a Florida legal publication. Berry called Lifecodes, and it ran the tests in August 1987. The results were impressive: the results matched Andrews to the Hodge sample, and Lifecodes claimed that the frequency of the pattern was one in ten billion. As Michael Baird said of Andrews at the time, "In a world population of just over 5 billion, he's the only guy who could have left his semen there."[24]

During the pretrial admissibility hearing, the prosecution brought in expert witnesses to discuss the evidence. Things seemed to be going the prosecution's way, and the defense attorney, Hal Uhrig, felt helpless. He tried to find experts to challenge the prosecution, but none agreed. Instead, he decided to challenge the DNA evidence on the most common-sense notion he had: with a world population of five billion, how could the possibility of a match be one in ten billion? The prosecution was caught off guard; Berry had not prepared for this challenge and could not convince the judge that the statistical evidence should be admissible. Without this evidence, the jury failed to reach a verdict, and the judge declared a mistrial.

Two weeks later, Andrews went to trial for the second rape. This time, the prosecution team, led by Ashton, had done its homework and convinced the court to admit the statistical evidence. Within just a few days, Andrews was convicted and sentenced to 22 years, becoming the first person in the United States to be convicted based on forensic DNA evidence.[25]

By late 1987, the trickle of cases in which DNA was a factor became a flood. Cellmark and Lifecodes aggressively marketed their technology, and the media provided positive coverage. At this point, it seemed that the acceptance of DNA would go unquestioned and without challenge from the defense.

The Wesley-Bailey *Hearing*

The Albany, New York, area was struck with two sexual assaults that eventually led to the first challenge of DNA evidence in which the defense actually called witnesses to combat the prosecution. The two cases—*People v. Wesley* and *People v. Bailey*—were similar in nature and time frame, prompting the court to hold a combined admissibility hearing that has been referred to as the "*Wesley-Bailey* hearing."[26]

George Wesley, a man in his mid-30s who had spent most of his life in institutions for the mentally challenged, was charged in the 1987 rape and murder of 79-year-old Helen Kendrick. Blood was found on Wesley's clothes, and the prosecution sought to use DNA fingerprinting to prove that the blood belonged to the victim.[27] Cameron Bailey was on trial for the rape of a 17-year-old girl. The victim had become pregnant and had an abortion; the prosecution believed that Bailey fathered the child and wanted to use DNA testing to prove it.[28] In both cases, the prosecution wanted to draw blood from the defendants to carry out the DNA tests that were crucial to securing convictions.

The admissibility hearing began in December 1987 to determine if the procedures used by Lifecodes, which would perform the tests, met the *Frye* standard, which asks whether novel scientific evidence is generally accepted in the relevant scientific community and thus admissible in court.[29] The prosecution had a network of scientists willing to testify in support of the technology. The main expert was Lifecodes' own Michael Baird, who explained the basic process and made the legal criteria for admissibility seem simple and clear. Other well-known scientists, Drs. Richard Roberts and Kenneth Kidd, agreed that Lifecodes' protocols were sound.[30]

Defense attorney Douglas Rutnik began his challenge by arguing that Baird's testimony was questionable because he had a financial stake in the outcome, but the judge quickly ended that discussion. Finding high-caliber expert scientists to challenge the prosecution was no small feat for the defense, but Rutnik found two: Dr. Neville Colman of the Mt. Sinai School of Medicine and Dr. Richard Borowsky of New York University. They challenged the foundations of Lifecodes' tests and argued that their methods had not been subjected to adequate peer review.[31]

The defense challenges were met head-on by the prosecution's experts. The decision of Judge Joseph Harris ultimately dismissed, even insulted, the defense experts, claiming they were underqualified to serve as experts on the issues at hand and severely overmatched by the prosecution's witnesses. He ruled in favor of admissibility of DNA, a technology that could "constitute the single greatest advance in the search for truth . . . since the advent of cross-examination."[32]

After failing to successfully challenge the DNA evidence in the Andrews case and the *Wesley-Bailey* hearing, the defense community was at a loss. By 1989, DNA test results had been admitted in more than 100 cases in the United States and had likely been used to acquire confessions in many more, all without substantial challenge from defense attorneys.[33]

Clearly, the strategies used in the previous cases were not working. As defense attorney Peter Neufeld put it at the time, "Mostly the evidence has come in without any objections, because the lawyers haven't known how to respond to it."[34] The prevailing wisdom that the tests utilized would either produce the correct answer or no answer at all—with no real possibility of a false positive—echoed throughout the early cases. Historian Jay Aronson has argued that this is due in part to the fact that both Cellmark and Lifecodes had multinational parent corporations that were willing to spend billions of dollars each year to spread the use of DNA profiling as much as possible. Furthermore, the techniques were still not well-known outside of these two private companies, making defense use of experts a tricky proposition. Still, the defense community knew that if it wished to successfully challenge DNA evidence, it needed to find highly qualified expert witnesses to match the scientists on the prosecution side and to convince the court that the knowledge of these experts was significant for the admissibility of DNA-profiling evidence.[35] It began to mount its first serious challenge to DNA evidence in early 1989, led by Barry Scheck and Peter Neufeld.

Scheck and Neufeld met in the 1970s while working as defense attorneys for the Bronx Legal Aid Society in New York. Their backgrounds were quite different, though both shared a passion for political activism and an aversion to inequality and injustice. Scheck came from an entertainment family; his father, George, was a tap dancer and manager for several celebrity entertainers. Scheck became a fierce debater in school and at Yale became involved in a number of political causes. Neufeld came from a politically active family; his parents, Muriel and

Stanley, were leaders in the secular humanist ethical culture movement, and his brother, Russell, worked with the Students for a Democratic Society (SDS), an organization that opposed the Vietnam War and racial discrimination.[36]

The pair quickly became close friends.[37] Both eventually left the Legal Aid Society, Neufeld for private practice, Scheck to be a professor and director of clinical education at the Cardozo School of Law at Yeshiva University, but they continued to work cases together. In retrospect, the most important one may have been that of Marion Coakley, as it sparked an interest that strongly influenced the next phase of their careers.

The Coakley Case

In 1984, Barry Scheck had been involved in a mistaken-identification case in which a man named Robert McLaughlin was shown to be innocent. A lawyer who worked with Scheck on the case, Richard Emery, then sent another one his way. It was from the same Bronx Legal Aid office where Scheck and Neufeld used to work and involved a man named Marion Coakley, who had been convicted of rape and robbery.[38] The serologist who was involved in the case, Robert Shaler, was going to work for Lifecodes and told Scheck and Neufeld about the company's DNA testing, suggesting that they try it in the Coakley case, but there was not to be enough evidence to get results.[39]

Although Scheck and Neufeld could not obtain DNA results to exonerate Coakley, other evidence pointed to his innocence, including a palm print that did not match, and Coakley was exonerated.[40] Still, the case was an important one. As Neufeld recounted, "It was at that time that we first learned about this new technology called DNA typing. . . . That was our first window into the power of DNA technology."[41] Scheck echoed these sentiments, saying that although DNA was not used for the Coakley exoneration, from that point on they "knew, from how that was set up, that there were some classic problems in the way they were trying to transfer this technology from medical and research purposes" to the forensic arena. They quickly realized the potential power of DNA testing and decided to focus their efforts on its use in courtrooms.[42] "We realized then that DNA was going to be extremely important, and it had not really been involved in the courts yet," Scheck said. "So we held a forum at Cardozo Law School involving DNA testing—the first one, I think, in any American academic institution for its forensic application."[43]

It is worth noting that neither Scheck nor Neufeld had anticipated becoming experts on a complex scientific technology. Neither had a background in science, according to Neufeld:

> In fact, like a lot of other lawyers, it was the difficulty in comprehending chemistry that moved us to law school in the first place. The last thing we ever wanted to see, as lawyers, was any kind of physics or chemical equation. But what happens is that you have a client whose life and liberty are at stake, and it forces you to learn particular disciplines. It might be biology or chemistry. It might be a law of physics. It might be toxicology. It could be any of those sciences. And you have no choice but to learn them, because if you don't learn them, then someone may abuse the information and send out an erroneous piece of information to the jury, and your client will suffer as a result.[44]

Despite their nonscientific backgrounds, Scheck and Neufeld became interested in DNA technology, and the 1987 forum at Cardozo garnered some attention. In mid-1988, both were named to the New York State panel on forensic DNA analysis.[45] Thus, when defense attorney Andrew Rossmer needed help in handling the DNA evidence in the case of Joseph Castro, Scheck and Neufeld seemed like the perfect choice.

The Castro Case

On February 5, 1987, Vilma Ponce, 20 years old and seven months pregnant, was found stabbed to death along with her two-year-old daughter. Ponce's husband found the bodies in their apartment in the Bronx. The husband told police that he had seen a man leaving the building with blood on his hands. The man turned out to be 38-year-old Joseph Castro, a janitor's helper and neighborhood handyman who lived in the adjacent building. Ponce's husband could not identify Castro in a photo array, but the investigation continued.[46]

The "grim but unexceptional homicide"[47] took a turn when detectives, questioning Castro several days after the incident, discovered on his watch a small spot of blood, which Castro claimed was his own. Risa

Sugarman, an assistant district attorney in the Bronx, ordered a genetic test. The watch, along with samples taken from the two victims, was sent to Lifecodes for analysis. The tests were performed, and on July 22, Lifecodes issued a definitive, unambiguous report to the Bronx District Attorney's Office: "The DNA-PRINT pattern from the blood of Ponce matches that of the watch with three DNA probes. The frequency of these patterns in the general public is 1:189,200,000."[48]

Castro was charged with two counts of second-degree murder, and prosecutors sought to have the test results admitted as evidence. Sugarman knew that this meant a *Frye* hearing to determine whether the evidence would be admissible in court. Until this point, DNA identification evidence had never been declared inadmissible under *Frye*.[49] There had not, however, been a substantial challenge to the evidence.

Castro's defense was originally being handled by court-appointed attorney Andrew Rossmer. Unfamiliar with the technicalities involved in genetic fingerprinting and feeling as though he was in over his head, Rossmer asked Neufeld and Scheck to handle the *Frye* hearing. As both lawyers were serving on a state panel studying DNA forensic analysis, they seemed to be the perfect specialists to do so.[50]

Neufeld and Scheck, unlike many of their colleagues in the legal and criminal justice worlds, were skeptical of the oft-praised DNA evidence, concerned about its use in the courts, and "decided to make the Castro case the first in which there would be a comprehensive inquiry into the various issues that comprise DNA typing."[51] So although case law seemed to be against them, they forged on.

For Neufeld and Scheck, a key issue was that the testing was carried out by private commercial companies—Lifecodes and Cellmark—and was thus unregulated. As Neufeld noted, "There was no accountability, and we were concerned with that as a matter of social policy."[52] One commentator described the work as a "black box," where samples went in and results were spit out, which basically meant convictions were ensured, given the claims of certainty and reliability made by the companies.[53]

The defense needed expert witnesses to challenge the evidence, but at first, experts were hesitant to work with Neufeld and Scheck because they were concerned that an attack on the new technology would harm its image, thus compromising its potential value. But that perspective began to change. According to Neufeld, eventually, "the experts reached the conclusion that it was the sloppy work of some of these laboratories that was going to give DNA technology a bad name" and realized that they had "a professional obligation to do some house-cleaning."[54]

In November 1988, just weeks after becoming involved in the Castro case, Scheck and Neufeld attended a symposium on forensic DNA typing at the Banbury Center at Cold Spring Harbor Laboratory on Long Island, New York. Neufeld described it as "the first conference where there was any discussion of potential problems with the technique. Previously, all you'd hear was how great it was."[55] The meeting included not only defense attorneys but also prosecutors, FBI representatives, molecular biologists, and other scientists.

At the conference, Lifecodes scientist Michael Baird, who had by then testified in more than 20 hearings in the United States, gave a presentation in which he showed several autoradiographs, or autorads—the x-ray images examined to determine if the patterns on two samples match—and claimed that he would sometimes call a match even when the patterns did not quite line up but were similar. Furthermore, he did not always conduct the proper control tests but knew from experience that the samples matched.[56] One particular guest at Baird's presentation was human geneticist and mathematician Eric Lander, of the Whitehead Institute in Cambridge, Massachusetts, who "was a little disturbed" by Baird's claim.[57]

Neufeld met Lander at the meeting and showed him one of the autorads from the Castro case. Lander called some colleagues over and asked them if they thought it was a match, to which two of the three replied, "Garbage."[58] Soon after the conference, Lander was asked to serve as an expert in the Castro case. Lander declined the invitation but agreed to help Scheck and Neufeld understand the technicalities of DNA typing. Throughout the initial hearings, they asked Lander questions, sent him autorads and other data presented by the prosecution, and sent transcripts of testimony. To Lander, it was immediately clear that there were issues: "I could see all kinds of problems. I thought I would simply give the defense lawyers questions to ask, that they would force the prosecution witnesses to admit the problems, and the case would fall apart."[59] But it was not so simple. "Distressed and appalled" by Baird's responses to the questions,[60] Lander reluctantly agreed to testify, though he declined to accept the expert-witness fees. He ended up dedicating more than 350 hours of work on the case, including six days on the witness stand and preparation of a 50-page report.[61] In Lander, Scheck and Neufeld knew they had found somebody "right up [their] alley"; Scheck described him as "this fast-talking New York Jew from Brooklyn who loved to argue and knew a lot of law."[62] Throughout the hearings, Lander and the defense team found several problems with the methods used by Lifecodes in the Castro case.

In late April, there was another meeting at Cold Spring Harbor on genome mapping and sequencing. Lander attended and met biochemist and molecular biologist Richard Roberts. The two discussed the Castro case; Lander explained his concerns and left his report with Roberts, who "quickly became rather concerned" and "soon realized that something had to be done."[63]

A few days after reading the full report, Roberts suggested that the expert witnesses from the case, both from the prosecution and defense, meet and discuss the issue as scientists, with "none of this lawyerly talk."[64] There were ten experts in total, five for each side; only four were able to attend the meeting, but the remaining six gave their approval.[65] Neufeld also approved of the meeting: "I was extremely surprised, but I thought it was a great idea."[66]

The experts met and ended up drafting a two-page consensus statement concluding that the Lifecodes tests in the case were "not scientifically reliable enough to support the assertion that the samples . . . do or do not match."[67] Nine of the ten experts agreed with this conclusion; Baird was the only holdout.[68] The report discussed the procedures for assessing the validity of novel scientific techniques: "All experts have agreed that the *Frye* test and the setting of the adversary system may not be the most appropriate method for reaching scientific consensus. The *Frye* hearing is not the appropriate time to begin the process of peer review of the data. Initiating peer review at this time wastes a great deal of the court's and the experts' time. The setting also discourages many experts from agreeing to participate in the careful scientific review of the data."[69] The report emphasized the "need to reach general scientific agreement about appropriate standards for the practice of forensic DNA typing" and encouraged the National Academy of Sciences to form a committee to do so.[70]

The meeting was described by Neufeld as "unprecedented in the annals of law."[71] The *Castro* decision basically followed the scientific conclusions, ruling that while DNA fingerprinting was generally acceptable and admissible, the specific analysis performed by Lifecodes in the case was not. That is, the theory underlying forensic DNA typing was accepted, and there were techniques that were accepted to produce reliable results; in this particular case, however, Lifecodes failed to perform all of the necessary tests, and the evidence was thus inadmissible.[72] The prosecution conceded that the test results were unreliable, with Sugarman noting that this outcome "was a better service to the criminal justice system." Speaking for both herself and Justice Gerald Sheindlin, Sugarman said they were both convinced that "you have to look at [DNA test results] very closely before you let it go before a jury."[73]

To have a legal actor, particularly a prosecutor, share such a sentiment was no small feat. After all, it had been only a few years since forensic DNA fingerprinting was introduced to the U.S. legal system with the promise of revolutionizing the search for truth, a new type of scientific evidence that was "incapable of giving a wrong answer" and that would "reduce to insignificance the standard alibi defense."[74] The *Castro* case was thus a major victory for the defense; the perception of DNA evidence shifted from an infallible crime-fighting tool to that which should be questioned deeply and systematically. As Neufeld pointed out, prior to *Castro*, no challenges had "addressed the problems of forensic DNA typing that distinguish it from diagnostic DNA typing."[75]

Still, Neufeld and Scheck were not fully satisfied. Although they had scored a major victory, the decision failed to account for the fundamental flaws with Lifecodes' methods and the potential implications of those flaws. As Neufeld told a reporter, the judge "says in the abstract DNA tests are fine, when in the only test he ever looked at, it wasn't fine, it was a shambles."[76] For Neufeld and Scheck, the troubling part was that Lifecodes had performed its tests in almost 1,500 criminal cases to that point, and the decision failed to mention that the flaws uncovered in *Castro* potentially tainted those earlier results. In what came to be an important part of the innocence movement's mantra, Scheck described this issue as "a fundamental civil liberties problem." Even if all of the scientific problems are fixed, "it is still wrong that these past cases are based upon unreliable science, and it is not inconceivable that some of these people have been unjustly convicted."[77] Some people, including Neufeld, thought challenges to previous Lifecodes cases might be one outcome of *Castro*. After the case, he and Scheck received numerous requests for help from attorneys around the country. Although they were unable to assist directly with most of the cases, they did make briefs and transcripts from *Castro* available through the National Association of Criminal Defense Lawyers.[78]

The *Castro* case, along with the *Schwartz* case in Minnesota in which Cellmark's techniques were challenged, also led the media to share some skepticism of DNA evidence.[79] While the cases did not disprove the potential power and reliability of DNA testing, they showed that the evidence must be carefully examined before being deemed admissible. As Eric Lander put it at the time, "No biologist questions the potential power of DNA typing. What is missing in forensics is a set of adequate guidelines."[80] Thus, perhaps the most important outcome of the *Castro* case was the push to establish national standards for forensic DNA testing.

Wanting to ensure that the reputation of DNA evidence was not further tainted, many people looked to the Federal Bureau of Investigation (FBI) to lead the development of standards for forensic DNA testing in the United States. The FBI began offering forensic DNA testing to law enforcement agencies in December 1988, and in the wake of *Castro* and *Schwartz*, it wanted to produce standards that would hold up to legal challenges. The FBI took the arguments used by Scheck and Neufeld—that forensic casework is fundamentally different from diagnostic work—to emphasize that only people within the forensic community could evaluate the scientific techniques. This served to protect the FBI against the challenge of many previously used defense experts.[81]

Heading into 1990, the FBI developed its own network of laboratories and scientists within the forensic science community, which developed techniques that became the standard in the industry. Certain aspects of the FBI's procedures, however, still came under fire, as Scheck and Neufeld took aim in *United States v. Yee et al.*

Yee *and the "DNA Wars"*

On February 27, 1988, David Hartlaub stopped to make a bank deposit from the music store where he worked in Sandusky, Ohio.[82] After parking his van, Hartlaub was attacked by a group of men who shot him, threw his body out of the vehicle, and drove off. The van was later found abandoned with the murder weapon inside. The bank bag containing nearly $4,000 was also left in the van, ruling out robbery as the motive for the crime. Police found three suspects: Steven Wayne Yee, Mark Verdi, and John Ray Bonds, all members of the Hell's Angels motorcycle gang. The investigators posited that the three men had mistaken Hartlaub for a member of the rival Outlaws Motorcycle Club whom they had planned to kill.[83]

A significant amount of blood was found in Hartlaub's van and the backseat of Yee's car. When arrested, Bonds had what appeared to be a severe ricochet injury on his right arm. The FBI performed an analysis on the samples and found that Bonds's DNA profile matched the blood samples from both vehicles. The FBI initially claimed that the probability of a random match was one in 270,000 but later lowered the figure to one in 35,000. With this crucial piece of evidence, both the prosecution and defense prepared for the admissibility hearing, expected to be a "showdown."[84] The importance of the decision was understood; while it would not be binding, it would likely be influential around the country. As one defense lawyer remarked at the time, "The decision . . . will be relied upon by judges all over the United States. I can't imagine any judges doing this twice."[85]

The defense was led by Scheck and Neufeld, who argued that forensic DNA testing was different from other uses of the technology, so the focus must be on the forensic setting as specifically as possible. They critiqued the procedures used by the FBI, which they suggested had not yet been subjected to scientific peer review. Rather than focus only on scientists from the human genetics research community, Scheck and Neufeld sought out scientists who had not been included in the FBI's review process to provide reviews of the procedures. The critiques focused on both the actual testing procedures and the probability calculations. The FBI's own experts responded and, in the end, won: the FBI's techniques were deemed admissible. The district court adopted this finding, saying that the problems presented with the DNA testing procedures were not issues of admissibility but issues of weight for a jury to decide. The defendants were ultimately convicted in 1991 and lost their appeal.[86]

Few judges disagreed with the *Yee* decision, and it had relatively little impact on later admissibility hearings. It did, however, spark debate and controversy in the scientific community. Eric Lander wrote an editorial in the *American Journal of Human Genetics* (*AJHG*) in which he offered a critique of the FBI's procedures that had been allowed in *Yee*.[87] The article was followed by a series of letters to the editor from academics, forensic scientists, lawyers, and corporate executives, all critiquing Lander for his initial article. One prosecutor suggested that he "leave law to the lawyers."[88] Lander was allowed to respond to these letters, and while he suggested that some of the criticisms were unfounded, he offered a reasonable conclusion: "Society needs both voices of advocacy and voices of caution to ensure that new technologies achieve their full potential. We are all on the same side."[89]

The exchange of letters in *AJHG* was significant and far more amicable than the one in *Science*. In a December 1991 issue, *Science* published two articles, one by Richard Lewontin and Daniel Hartl criticizing the common probability statements made regarding forensic DNA matching (such as those made by the FBI in the *Yee* case) and one by Ranajit Chakraborty and Kenneth Kidd suggesting that the methodology was sound and generally accepted.[90] The debate between the two sets of scholars was fierce, but it was the circumstances surrounding the publications that really showed just how contentious things were.

Lewontin and Hartl's article had been accepted by the journal first. When word of the upcoming publication got out, rumors flew that members of the FBI planned to halt publication of the paper. James Wooley, the prosecutor in the *Yee* case, called Hartl and expressed his concerns about the article being published. Lewontin then wrote Wooley, suggesting that it was inappropriate for a state official to try to intimidate a citizen. The editor of *Science*, Daniel Koshland, was aware of the controversy and took another look at the paper. He asked Lewontin for revisions, which upset the original authors. Koshland also solicited the rebuttal from Chakraborty and Kidd.[91]

Accusations were thrown from every direction. The scientists criticized one another, suggesting that philosophical and ideological beliefs were getting in the way of the science. But the lawyers were also involved. Neufeld and Scheck accused numerous scientists and federal law enforcement officials of "meddl[ing] in the peer-review process at leading scientific journals" and suggested that the journal editors were in cahoots with the FBI. They also accused Wooley of unethical behavior.

Wooley's allies fired back, suggesting that the scientists supporting the defense were simply hired guns.[92]

The debate over DNA evidence remained heated as Congress debated the DNA acts of 1991 that addressed the lack of funding and proficiency testing in state labs and the establishment of a national DNA databank. Scheck testified before congressional committees, focusing on the need for blind proficiency testing and suggesting that the FBI would not adequately regulate itself.[93]

The remainder of the debate in Washington involved a National Research Council report with which the FBI and others from the prosecution community were unhappy. A second panel was convened to draft another report, which was not seen until 1996.[94] Much of the argument centered on technical issues that are beyond the scope of this discussion.[95] Suffice it to say that by mid-1993, "almost all of the trial court decisions denying the admissibility of DNA evidence because of the population genetics controversy were overturned at the appellate level,"[96] and DNA profiling was generally considered valid and reliable by the courts. The burden to decide whether particular case results were sound mostly shifted to the jury, due in part to the decision in *Daubert v. Merrell Dow Pharmaceuticals*, in which the Supreme Court made judges the "gatekeepers" of scientific evidence (rather than relying on *Frye's* "general acceptance" standard). In other words, rather than count how many scientists accepted a certain type of scientific evidence, judges would determine whether the evidence was relevant and whether it was reliable enough to be heard by a jury. The post-*Daubert* years saw widespread acceptance of DNA evidence, and although DNA was generally seen as a prosecution tool to establish guilt, two important cases demonstrated its utility for uncovering errors, setting the tone for what later became the innocence movement.

The Dotson Case

On July 9, 1977, Cathleen Crowell was standing on the side of a road in the Chicago suburb of Homewood when a police officer passed by. He noticed her dirty clothes, and the 16-year-old recounted the story of being thrown into a car by three young men and raped as she was leaving work at a local mall. The rapist, she said, had scratched letters into her stomach using a broken beer bottle. Crowell was taken to a nearby hospital, and a rape examination was performed. Clothing containing what was believed to be a seminal stain was collected, along with several pubic hairs and a vaginal swab.

Cromwell worked with police to develop a sketch of the rapist. When shown a book of mug shots, she identified Gary Dotson, who was arrested the next day and identified in a lineup.[97]

Dotson went to trial with two key witnesses against him. The first was Cromwell, and the second was a forensic specialist who claimed that the stain from the victim's underpants came from a type B secretor, which Dotson was. Since only about 10% of the population fits this profile, there was a good chance that Dotson was the source. The specialist also testified that the hairs recovered from the victim were "microscopically similar" to Dotson's; the prosecutor later claimed that they actually matched.[98] The evidence was enough to persuade the jury; Dotson was convicted of rape and aggravated kidnapping and given concurrent sentences of 25 to 50 years.

With the case seemingly closed, the victim moved on. She married (now Cathleen Webb) and moved to New Hampshire. It was not until March 1985—nearly eight years after the initial incident—that Webb expressed her guilt to her pastor. She informed him that she had fabricated the rape allegation as a cover story because she and her boyfriend at the time feared she was pregnant. She contacted a lawyer to represent her, but the Cook County prosecutors wanted little to do with the old case. She eventually went to the press, and the *Chicago Sun-Times* covered the story. The *Chicago Tribune* also provided limited coverage, though it mostly drew on information from the state attorney's office, which tried to discredit the story. Dotson was released on bail the next month, but it was soon revoked.[99] A clemency hearing was forthcoming, and the decision was far from a sure bet, as witness recantations rarely resulted in overturned convictions. Some people in the legal community, while respecting the precedent for not believing recantations, questioned the court's logic in this case, which was different from similar scenarios, since there was neither a threat nor money involved. One prominent Chicago lawyer bluntly stated, "The law has made an ass out of itself and the judge has helped it out, if you want to know the truth."[100]

The national media picked up on the story; a *New York Times* article suggested that the case could have wide ramifications for the criminal justice system: "Confidence in American justice cannot rest easily when [Dotson] is sent back to jail on the word of a woman who is, one way or the other, an acknowledged liar."[101] Webb even said she would stand trial for perjury if it meant Dotson would be freed.[102]

The following weeks were littered with stories in the *Chicago Tribune* that seemed to support the prosecution, but the public continued to support Dotson, circulating several petitions for his release. Judge Richard Samuels, however, believed the recantation to be "implausible"[103] and denied clemency after a three-day hearing that was covered by the international media. In response to his decision, Judge Samuels was the target of public outcry, including death threats. The governor ultimately commuted Dotson's sentence to time served as a matter of "basic justice"[104] and placed him on parole, a move that garnered the governor some praise.[105]

Once released, Dotson made several national television appearances together with Webb, including *Today* and *Good Morning America*, to declare his innocence.[106] The newfound freedom was difficult to manage for Dotson, however, and after struggling with alcoholism, unemployment, a strained marriage, and being a parent, a domestic incident landed him back in prison.[107]

Journalist Civia Tamarkin believed in Dotson's innocence and recruited former assistant state's attorney Thomas Breen to take up the case on his behalf. Breen saw an article in *Newsweek* about the new DNA fingerprinting technology and pursued it on Dotson's behalf. The prosecution was open to DNA testing. The governor's office contacted Sir Alec Jeffreys, who agreed to conduct the test, but the technology at the time could not produce a result because the sample was degraded. But newer tests, pioneered by Berkeley-educated forensic serologist Edward Blake, could work on degraded samples. Rob Warden brought Blake, whom Warden described as "the number-one forensic geneticist in the country," onto the case,[108] and a new test was conducted on the seminal stain and blood samples from Dotson and the victim's old boyfriend, David Bierne.[109]

In August 1988, the test results excluded Dotson as a potential source of the semen. The governor, however, refused to grant clemency before being assured of the test's scientific reliability, though the Prisoner Review Board unanimously recommended a pardon.[110] Nine months later, still with no action, the state attorney's office supported a motion in opposition to a new trial. It did not necessarily believe in Dotson's innocence but that the trial outcome would have been different had the forensic evidence been available at the time.[111] The motion was granted, charges were dropped, and Dotson was finally exonerated ten years after his original conviction.[112]

Gary Dotson's case is usually cited as the first example of an American being exonerated through DNA testing. There were, however, two exonerations that year, and Dotson's was the second of them.

The Vasquez Case

Seven months before Dotson was exonerated, in January 1989, David Vasquez was freed after DNA suggested he had not committed the rape-murder for which he had been imprisoned.[113]

The victim was 32-year-old Carolyn Jean Hamm, a lawyer who was raped, bound, and hanged in her home in Arlington, Virginia, on January 23, 1984. Vasquez, a 38-year-old who was described as "borderline retarded,"[114] was placed in the neighborhood by two eyewitnesses, who described him as "creepy" and "strange."[115] Also found at the scene was a hair fiber that was said to be consistent with Vasquez's.[116] He was arrested and interrogated three times by the police. During the first interrogation, before which he was not advised of his *Miranda* rights, Vasquez gave a shaky statement with facts supplied by the detectives. During the second and third interrogations, he provided a "dream statement," describing the incident as he had envisioned it in his sleep.[117] He was charged with murder, rape, and burglary. Confused, frightened, and threatened with a death sentence, Vasquez entered an *Alford* plea— essentially, a no-contest plea that allows the defendant to maintain his innocence while acknowledging that the prosecution's evidence could still convince a jury to convict—on the day before the trial.[118]

Nearly three years after Vasquez began his prison sentence, another rape-murder occurred in the same neighborhood that bore several similarities to Hamm's. Detectives initially believed it was a co-conspirator of Vasquez's from the Hamm case, but when Vasquez was offered an early release if he would identify such a person, he refused and again asserted his innocence. Investigators soon realized that a series of murders seemed to follow a similar pattern, and they began to think they might have a serial killer on their hands.

After realizing that none of the crimes in question had occurred between 1984 and 1987, the police examined criminal records to identify potential suspects, and one emerged: Timothy Spencer had been imprisoned in 1984 for a burglary and released in September 1987 to a halfway house mere months before the most recent killing. The detectives, aware of the recently developed DNA technology, pursued scientific testing of the evidence. Spencer provided blood samples, which matched the samples from numerous cases. There was not enough evidence from the Hamm case to test, but an FBI report found that the same offender had committed the string of murders.[119] On July 16, 1988, Timothy Spencer was convicted of the most recent murder. He was later convicted and sentenced to death for three additional murders.[120]

Vasquez, meanwhile, had no judicial remedy under Virginia law. The DNA testing, however, had convinced the commonwealth attorney Helen Fahey that Vasquez was not involved in the Hamm murder, and she asked the Virginia governor for a pardon.[121] His application was granted on January 4, 1989, making Vasquez the first exoneration in the United States based on DNA evidence.[122]

Unlike Gary Dotson's case, which received national media attention, the Vasquez exoneration was mostly a local event. Searches of newspaper databases reveal coverage of the Dotson exoneration ranging from local papers to the *New York Times*. The Vasquez case, on the other hand, was covered by one writer for the *Washington Post*, a national newspaper, but essentially a local one for the events.[123] Perhaps because of this, innocence lore sometimes overlooks Vasquez and points clearly to Dotson as the beginning of the DNA-exoneration era.[124]

One potential reason for this assessment is that some people may not consider Vasquez's a DNA exoneration; DNA testing was not actually possible in the murder for which Vasquez was convicted, so it did not directly indicate his innocence. Rob Warden has suggested that this is the case, although one can argue either way.[125] Still, Vasquez is listed by the Innocence Project as a DNA exoneree.[126] Furthermore, there even seems to be some confusion, or at least lack of clarity, within the innocence movement as to which case constitutes the first DNA exoneration. Innocence Project data from mid-2014, for example, listed Dotson first and Vasquez second in exoneration order, yet the dates of exoneration in that same database clearly show Vasquez as being the earlier one.[127]

Despite this lack of clarity, these two cases together mark 1989 as the beginning of the DNA-exoneration era. Several more cases followed in the next few years: Edward Green was exonerated in March 1990, less than a year after being convicted of rape in Washington, D.C.; Centurion Ministries had its first DNA exoneration in the summer of 1991, when Charles Dabbs was cleared for a wrongful rape conviction in New York; and Bruce Nelson was freed a month later after being wrongly convicted of rape and murder in Pennsylvania.

These early DNA exonerations were crucial, and two entrepreneurs immediately recognized their importance. Barry Scheck and Peter Neufeld, having experience with wrongful conviction cases and recognized as legal experts with knowledge of DNA technology, followed the early cases closely.

The Innocence Project

In retrospect, it does not seem surprising that Barry Scheck and Peter Neufeld emerged to pick up the torch and spark the innocence movement. Both had formative experiences that made them ideal candidates to lead such a campaign.

Both had progressive parents who encouraged political activism. Scheck said his father "was always part of a progressive political movement, . . . so I grew up in a household where this tradition of political activism was alive." He described himself as "a child of the 60s," saying he "was pretty active in the civil rights and anti-war movements as a teenager." He went to Yale University, carrying the activist spirit with him and engaging in a number of political activities.[128]

Similarly, Neufeld described his parents as "very inquisitive," getting him and his brother involved in the civil rights movement when they were young; "From a very early age, we always thought about doing public-interest work."[129] Even in his preteen years, Neufeld's parents engaged him in progressive activism, taking him to support the southern freedom schools during the civil rights movement.[130] Like Scheck, Neufeld carried his activist spirit with him when he attended college at the University of Wisconsin. As a student, he was suspended for participating in a demonstration in 1969 involving the Black Student Union and later got in trouble for taking part in an antiwar protest.[131]

In addition to having backgrounds influenced by political activism, by the time the DNA wars came about both Neufeld and Scheck had been exposed to wrongful convictions. The issue entered Neufeld's consciousness in the 1960s, when he was young and engaged in civil rights activism with his parents: "Basically from the time I was ten, I would hear stories about black men being wrongfully convicted, so it was a part of my zeitgeist, or consciousness, in my prepubescent days." In the 1970s, as an attorney in the Bronx, he gained experience working on exoneration cases: "When I was a public defender, 1976 to 1977, I handled cases of people who had been sort of pressured or coerced into pleading guilty to crimes they didn't commit, and I reopened their cases. So I was very much aware of wrongful convictions in that sense years before [Barry Scheck and I] ever did anything."[132]

Scheck's first wrongful conviction case was that of Robert McLaughlin, who had been convicted of taking part in a string of robberies and a murder in Brooklyn in 1979. The police had found the primary suspect and were looking for his supposed associate, Robert W. McLaughlin. Instead, however, they found Robert K. McLaughlin—who went by Bobby—and he was mistakenly picked out of a lineup by a 15-year-old witness. Despite a lack of physical evidence, a statement from a victim who said Bobby was not one of the offenders, and statements from others saying that Bobby had been elsewhere at the time of the crime, he was convicted and sentenced to 15 years to life.

Bobby McLaughlin's foster father convinced prominent civil rights attorney Richard Emery to take up the case. Emery and Scheck mounted a media campaign with help from Jack Newfield, "a crusading journalist with the *Village Voice* when it was an extremely influential paper," and John Miller of the local NBC News affiliate. They uncovered the mistaken identification and eventually secured McLaughlin's freedom in 1986.[133] The case was "a formative experience" for Scheck, who gained experience wrestling with the postconviction issues involved in securing exonerations but also expanded his knowledge of the social scientific research on eyewitness errors and gained a greater understanding of "the power of the press."[134]

Thus, it was only natural that when Marion Coakley's case came around, Scheck and Neufeld—who had been close friends since they worked together at the Bronx Legal Aid office—would work the case together. As noted earlier, they were unable to secure Coakley's exoneration through DNA testing but freed him using more traditional evidence. Regardless of the means, the Coakley case was the first exoneration that Scheck and Neufeld secured together.[135] Equally important, it was their first real introduction to DNA technology. It made sense, then, that they recognized the potential of DNA and engaged in the legal battles over its use.

Although Neufeld and Scheck were on the side challenging the scientific evidence throughout the *Castro* case and the DNA wars, they did so not out of an aversion to the technology but because they, along with other lawyers and scientists involved, recognized its potential: "In terms of how the innocence movement, through at least our work, began to form, there was a focus at the very beginning on . . . the power of DNA technology. And we knew from the very beginning the power of this technology, not just to exonerate the innocent but to identify those who had committed crimes, and that would really begin to expose all these other causes of wrongful convictions. We really did understand that potential of it from the very beginning."[136] Their founding of the Innocence Project, then, was not a spontaneous moment of genius but a logical progression from the work they had been doing for years. What they realized by the late 1980s, "about the same time that the FBI opened up the first major DNA laboratory in the country to handle criminal cases, is that this is a much more robust technology than what they've been using for the last 30 years." They already believed that some types of evidence, such as eyewitness identifications, might not be reliable and that this technology would allow them to go back and examine old cases. While they had technical issues with the ways in which DNA was being handled, they never questioned its utility for exonerating innocents who had been wrongly convicted. Scheck even discussed this point during his testimony to Congress about the DNA acts of 1991 when he pointed out that, just as DNA was a powerful investigatory tool that could be used to secure convictions, it could also be useful in freeing the innocent; it was "an amazing tool to revisit old cases where people had been dragged out of the courtroom screaming, 'I'm innocent! I'm innocent! I'm innocent!'"[137]

Scheck and Neufeld were taking potential innocence cases on an ad hoc basis and had some early successes, and as word of their exploits spread, the letters piled up:

I think we were, even before [the Innocence Project] was formed in '92, already thinking about doing a lot more with these cases. And to do a lot more with these cases, we would need an infrastructure, because up until then, we were basically doing things out of our hip pocket, and that's not a great way to do something. Also, we all had other responsibilities and couldn't do it that way. And so, frankly, when we first started thinking about the problems in DNA yet the advantages of DNA, to reopen old cases, you immediately understood that this was not going to be anecdotal like it had been in the '70s or '80s [but] that this was going to be something actually very substantial numerically, with much greater potential. And as soon as we realized that, which was in '89 or thereabouts, we realized we had to develop an institution.[138]

So, in 1992, Scheck and Neufeld officially founded the Innocence Project as a clinical program at Cardozo Law School, creating an organized, systematic way to investigate old cases and use DNA to exonerate prisoners when possible. At first, the organization was a small outfit, and the massive number of incoming letters from prisoners was overwhelming. The staff was just four people "processing thousands of letters." Neufeld added, with a laugh, that they were just "trying to hold the whole thing together with bubble gum and aluminum foil."[139]

Today, when people want to establish an innocence organization, they often follow the Innocence Project's model; in 1992, however, no such model existed. Centurion Ministries was the only organization dedicated to wrongful conviction cases, and Neufeld says he and Scheck were "totally aware" of what Centurion was doing.[140] Scheck, in fact, had reached out to Centurion to introduce himself and explain that he and Neufeld were interested in DNA, had been working on some cases, and might be interested in working with Centurion if it needed lawyers. Indeed, Scheck and Neufeld did work with Centurion on several early cases together, including the case of Edward Honaker.[141] When the Innocence Project was being formed, Kate Germond from Centurion shared its processes and practices with Scheck and Neufeld: "I spent a lot of time with Barry and Peter in the early days. I went up to New York a whole bunch and gave them everything about how we did it, the letters we sent out, why I did, where I looked for evidence . . . total open book. I was very excited about it."[142]

Working with Germond and Centurion, which had already been a formal organization for nearly a decade, must certainly have been helpful for the formation of the Innocence Project, but the two organizations looked quite different. Centurion focused solely on casework, reinvestigating cases and exonerating individuals. From the start, the Innocence Project had broader goals; Neufeld and Scheck had a vision for reform that stretched beyond their cases. From the outset, they decided to focus only on DNA cases, hired a staff attorney, and "began slowly but surely building out the Innocence Project and the use of DNA testing."[143]

The decision to focus only on DNA cases was a strategic one made, at least in part, on the basis of a long-term aspiration to become involved in policy reform: "If you want to do policy and not just do the exonerations," Neufeld said, "you want cases that are simply non-controversial, where everybody agrees—prosecutors, judges, the defense—that these people are stone-cold innocent." Neufeld spoke of the importance of establishing a "data set" to influence policy, specifically, a data set of indisputable cases:

> One of the things I remembered going back into the '80s was that a lot of people felt like, there in New Jersey, that Rubin "Hurricane" Carter—although as far as I was concerned he was innocent, and my reading of all the material was that he was clearly exonerated—there were tons of people in New Jersey who thought he was guilty. And one of the reasons you could have that kind of debate was because you didn't have irrefutable evidence of innocence, scientifically irrefutable. So, beginning in '89, with the first DNA exoneration, and then proceeding into our emphasis on DNA exonerations, our focus, you then would be able to build up a group of cases. So you had data, a group of powerful narratives, which is how things really change—people love a powerful story—all of which involve cases where there was no doubt that the person was innocent. And also, using DNA meant you could very quickly get a whole bunch of cases where there was no doubt that people were innocent. And so that gave us

the ability then to think about reform and change that we couldn't think about with whether it was Barry getting involved with Bobby's case or me doing those cases in the public defender office in '76, '77.[144]

The data set of DNA cases developed substantially in the first few years of the Innocence Project's existence. Scheck and Neufeld had a number of early successes, including the exoneration in late 1992 of Kerry Kotler, who had been convicted of rape 11 years earlier. The Kotler case received some media attention, including coverage in the *New York Times*.[145] But perhaps the most important DNA exoneration of this era involved a Maryland man, a former marine convicted and sentenced to die for a most brutal crime.

DNA Meets the Death Penalty

The morning of Wednesday, July 25, 1983, was a pleasant one in eastern Maryland. Thomas Hamilton kissed his daughter, nine-year-old Dawn, goodbye before heading out for work shortly after six o'clock. They were staying with friends, Gary and Elinor Helmick, and their two children, Gary and Lisa, at their apartment in Rosedale.[146]

That morning, Elinor was not only watching her two children and Dawn but also looking after her niece, Missy, and nephew, John-John. She sent them outside to play but was soon informed that Lisa and John-John had gone into the woods, which were off-limits. Elinor asked Missy and Dawn to call them back into the house. Missy, Lisa, and John-John soon returned without Dawn.

Dawn had gone to nearby Bethke Pond and saw two boys she knew, Christian and Jackie. While there, a man approached her and asked what she was doing. After she told him she was looking for her friend Lisa, she went with the man into the woods. According to one report, the man said that he and Lisa were playing hide-and-seek and that Dawn could play with them; another suggested the man just offered to help Dawn search.

Elinor went looking for Dawn. When Christian and Jackie informed her that Dawn had gone into the woods with a man—described as an approximately 30-year-old white man with blond hair and a mustache—she became worried. Unsuccessful in her search, Elinor soon called the police. Within hours, more than 100 police officers were searching for the missing girl. Shortly after finding Dawn's shorts and underwear hanging from a tree, her body was found lying face down, her head bloodied by a rock and with a stick penetrating her vagina.

The boys from the pond, Christian and Jackie, just ten and seven years old, respectively, were questioned by police and asked to construct a composite sketch. Christian went first and, though he was uncertain about a number of the man's features, put together a sketch. Jackie gave a different description of the man but was unsure of his features and ultimately agreed with Christian's composite.

The crime was front-page news in the local papers and sparked a manhunt. Tips poured in, theories were developed, and leads were followed, but none stuck. On July 28, an anonymous caller said that the composite looked similar to a local man named Kirk Bloodsworth. When police followed up, they found that Bloodsworth had left work, and his wife, Wanda, had filed a missing-person report. Wanda confirmed that Kirk had left town on August 3 and had been sick for a few days before leaving.[147]

Police found Kirk in Cambridge, Maryland, where he had been staying with friends. Christian identified Bloodsworth in a lineup—though the boy did not remember the man having red hair like Kirk's—but Jackie failed to identify a suspect. Nonetheless, Kirk was arrested two weeks after the murder.[148] He never confessed to the crime, though he was duped into mentioning the murder weapon.[149]

Over the course of the investigation, police found five witnesses who claimed to have seen Bloodsworth either with the victim or near the crime scene. There was also a pair of shoes that the prosecution said could have belonged to Kirk, and an expert testified that marks on the victim's body may have come from them. Prosecutors also emphasized Bloodsworth's comments that he had "done something terrible"[150] and his mention of the murder weapon in building their case against him.

Despite a number of alibi witnesses who testified that Kirk was at home or with other people on the day of the murder,[151] he was convicted on March 8, 1985, and sentenced to death. The conviction was overturned the next year by the Maryland Court of Appeals when it found that the prosecution had failed to tell the defense that there were other suspects.[152] Bloodsworth was retried and convicted again, this time sentenced to two life terms.

Kirk maintained his innocence from the outset. After the 1988 appellate decision affirming his conviction, the case was taken over by Robert Morin, who in 1992 requested that all key evidence be reexamined.[153] Forensic Science Associates, a California-based lab, discovered a small spot of previously undetected semen on Dawn's underwear.[154] The prosecution signed a letter to the defense saying that it would "agree to [Bloodsworth's] release" if a laboratory ever "determines with scientific certainty" that any sperm found did not come from him and it was able to confirm the results.[155]

On the day before Thanksgiving in 1992, Morin received a call to inform him that the sample had been tested and Bloodsworth was excluded. He told Kirk on Thanksgiving Day. The FBI confirmed the results, and prosecutors joined the defense in asking for charges to be dropped. Bloodsworth was released on June 28, 1993, after a five-minute hearing,[156] and in December, he was given a full pardon by Maryland governor William Donald Schaefer.[157]

Bloodsworth was the first person in the United States to be exonerated through DNA evidence after being sentenced to death, and his case made national headlines. At a time when the death penalty was increasing in use—there were more executions in 1992 and 1993 than in any years since the practice was reinstated in 1976[158]—the fact that it had been proven, with near certainty, that a man had been wrongly sent to death row was a monumental occurrence. Bloodsworth, however, was just one of the individuals who had been wrongly sent to death.

Innocence and the Death Penalty

Richard Dieter was finishing up law school when the perfect opportunity came along. Michael Kroll was stepping down as executive director of the Death Penalty Information Center (DPIC), an organization founded in 1990 to provide information and analysis on a variety of issues surrounding capital punishment, and the organization was looking for someone to fill his position. Dieter was looking for a job and "welcomed . . . being able to work full-time on the death penalty right out of law school, which isn't always possible."[159] He became the director of DPIC in 1992.

Initially, innocence was on DPIC's radar only in a roundabout way: "We were looking at problems with the death penalty, and obviously this problem is, like, poor counsel or racial bias might lead to a wrong person being convicted," Dieter said; but it was still the early days of DNA exonerations, and "it wasn't clear that we would focus on innocence, . . . but we were open to such things."[160]

Shortly after Dieter became director of DPIC, the organization received a request from the House Judiciary Committee's Subcommittee on Civil and Constitutional Rights. Earlier that year, the subcommittee had heard testimony from death row exonerees and wanted to know more. The chairman of the subcommittee, Don Edwards, called DPIC and asked it to prepare a report on the risks of executing the innocent. The report suggests that the subcommittee asked DPIC to "compile information on cases in the past 20 years where inmates had been released from death row after their innocence had been acknowledged,"[161] though Dieter told me that the organization had leeway in preparing the report and was responsible for making decisions about how to do so.

DPIC agreed to prepare the report and began compiling a list of those who had been freed from death row who otherwise may have been executed. In addition to a simple list, it explained how these errors occurred. It drew on news reports and files from the National Coalition to Abolish the Death Penalty, as well as the work of Bedau and Radelet, who had extended their earlier work and just published a book on the topic, *In Spite of Innocence*.[162] DPIC decided, however, to place stricter limits on its cases than Bedau and Radelet had done. First, it chose to start its list at 1973, which although "somewhat arbitrary" was "a good year to start." It also placed stricter limits on who would be included on its list. Bedau and Radelet had included a number of cases in which they believed an innocent person had actually been executed, but Dieter said DPIC "decided not to get into that. It's a little hard to say who has been executed with definitive proof. But you could, with objective analysis, say how many people had received a death sentence and then were freed, all charges dropped, or were acquitted at trial." This also marks a major departure from Bedau and Radelet, who had personally determined the probability of innocence; DPIC tried to remove this element of subjectivity: "We decided to make it a little tighter criteria for who would be on the list. We wouldn't make any subjective judgments about innocence, but rather we would say, if a person had all charges removed for the crime that sent them to death row, then . . . their innocence would be restored. Their presumption of innocence would be restored. They would be exonerated. Despite having had a conviction, it was a wrongful conviction."[163] DPIC had gathered more than 40 cases in which DNA was used to clear someone who had been convicted and sentenced to death. Kirk Bloodsworth was exonerated as DPIC was preparing its report. Incidentally, Kirk's attorney, Robert Morin, had been a professor of Richard Dieter's in law school. Morin was aware of what Dieter was doing with DPIC and asked him to help get some publicity for Bloodsworth's exoneration, to which Dieter agreed: "I said, 'Sure.' So [we] helped put out a press release, and there was a lot of media at the actual release, pictures of him, and, you know, he's a gregarious person, and some of the news radio stations in Baltimore had supported him. . . . So it was kind of an event when he got released, and it blossomed into a huge media event. I mean, he traveled the whole circuit, national TV, and it continues, actually, to this day."[164] Bloodsworth, whose exoneration "triggered . . . a whole other way of looking at this issue through science," made DPIC's final report, along with three other 1993 exonerees. DPIC had 48 cases in its final report, *Innocence and the Death Penalty: Assessing the Danger of Mistaken Executions*. The House subcommittee released the document as a staff report on October 21, 1993, and DPIC released it on its own to the media and the public.

According to Dieter, the report "got a very big reaction."[165] This was due, in part, to its timing. In January of that year, the United States Supreme Court decided *Herrera v. Collins*, which addressed the issue of innocence and the death penalty. Lionel Herrera, who had been convicted and sentenced to death for a 1982 murder in Texas, claimed that he was actually innocent and thus his execution would violate the Eighth and Fourteenth Amendments. While the Court did not expressly say that the Constitution permits executing the innocent, it ruled that without evidence of other constitutional violations, new evidence of innocence is not grounds for a new trial.[166]

Herrera gave increased attention to the issue of wrongful convictions and the death penalty, which "suddenly was on a lot of people's minds."

Thus, Kirk Bloodsworth's exoneration came at a time when people were thinking and talking about innocence and capital punishment, and DPIC's report added significant weight to the conversation. "I think just having a list," Dieter said, "having something concrete, having names and faces of people, really crystallized the issue."[167]

DPIC did not just release its report and move on; it has maintained a list of death row exonerations since, a popular aspect of the organization's work, though Dieter points out that it was not a great scheme or plan: "We've kept the list . . . since then. And we never intended to have a list, but it's one of our signature things that we keep monitoring when people are freed and have followed that issue closely ever since."[168] DPIC's list has been an important resource for both innocence and anti-death penalty advocates; as Samuel Gross pointed out, at that time in the 1990s, nobody had assembled, organized, and maintained information about exonerations.[169] DPIC has produced follow-up reports, which remain popular. "We've done a number of other innocence reports since [the 1992 one]," Dieter said, "and each time the innocence issue captures the public's and the media's attention more than some other issues here."[170] DPIC's reports and list became widely cited, and the organization became the key source for information regarding wrongful capital convictions.[171]

The importance of events like Kirk Bloodsworth's exoneration and DPIC's report to the history of the innocence movement is immense. As Jim McCloskey put it, quite simply, "Guys like Kirk have had quite an impact."[172] In fact, the DNA exonerations from death row in the mid-1990s even prompted Supreme Court Justice John Paul Stevens to take notice, as he said that reliable evidence "has made it possible to establish conclusively that a disturbing number of persons who had been sentenced to death were actually innocent" and that those errors "raise the question whether either the deterrent value of the death penalty or its therapeutic effect on the community outraged by a vicious crime justifies its continued popular support."[173]

It was not just death penalty exonerations, however. By the mid-1990s, Bloodsworth was joined by more than two dozen others on the growing list of DNA exonerees, mostly from non-capital cases, as the technology was generally accepted as valid and reliable and was being used on a consistent basis. DNA was, in short, part of the legal landscape, but it had not yet become the public phenomenon it is today. That began to happen with the sensational media coverage of the O. J. Simpson murder trial, in which DNA grabbed the public eye.

DNA in the Spotlight

On June 12, 1994, Nicole Brown Simpson and Ronald Goldman were found dead outside Brown's townhome near Los Angeles, California. They had been stabbed, and police found a significant amount of forensic evidence: blood on a hat and a single leather glove, bloody shoe prints, and several drops of blood away from where the bodies were found. Brown's ex-husband, former football star O. J. Simpson, was not in town, having left for Chicago on the night of the murders. The detectives, however, found blood on the door of Simpson's car, a white Ford Bronco. Police entered Simpson's property without a warrant, finding blood on the walkway and in the foyer of his house. They used this evidence to obtain a warrant and searched Simpson's home. The only evidence seized was a pair of socks from Simpson's bedroom; at the time, there was no mention of blood, though weeks later, the Los Angeles Police Department (LAPD) crime lab reported that a thick blood stain on the socks matched the profile of Simpson's ex-wife, Nicole. Simpson was notified and flew home from Chicago immediately.

Upon questioning Simpson, police noticed he had a cut on his left hand. An LAPD nurse drew a blood sample from Simpson, which was turned over to detectives. The sample was not entered into evidence until later in the day, and the LAPD seemed unable to account for the entire sample: the nurse claimed to have drawn eight cubic centimeters of blood, but only six and a half cubic centimeters were accounted for. This became a source of fierce dispute, the defense claiming that the missing amount was used to manufacture evidence against Simpson, the prosecution arguing that it was simply a measurement or memory error on the part of the nurse.[174]

Simpson prepared for the ensuing trial by hiring a "Dream Team" of defense lawyers. Scheck and Neufeld initially became involved as consultants to assist and advise the defense team about the technicalities of the DNA evidence. "We had no intention of ever doing anything with the trial," Scheck once said. "We were just telling them, 'This is what it means. These are the potential problems.' And then slowly but surely, in a very strange, inexorable way, we got drawn in as lawyers in the case."[175]

The trial began in early 1995 and was followed incessantly by the media and general public. Although there was some criticism of Cellmark, which performed the DNA tests, much of the discussion regarding the evidence was about the way in which it was handled by police.[176] In the end, the defense was able to cast enough doubt to convince the jury to acquit, and the verdict led to an uproarious, divided reaction among the public.[177]

In retrospect, images from the O. J. Simpson case often come first to mind when thinking about DNA in the criminal justice system. As Jay Aronson has written, "visions of white Ford Broncos, bloody gloves that don't fit, and footprints from 'ugly-ass' Bruno Maglia shoes dominate our perceptions," but the debate over DNA technology was largely over by that point.[178] Still, several things emerged from the O. J. Simpson trial that are relevant for the innocence movement.

First, while the people involved in the case reaffirmed their belief in the power and potential of DNA testing, the case also emphasized, as Neufeld has pointed out, the healthy dose of skepticism and caution needed when working with the technology:

> One legacy of the Simpson case with respect to DNA typing is it highlights, on the one hand, the tremendous potential of this technology, that it is a science that can be equivalent of the videotape of the commission of the crime. Yet, on the other hand, . . . we're talking about applied science, . . . and whenever people get involved in the application of science, [there] is much opportunity for mistake, error, and for much worse. And so we have to be very rigorous in the kinds [of] controls that we exert when we utilize this tremendously powerful new technology to make sure that it's used wisely and cautiously.[179]

Scheck seconded this notion, suggesting that the case influenced crime labs to be more diligent in doing a sound job with the technology, wanting to be certified and accredited.[180] As he said, "They were using 19th-century evidence-collection techniques for 21st-century technology, which had more than the potential but the reality of producing contaminated results." But the attack angle taken in the Simpson case "actually changed forensic science in a very profound way, because everybody understood that if you're going to get anything out of DNA testing, you have to collect the evidence correctly [and] you have to make sure that the labs are handling it correctly so that you don't screw up these results."[181] Scheck even worked with some of the defense's opponents from the case, including Woody Clark, to later issue guidelines to help law enforcement learn what to do and what not to do with DNA evidence—in short, "to learn the lessons from the Simpson case."[182]

A second impact of the O. J. Simpson case was on the public's view of DNA. While some people outside the legal and scientific communities may already have been aware of DNA and its potential power in criminal justice, the Simpson case planted it firmly in the public consciousness. It was, in fact, impossible to avoid: the term "DNA" was used more than 10,000 times throughout the trial,[183] and well over 100 articles appeared in the *New York Times* alone discussing DNA in conjunction with the case between June 1994 and October 1995.[184]

Finally, although Scheck and Neufeld were already well-known within the legal and scientific communities, their involvement in the O. J. Simpson case provided a new level of publicity, which was both a blessing and a curse.[185] There is no doubt that their participation in the O. J. Simpson case increased their public exposure and cemented their reputations as all-star advocates and high-power legal experts, but it also brought with it some questions, given that their innocence work was growing. "Having long argued that DNA is reliable enough to free convicted rapists," one *Washington Post* article asked during the trial, "can they now credibly argue that DNA evidence should not be admitted against O. J. Simpson? Experts will follow their reasoning, but the public may merely hear that the defense duo is 'attacking' the evidence, but not understand why or how."[186] Others more blatantly accused Scheck and Neufeld of hypocrisy; how could they on the one hand use DNA as a powerful tool for exoneration yet try to obstruct its use by the prosecution on the other? These accusations were accompanied by claims that they had "sold their public-interest souls for fame," abandoning what was important to them in order to assist a wealthy client.[187] For their part, Scheck and Neufeld have claimed that their principles had not changed but that it was important to ensure that the use of DNA by authorities remained honest; indeed, they did not attack the technology itself but its handling. They were, after all, believers in DNA. Furthermore, they had always maintained that the certainty behind an exclusion—showing that someone did not match—was higher than that of an inclusion.

For some observers, Scheck's and Neufeld's involvement in the O. J. Simpson case might be seen as their defining professional moment, and there was some concern that it might have a negative impact on the innocence work. As one reporter noted, "Here and there, people who've worked with Scheck and Neufeld on DNA issues worry about the impact of the Simpson trial."[188] Similarly, one interviewee remarked to me that Scheck was at least somewhat concerned that "their involvement in that case might have hurt the [innocence] movement,"[189] though this did not come to pass. By the end of the Simpson trial, the debates over whether DNA profiling was a reliable and accepted science were mostly over. Now, the public was aware of the technology, and it had been used to develop a significant database of known wrongful convictions. By mid-1995, there had been nearly 30 DNA exonerations, and innocence was gaining momentum.

Convicted by Juries, Exonerated by Science

The string of DNA exonerations in the early 1990s captured the attention of the United States attorney general, Janet Reno, a position she had come to almost by chance in 1993. President Bill Clinton had first nominated corporate lawyer Zoe Baird, but she withdrew after admitting that she had hired illegal immigrants and had not paid their Social Security taxes. Clinton then looked toward district court judge Kimba Wood, who backed out before being officially nominated for reasons similar to Baird's.[190] Unsure of where to turn and desiring to appoint the nation's first female attorney general, Clinton's attention shifted to Reno, of whom he knew because his brother-in-law, Hugh Rodham, was a public defender in the drug court that Reno had helped establish.[191]

Reno had been the state's attorney in Miami since 1978, the first female state's attorney in Florida's history. Her reputation was that of "a straight-shooting and tough law-enforcement advocate"[192] whom Clinton described as "'a front-line crime fighter' of 'unquestioned integrity.'"[193] Reno showed a commitment to justice during her time as a prosecutor, making "a career of going after crooked police officers, judges, and other public officials," and was "aggressive in controversial civil-rights cases."[194] She was best known for her prosecution of William Lozano, a police officer who had killed two black motorists in 1989, a crime that sparked riots in Miami.[195]

Reno's time as a state's attorney also included her involvement in an exoneration. James Richardson was convicted of murder in 1968 after his seven children died from eating food poisoned with a powerful insecticide. Richardson was sentenced to death but was spared the electric chair when the Supreme Court placed a moratorium on capital punishment in the 1972 case *Furman v. Georgia*.[196] After evidence surfaced of Richardson's innocence, Florida governor Bob Martinez appointed Reno as special prosecutor to examine the case, which soon made national news.[197] After several months of review, Reno concluded that Richardson had been the victim of a miscarriage of justice. His conviction and sentence were vacated on April 25, 1989, and he was granted a new trial. He was not retried. Reno suggested that the state did not even have enough valid evidence to charge Richardson. She filed a memorandum saying, "James Richardson was probably wrongfully accused"[198] and on May 5 announced the dismissal of the case.[199]

It may just be serendipity that someone who thought about criminal justice in such a progressive fashion, someone so dedicated to the pursuit of justice, was serving as the United States attorney general at the beginning of the DNA-exoneration era, but given her background and experiences, it is not surprising that wrongful convictions caught her attention. Reno made a phone call to the director of the National Institute of Justice, Jeremy Travis. She was intrigued by the idea that there was now a way to scientifically assess whether a convicted person was actually guilty of the crime and wondered how many cases there were in which DNA had been used to uncover an error, so Travis and a team of researchers began exploring the topic.

Travis and his team began by searching newspapers. Travis also reached out to Barry Scheck to see what cases he had on file. By early 1996, they found 28 cases in which people had been exonerated through DNA testing. In a June 1996 report, *Convicted by Juries, Exonerated by Science*,[200] the authors described the cases and some basic patterns they found: the types of crimes, time served, the types of evidence presented, and so forth.[201] The study also included a brief survey of DNA laboratories, asking them how many cases they handled and how often suspects were excluded.

The study's findings are interesting on their own, but it is perhaps the next section, covering the policy implications of the cases, that is most important. The chapter describes "the need in the legal system for improved criteria for evaluating the reliability of eyewitness identifications," drawing on the work and words of psychologist Elizabeth Loftus, who had long been critical of eyewitness evidence.[202] Several pages are also dedicated to forensic evidence, including the reliability of non-DNA evidence, the competency of the labs that carry out the testing, the preservation of evidence, the training of attorneys on the forensic uses of DNA testing, and the complications that come with using DNA in criminal cases. This policy discussion was significant; Marvin Zalman suggests that the report "was obviously designed to be as much a popular policy tract as a scholarly study."[203] The policy discussion was indeed by design. When Reno had first requested to Travis that NIJ study this issue, her request "was not just to get a number, but she was—this says a lot about her—she was always interested in, what can we learn about the system by reviewing the cases of individuals who had been exonerated? In essence, what went wrong?"[204]

In addition to analyzing and presenting the cases and describing what went wrong, the report was also "positioned . . . as a discussion document." The report brought together key minds from inside and outside the system, individuals who were known in their respective fields, to comment on the cases and offer their perspectives. Nearly one-fifth of the document is made up of commentaries from various people who were not involved in the actual study, including several professors, prosecutors, a judge, and a police chief. The issues covered in these commentaries vary but include, among others, the admissibility rules governing the introduction of forensic evidence in court, expert witnesses, collection and preservation of evidence, and training to ensure that forensic evidence is handled properly. This was important for Travis and his team; as the research entity of the Justice Department, it was their job "to use their research to promote better policy formation," and they wanted to spark discussion to that end.[205]

Perhaps the most significant commentary was that offered by Neufeld and Scheck. In four carefully worded pages, they discussed the systemic nature of wrongful convictions and the need for change. They painted a picture in which wrongful convictions are a fairly widespread problem, describing the 28 cases in the report as "just the tip of a very deep and disturbing iceberg" and citing data from the FBI's DNA testing that suggests an extraordinarily high exclusion rate.[206] These known cases imply that the error rate in criminal justice is "much greater than anyone wants to believe."[207]

As Neufeld and Scheck had done since founding the Innocence Project, they emphasized the incredible opportunity that DNA provides to reexamine cases and to learn about the flaws in the criminal justice system. They mentioned that the factors found to contribute to the wrongful convictions in the report's cases "do not seem strikingly different" from those found by Edwin Borchard more than 60 years earlier, suggesting that the time had come to finally implement reforms to prevent such errors from occurring. "Are there systemic weaknesses that can be identified in DNA laboratory tests (hair, fiber, etc.), police interrogation techniques, or other investigatory methods used by police and prosecutors that are conducive to false or true arrests and convictions?" they asked. "Perhaps there has never been a richer or more exciting set of cases for criminal justice researchers to explore in terms of shedding light on how law enforcement methods impact the crucial problem of factual innocence."[208] They were also careful, somewhat defensive even, in saying that, while it is absolutely possible for laboratory error to lead to incorrect results in both inclusion and exclusion cases, the DNA testing in exoneration cases is done in such a way as to minimize the risk of this occurring.

While the National Institute of Justice report received fairly little coverage in the general press, it did receive its fair share of attention among criminal justice practitioners.[209] The report represents an agency of the federal government recognizing wrongful conviction as an issue worthy of attention; for the first time, errors were viewed on a national level as a problem, and a call for reform was made. Zalman suggests that Neufeld and Scheck's commentary "can be viewed as the most public, and perhaps the first clarion call, of an innocence paradigm manifesto,"[210] but this is true of the entire document, not just their commentary. Throughout the various commentaries and the chapter on policy implications, a number of issues are raised that became staples in the innocence reform agenda. *Convicted by Juries, Exonerated by Science* thus stands as an important component of the innocence developments in the 1990s; as the Innocence Project's current executive director, Maddy deLone, put it, "it was a moment,"[211] and it came as part of the larger development of DNA as a tool for justice.

* * *

The importance of DNA to the innocence movement cannot be overstated. The development of DNA profiling and its use in the legal system was not the result of a simple process. The way in which it developed—from its discovery and use in Great Britain to its initial use in the United States as a powerful tool to solve crimes, through the legal battles over its validity, reliability, and admissibility—provide important context for understanding the innocence movement. After all, Barry Scheck and Peter Neufeld, who became leaders of the movement, developed their scientific knowledge base during this period. As Scheck once recounted, "We got involved at the ground floor with the leading scientists, trying to think through how to use this technology correctly, how to develop standards for it, how to think about civil liberties implications of its use. That was a great place to be. We got in on the ground floor of the application of this technology with the criminal justice system. I didn't know anything about DNA, neither did Peter, and we got educated by the best teachers in the world in the context of litigation. It's extraordinary."[212] From the outset, Scheck and Neufeld saw that DNA evidence had unique and powerful potential for reevaluating convictions and made it their focus. If innocence work had first become a nonprofit industry with the work of Centurion Ministries, its first major step toward becoming a movement for broader change happened with the Innocence Project.

This period from the first DNA exonerations in 1989 to the National Institute of Justice report in 1996—the beginning of the DNA-exoneration era—is one of the most important formative periods for the innocence movement. As noted earlier, 1989 is often considered the beginning of the movement, and it is easy to understand why. These developments mark the penetration of DNA into the legal and criminal justice world as a tool not only for capturing the guilty but also for exonerating the innocent. In short, innocence was beginning to enter the spotlight.

What existed at that point, however, was certainly not what anyone would call a "movement"; a handful of successful cases, a small circle of supporters and crusaders, and two organizations with disparate goals and aspirations would hardly satisfy any definition of a movement. But over the next decade, a series of events led to an expansion of the advocacy network, greater attention on wrongful convictions, the formulation of an agenda, and ultimately, the emergence of the modern innocence movement.

3

"We're All Together on This"

Expanding the Network, Becoming a Movement

By the mid-1990s, the pieces were falling into place: the future leaders of the movement had developed an organizational model, DNA was an established part of the legal system, and wrongful convictions were becoming recognized as an important criminal justice issue. What existed at that point, however, could hardly be considered a movement. As Peter Neufeld said about the early innocence work, "They're just cases . . . helping people, but they're not part of—they're not even the beginning of a movement. And frankly, there wasn't a movement in the '80s."[1]

Given that the Innocence Project has been at the center of the innocence movement, we might expect to find that the early movement was based out of New York. However, it was in Chicago—a historical rival to New York whose "Windy City" nickname is often attributed to a popular (but false) myth that traces it back to derogatory remarks made about the city by New York editor Charles Dana[2]—that the innocence movement found some of its closest and most important allies. A series of events in Chicago during the late 1990s and early 2000s led to popular widespread attention on wrongful convictions and, ultimately, the development of the advocacy network that became the modern innocence movement.

Capital Punishment Takes Center Stage

After the Death Penalty Information Center released its 1993 report, a number of high-profile exonerations generated widespread attention on issues about wrongful convictions and the death penalty. The next several DNA exonerations from death row came out of Illinois. In 1995, Rolando Cruz and Alejandro Hernandez were exonerated after spending ten years in prison for murder.[3] The next year, Verneal Jimerson and Dennis Williams, two of the four men wrongly convicted in the infamous Ford Heights Four murder case, were exonerated through DNA.[4] These cases received attention nationwide and added fuel to the conversation about innocence and the death penalty.[5] In Illinois, at least, wrongful convictions, or more precisely, exonerations, and the death penalty became "inextricably linked."[6]

Rob Warden immediately recognized the importance of the relationship between exonerations and the anti–death penalty movement. In addition to Kirk Bloodsworth, Cruz-Hernandez, and the Ford Heights Four, he mentioned the earlier case of Clarence Brandley, a Texas death row exoneree whose case had been investigated by Centurion Ministries,[7] and the work of Bedau and Radelet as important milestones. Together, this collection of exoneration cases "gave . . . a great new salience to this issue."[8]

Warden also recognized the importance of keeping the innocence lens focused on the death penalty, as it tends to be a powerful lens through which many people view criminal justice generally: "When I started looking at this, I thought, we need to keep . . . the focus on the death penalty cases," Warden said. "It's important because that is what really, you know, people glob onto that. It fascinates people." With this recognition and a desire to make some headway on abolishing the death penalty in Illinois, Warden helped set in motion an event that was one of the most significant for the innocence movement.

"An Extraordinary Gathering"

Rob Warden was working as a consultant for the MacArthur Justice Center, which at the time was at the University of Chicago. Illinois had nine death row exonerees by the end of 1996, and Warden had an idea.

When the Chicago Bears had won Super Bowl XX after the 1985–1986 season, there was a poster produced featuring nine Bears players in fedoras and dark sunglasses, with a caption that read, "The Black and Blues Brothers." Being in Chicago, Warden was inspired to get Illinois's nine death row exonerees together for a similar picture. The exonerees were scattered around the country, and getting them together proved difficult; so Warden sent a photographer to take individual photos. They ended up with a poster that read, "Nine Reasons to Abolish the Death Penalty."[9]

While working on the poster, Warden got a call from Lawrence Marshall, a law professor at Northwestern University, who invited Warden and Locke Bowman, the legal director of the MacArthur Justice Center, to breakfast. Marshall had an idea to hold a conference featuring those who had been exonerated from death row across the country. Warden expressed his concern about the difficulties of getting them all together—he recalls that there had been about 74 death row exonerees at the time—given the struggles he had recently faced with his poster. Marshall, however, pushed on: "He said, 'Well, we don't need to get 'em all. We just need to get some respectable number,'" Warden said. "And, yeah, we sort of saw the wisdom in that, and we decided to cooperate with him."[10]

Warden and Marshall "began to work fairly closely" in putting the conference together.[11] The goal of the conference was to bring great attention to flaws in the capital punishment system and generate discussion and, ultimately, reform. Marshall was sure to point out, however, that reform did not necessarily mean abolition. As he told a journalist at the time, "There are a lot of areas where we can make significant changes that would not destroy the death penalty but would improve it by making it far less error-prone, far less arbitrary, far less racist and far less classist."[12] The hope was that it would prompt changes to practices regarding jailhouse snitches, interrogations, eyewitness identifications, and the postconviction presentation of new evidence. One *Washington Post* editorial also suggested that a goal was to increase media access to inmates: "Prison officials prefer that the faces and histories of the condemned not be widely known. Capital punishment functions best when it becomes routine and hardly anyone knows the names of the departed."[13] According to Marshall, exonerees "speak to the emotional, human side as opposed to the intellectual side" of the capital punishment discussion.[14]

The conference, called the National Conference on Wrongful Convictions and the Death Penalty, was held November 13–15, 1998. More than 30 exonerees attended, including eight of the nine from Illinois; as Warden told me with a laugh, "Alex Hernandez couldn't make it, telling us later that he came and couldn't find a parking place. That was stunning."[15] They were joined by as many as 1,200 lawyers, death penalty activists, investigators, journalists, professors, and law students.[16]

The "unprecedented three-day meeting"[17] was the first time death row inmates had gathered formally and was the largest capital punishment event since the practice was reinstated in 1976.[18]

During the conference, panelists discussed flaws in the criminal justice system that led to wrongful convictions, including "nuts-and-bolts" issues such as forensic evidence and investigative practices.[19] The "emotional climax of the event,"[20] however, came when the exonerees took the stage. The formula was systematic yet incredibly powerful. Journalist Andrew Gumbel recounted the speech of one exoneree: "My name is Joseph Burrows. The state of Illinois sought to kill me for a murder I did not commit. I was put on death row in 1989. I was released in 1994. If the state had its way, I'd be dead today."[21] One by one, the exonerees stood in front of the audience and followed this protocol. After saying their part, each placed a sunflower in a vase "to symbolize the life they regained."[22] They then sat together onstage; one exoneree referred to it as "a living graveyard," and one attorney called it "a stage of honor."[23]

By all accounts, the moment was moving. The exonerees wept and hugged one another as they received a standing ovation from the audience, a sea of emotional supporters.[24] As one reporter put it, the scene "was a chilling flesh-and-blood reminder of the greatest fear of opponents and supporters of the death penalty";[25] another, Jim Dwyer, called the proceeding "a living, walking demonstration of the creaking floorboards on which capital punishment rests."[26] When asked about the event, Kate Germond simply replied, "Yeah, that was amazing."[27]

Other key speakers drove home the conference's messages. Prominent lawyer and legal activist Bryan Stephenson said, "What we are witnessing here today is a great American tragedy."[28] Stephen Bright, a lawyer and the director of the Southern Center for Human Rights, emphasized the importance of "educat[ing] the American people about how rough and crude our judicial system is. . . . Having twelve people in the jury box is better than fighting a duel, but only a fool would believe that system is infallible."[29]

The conference had a profound impact that stretched beyond the attendees and their immediate gathering, and it proved to be important for both the innocence and anti–death penalty movements.

Michael Radelet, who spoke at the conference, described its importance. While he did not want to go so far as to say it was responsible for putting innocence on the map, he described it as "a monumental event" for the press attention it received and suggested that it really brought innocence to the attention of a wider audience.[30] Rob Warden agreed, saying the conference "was the first time that we ever really got the national and international media to see that this was really a systemic problem and not just this anomaly. The media was able to see these people, touch them, shake hands with them, and interview them."[31] Similarly, Steve Drizin said that the conference "increased awareness generally about the causes and consequences of wrongful convictions."[32]

Richard Dieter said something similar, pointing out that the conference was covered in the *New York Times* and other papers around the country; it also generated international media attention.[33] At the time, he said, people knew much less about wrongful convictions than they do today, which contributed to perceptions of the event: "I mean, it is much more common now to be aware of this issue. But it was not that well-known at that time. . . . Each exoneration was a big story. People were waiting for the next one." He also pointed to the importance of the location in generating attention: "If this had all happened in Iowa or something, it might not have [had the same impact]. But Chicago, they had law firms, they had some law schools and law firms [that] are some of the best in the country, that were going after cases and finding not only cases, but prosecutorial misconduct and police misconduct, and exposing a really flawed system."[34] In addition to providing increased awareness and discussion about wrongful convictions on a national scale—a feat that should not be taken lightly—the conference provided hope for an anti–death penalty movement that had relatively little to celebrate at that time. This was a crucial moment for anti–capital punishment activists. In the late 1990s, executions were at an all-time high; 74 inmates were put to death in 1997, followed by 68 the next year. The peak was reached in 1999, when 98 inmates were executed.[35] Public support for capital punishment remained steadfast, and political capital was gained by heavily supporting the practice. In other words, all signs pointed toward the continued expansion of the death penalty in the United States. The public strongly supported the practice, and on both sides of the political aisle, "candidates for the city council to the White House" would "argue about who supports it more." Indeed, "the march to the death chamber continue[d] to pick up speed."[36]

The conference, however, allowed anti–death penalty activists to "mount[] a public relations counterattack."[37] Conference organizers wanted to make people aware that in a time of such expansion and support for the death penalty, the possibility of wrongly executing innocent people was very real,[38] and having the exonerees present in one room was important for driving that point home. "We want to start a dialogue with the rest of the country," Marshall told one reporter. "We want to bring the faces of these wrongfully convicted men and women who could be dead right now into every village and hamlet in the country."[39]

The tactic was effective. One journalist wrote that exonerees "represent perhaps the greatest challenge to use of the death penalty."[40] An editorial in a Portland, Maine, newspaper opened, "An extraordinary conference this weekend in Chicago should be the beginning of the end of capital punishment in America. That doesn't mean it will be, but after Sunday, when the conference ends, no one can say he and she didn't know that we execute innocent people in this land of the free."[41] The value of seeing exonerees onstage to the larger anti–death penalty movement was not lost on conference attendees. Steve Drizin called it "a watershed moment": "I think that the image of more than 30 men and women from all over the country who had been wrongfully convicted and sentenced to death, all on one stage, was seared into the consciousness of many people, not only in the United States but around the world. And it reframed the debate about the death penalty in this country."[42] The conference thus provided fuel for a dwindling anti–death penalty fire and gave advocates a reason for optimism. Warden described a "pivotal moment" after the exonerees had walked across the stage: "At the end of that, there was this standing ovation in Thorne Auditorium. It holds about 700 people, and I'm sitting in the front row with my wife, and I said, 'Oh my God, we can abolish this thing. We can do this!' And it was really exhilarating. It was the first time that I really saw hope for abolishing the death penalty."[43] The exonerees were energized as well. Gary Gauger, for instance, was "heartened by the conference," telling one reporter, "The justice system is evolving right here."[44]

While reforms to the capital punishment system short of abolition were suggested, and despite Marshall's comments about the goal not just being to do away with the practice, "most at the conference thought the death penalty has failed,"[45] and thus "the overwhelming thrust of the weekend was the abolition of the death penalty."[46] As exoneree Randall Dale Adams put it, "We came together for one reason and one reason only—to speak out and stop executions in America."[47] Marshall himself invoked the names of exonerees in a "call to abolish the death penalty."[48]

The conference not only provided hope for anti–death penalty advocates but, along with continuing exonerations, gave death penalty supporters a crucial reason to pause.

Governor Ryan Reacts

In late 1998, Anthony Porter was on death row; it had been his home for 15 years. His appeals exhausted and his execution only 50 hours away, he was measured for his burial suit, he ordered his last meal, and his family made funeral arrangements. The Illinois Supreme Court, however, granted him a stay due to his low IQ. They were unsure whether he fully understood what was about to happen.[49] This gave investigators a chance to explore the case, and they obtained a confession from another man, Alstory Simon.[50] In February 1999, Porter was freed.

Porter's exoneration, coming hot on the heels of the National Conference on Wrongful Convictions and the Death Penalty, created a stir in Illinois, according to Rob Warden: "And just the salience of that . . . Here's a guy, two more days and he would've been dead. And now, here's this overwhelming evidence that he's innocent. . . . That case then—just really, the synergy of the conference, followed by that, were just really amazing, and that's what really got us off the ground and linked us, the whole innocence movement, with the death penalty."[51] Death penalty supporters were frustrated with the focus on innocence, as conservative writers suggested that opponents were blowing wrongful convictions out of proportion and using them to undermine capital punishment.[52] Still, the issue was gaining traction and even reached into the hearts and minds of some death penalty proponents.

One of those supporters was Illinois governor George Ryan. A Republican proponent of capital punishment and a supporter of George W. Bush,[53] Ryan was shocked at the spate of exonerations in Illinois. He was aware of the Northwestern conference, and the exoneration of Anthony Porter shortly thereafter struck a chord with him. "George Ryan was aghast," Warden said. "He could have signed off on Anthony's execution and would have had the blood of an innocent man on his hand. This profoundly shook George Ryan. It was really an epiphany for him, because he trusted the system."[54]

A series of articles in the *Chicago Tribune* then caught the governor's attention. The authors had examined nearly 300 capital cases in Illinois and found that half had been reversed on appeal. The reasons included representation from defense attorneys who had been disbarred or suspended, prosecutors' reliance on jailhouse informants, recanted witness testimony, improper judicial rulings, and prosecutorial misconduct. Another revelation particularly grabbed Ryan's attention: the state of Illinois had more death row inmates exonerated (13) than executed (12) since the reinstatement of the death penalty in 1976.[55] In Ryan's mind, there was a clear conclusion: "I cannot support a system which, in its administration, has proven so fraught with error and has come so close to the ultimate nightmare, the state's taking of innocent life. . . . Until I can be sure that everyone sentenced to death in Illinois is truly guilty, until I can be sure with moral certainty that no innocent man or woman is facing a lethal injection, no one will meet that fate."[56] While Ryan did not go so far as to immediately declare himself against the death penalty, he believed that the system in Illinois had a "problem that's too big for case-by-case review."[57] Rather than continue down a flawed path, Ryan wanted to confront the problem. "I'm going to put a stop to this," he told the Illinois attorney general. "The system is broken. It's time we take a look and see what's wrong."[58] His solution was a bold one: in January 2001, Ryan placed a statewide moratorium on executions, the first in the United States.

Ryan's decision drew mixed reactions. A number of prosecutors in Illinois were critical, believing it to be an abuse of authority by the governor, and some were confused as to whether they were to continue pursuing capital cases. Defense attorneys were generally supportive of the moratorium.[59] A number of politicians also supported the decision, including President Bill Clinton, who called the move "courageous" but refused to act in kind at the federal level,[60] and Chicago mayor Richard Daley, who incidentally was Cook County's attorney in the 1980s and had prosecuted a number of the cases that were later overturned.[61] Ryan's move was seen by some people as "show[ing] political courage and integrity. . . . Even talking about the system's mistakes shows an honesty that many pro-death penalty politicians refuse to acknowledge."[62]

Of course, the moratorium decision was lauded by the anti–death penalty community, such as the Illinois Coalition to Abolish the Death Penalty[63] and local Catholic organizations that saw the move as "a bold step."[64] It was used as a rallying call for other governors to follow suit, including George W. Bush in Texas.[65] Many death penalty supporters were critical of the decision, but some took a pragmatic approach. David Frum, for example, cited the high public support for the death penalty in saying that "death penalty opponents have helped corrode American trust in the democratic system." However, he followed by saying that Ryan "acted properly. If state justice seems to be miscarrying, it's a governor's job to find out why and right it. But once Mr. Ryan has found the answer, the criminal laws of Illinois must be honored."[66]

In Illinois, the general public was not heavily critical of the decision, which one reporter suggested was "a measure of how public outrage over the wrongful convictions has changed the political landscape on the [death penalty] in this state."[67] At the very least, it generated significant discussion about the topic, a key goal of the decision according to Ryan, who "believe[d] that a public dialogue must begin on the question of fairness of the application of the death penalty."[68]

In addition to halting executions, Ryan appointed a committee to review the capital punishment system in Illinois and recommend adjustments to increase its efficacy. The commission was led by former federal judge Frank McGarr, former United States attorney Thomas Sullivan, and former Democratic senator Paul Simon. William Webster, the former director of the FBI, served as special adviser to the group. It also included law enforcement officials, prosecutors, defense attorneys, a businessman, and lawyer-novelist Scott Turow. The 14-member panel, most of whom supported capital punishment, was tasked with examining a variety of issues with the death penalty system, including a review of the state's exoneration cases, and suggesting reforms, with a particular focus on indigent representation for death row inmates. Although Ryan did not expressly support abolition, he said he would not proceed with executions without a guarantee from the commission that erroneous convictions would not occur. Thus, in Ryan's opinion, it was unlikely that any executions would be carried out during his tenure.[69]

Ryan's decision in 2000 made major waves in the legal world. "It was huge," Rob Warden said. "It was really huge."[70] It was, in fact, the top news story of the year in Illinois,[71] but its reach was nationwide, as it prompted a discussion in the broader criminal justice community. This was due in part, as Richard Dieter pointed out, to who and where it was. It was initiated by George Ryan, a Republican who had favored capital punishment. And it was in Illinois, "a state that had carried out executions, that had close to 200 people on death row. This was not New Hampshire. This was a real death penalty state."[72]

The timing of the decision also contributed to the extent of coverage it received. As noted earlier, this was a time of expansion for the death penalty, a point not lost on Dieter: "Nobody really was stopping the death penalty at that time. No state was abolishing it. They were adding it. New York added the death penalty, Kansas added the death penalty in the '90s. No states were about to abolish it. So for him to just put a hold on it and do it publicly, it was evening-news sort of stuff."[73] At a time when the possibility for abolition "seemed very remote," a moratorium was "the best people were hoping for." Ryan's maneuvers reenergized the anti–death penalty movement at a time when it sorely needed it and created "dramatic new momentum" against capital punishment.[74]

Many people at the time saw the decision as single-handedly changing the death penalty discourse in the country, sparking a new debate about an issue that had seemingly been settled. But as law professor James Liebman has pointed out, there was "a second catalyzing event" in 2000.[75]

Actual Innocence

In 1992, Barry Scheck and Peter Neufeld helped exonerate Kerry Kotler, who had been convicted of rape, burglary, and robbery in 1982. It was their first DNA exoneration and had come about in part due to the work of *Newsday* columnist Jim Dwyer, who had obtained case filings and drove public pressure that helped lead to Kotler's exoneration.[76]

For years after the Kotler case, Scheck, Neufeld, and Dwyer discussed the possibility of writing a book. Scheck and Neufeld continued their casework with the Innocence Project, and Dwyer continued to cover wrongful conviction cases in New York. In discussing "what it all meant," they came to the conclusion that it was more important to understand how people got into prison than how they got out, and they decided to lay out the reasons for wrongful convictions in a published form.[77] They signed a contract in 1998, and in 2000, *Actual Innocence: Five Days to Execution and Other Dispatches from the Wrongly Convicted* was published.

The book was a commercial and critical success. Similar in nature to much of the scholarship on wrongful convictions that existed at the time—narrative and descriptive but written for a general audience— "*Actual Innocence* is the rare book that has been both an influential work of legal scholarship and a popular best-seller."[78] In what was described by one reviewer as "a heartbreaking and infuriating compendium of stories of lives ruined,"[79] the authors used tales of wrongful convictions to highlight the factors that cause them: eyewitness errors, false confessions, forensic misconduct, prosecutorial and defense issues, jailhouse informants, and racism. They also described how some of the errors were discovered, discussed what can be learned from the cases, and suggested policy reforms.

The book was powerful, "as powerful as the DNA science it reports on."[80] A "very readable and dramatic narrative,"[81] *Actual Innocence* is in the style of the most gripping fiction. One reviewer described it as "a riveting collection of judicial horror stories" that "can make your palms sweat and your teeth grind."[82] In addition to being a gripping story, however, the book was also "enormously influential,"[83] a powerful agent for changing the minds of readers. *Publishers Weekly* described it as "an alarming wake-up call to those who administer our justice system that serious flaws must be addressed to protect the innocent."[84]

Actual Innocence was yet another tool to stoke the fires of the death penalty debate. Importantly, it was not just traditional abolitionists who heeded its messages. In a review of the book, conservative commentator and death penalty supporter George Will called it "frightening," saying, "It should change the argument about capital punishment and other aspects of the criminal justice system." From the "appalling" stories, Will drew the conclusion "that many innocent people are in prison, and some innocent people have been executed."[85] The fact that a conservative writer so publicly addressed these issues was not lost on anti–death penalty advocates; in a memo to DPIC board members, Richard Dieter described this piece as "a ringing endorsement of the importance of the innocence issue."[86]

The Changing Death Penalty Debate

By early 2000, innocence was fundamentally changing the death penalty discussion in the United States. While most people recognized, like Dieter, that there was unlikely to be widespread support for abolition, people across the ideological spectrum began to consider it. For politicians on both sides of the aisle, it became "politically acceptable" to "rethink capital punishment."[87] In a shifting political climate, while it was still unlikely that conservatives would call for abolition to the extent that many liberals did, the events in Illinois led to widespread skepticism about the system that was in place, from members of both political parties.[88] And questions about a potentially flawed system, rather than moral ones on the death penalty, were ones that politicians were open to discussing.[89] In fact, bills to stop executions were pending in 12 states at the time, and in Oregon, a group led by the former Republican senator and governor Mark Hatfield was working to put abolition on the ballot.[90] At the national level, Democratic senator Russell Feingold proposed the National Death Penalty Moratorium Act to expand Ryan's moratorium to all state and federal executions. He also called for a national commission to examine the safeguards in place to prevent wrongful convictions.[91]

In 2000, the debate over capital punishment also reentered presidential politics, where it had essentially been a one-sided affair.[92] Al Gore, the Democratic nominee for president and longtime supporter of capital punishment, was open to rethinking the practice. "If there is a study that shows a large number of mistakes," Gore said, "that has to make you uncomfortable. I have assumed up until very recently that the mistakes were rare and unusual."[93]

It was not just political figures who began questioning the death penalty in the face of exonerations; the media and public also took notice. Scores of news reports discussed the matter, and several clever political cartoons offered innocence-centric critiques of the death penalty. In terms of public opinion, a February 2000 poll showed national support at 66%, which, while still high, was the lowest it had been in two decades.[94] Furthermore, a poll that summer found that 80% of Americans believed that an innocent person had been executed in the past five years, and nearly half believed that such an error had occurred in Texas during George W. Bush's term as governor.[95]

On a number of fronts, Americans were again wrestling with the death penalty, and innocence was a main reason. Opponents and supporters alike were troubled by the flaws in the system that led to such egregious errors, causing the nature of the entire debate to shift. The tone of the death penalty debate changed dramatically, such that issues of fairness and innocence became the leading theme of media coverage in the late 1990s and into the 21st century.[96]

Thus, 2000 is considered by many people to be a "watershed" year in terms of changing opinions on capital punishment.[97] Ryan's moratorium and the resulting frenzy was the climax in a string of events—from the DNA exonerations of death row inmates to the DPIC report to the 1998 conference to the publication of *Actual Innocence*—that brought innocence forcefully into the national death penalty conversation.

In the years following his moratorium, Governor Ryan and his commission continued to review death penalty cases. They made a number of proposals for reform, but none were adopted. With Ryan nearing the end of his term, he felt that he must act, and in 2003, just days before leaving office, he opted for blanket commutation. After granting pardons to four men he believed to be innocent, Ryan granted clemency to the other 167 death row inmates in Illinois; three had their sentences commuted to 40 years, while the rest were given life without parole.

Ryan's commutations came a decade after Kirk Bloodsworth became the first death row inmate to be exonerated through DNA testing. Given all that occurred in this period—DNA exonerations, the reports by the National Institute of Justice and the Death Penalty Information Center, the 1998 National Conference on Wrongful Convictions and the Death Penalty, the publication of *Actual Innocence*, and Ryan's moratorium— his commutation decision does not seem too surprising. Rather, it seems more like a logical, albeit politically risky, step amid a shifting debate over capital punishment.

Still, the decision drew criticism from many directions. One writer described the decision as "a public circus that serves no legitimate purpose" and accused Ryan of caring more about his legacy than about justice.[98] In particular, some people criticized his death penalty moves as being nothing more than a way to save face for his other unholy dealings; Ryan and his administration were embroiled in a corruption scandal, for which he was later convicted and served more than five years in federal prison.[99]

Prosecutors in the state were also staunchly against blanket clemency and believed that each case needed to be handled individually on its merits.[100] The DuPage County state's attorney Joseph Birkett even filed a lawsuit to reinstate the death sentences, arguing that Ryan violated the Constitution's separation of powers; Ryan was "making public policy," according to Birkett, and "seizing control of the function of the General Assembly and the courts."[101]

Other political figures also criticized the decision. The incoming Illinois governor, Democrat Rod Blagojevich, disagreed with Ryan's commutations,[102] and House Republicans introduced a bill less than a week after the announcement to make it more difficult for other governors to follow Ryan's example by slowing the clemency process.[103]

Perhaps the most powerful criticism came from the families of murder victims. Ryan was accused of enhancing their suffering, which critics said was "callous."[104] Many victims' families felt especially "cheated" because, just a month before announcing blanket clemency, Ryan indicated to them that he was leaning against that approach.[105] Thus, upon hearing his announcement, many were angry and felt victimized. "Every one of the victims," one mother said, "[Ryan] has killed them all over again."[106] The partner of a police officer who had been killed by a man on death row said that Ryan "has shown no respect to the victims' families, to police, prosecutors, judges. What he's done is a tragedy and it's based on a personal agenda."[107] Ryan wrote to victims' families and explained that his decision was made because he could not risk a wrongful execution. This reasoning was criticized by prosecutors, who pointed out that most of the death row inmates who petitioned for clemency did not contest their guilt.[108] While many family members were angered by Ryan's commutations, some accepted it, so long as the alternative was life without parole.[109]

Ryan did find a number of supporters in Chicago and elsewhere. In an open letter to the governor, more than 400 law professors supported blanket clemency.[110] Death penalty opponents, including several exonerees, rallied in downtown Chicago in the days leading up to Ryan's announcement.[111] The Reverend Jesse Jackson spoke in support of blanket clemency, saying, "There are those here who are guilty and there are those here who are innocent. They often cannot be distinguished." He described the system as "fatally flawed" and was joined in his support by family members of ten death row inmates. He took them to the prison in Pontiac, where he was also joined by Rob Warden.[112]

In delivering what was described as "the sharpest blow to capital punishment since the U.S. Supreme Court declared it unconstitutional in 1972,"[113] Ryan expected a wide array of responses. He expected to face anger and ridicule, but, he said, "the people of [Illinois] have vested in me the power to act in the interest of justice. . . . And even if the exercise of my power becomes my burden, I'll bear it." In announcing his decision, Ryan cited his "frustrations and deep concerns about both the administration and the penalty of death."[114]

Although Ryan cited a number of issues in his announcement, including international trends against the death penalty, its lack of deterrence, prosecutorial politics, and the impact on offenders' families, he said his concern about the issue started with innocence, citing the Anthony Porter case and the *Chicago Tribune* series that had influenced his earlier moratorium. By January 2003, when announcing his commutations, Illinois had 17 death row exonerations, which Ryan described as "an absolute embarrassment" and "nothing short of a catastrophic failure."[115]

While Ryan focused not only on innocence but also on other issues of fairness and equality—how geography, race, and socioeconomic status influence who does and does not get the death penalty—he was driven by a concern about wrongful convictions. And like his moratorium in 2000, the 2003 clemency decision created major waves in the legal and political worlds. It also highlights the ever-important connection between innocence and the death penalty, a connection that strongly influenced legislation at the federal level.

A National Conversation: The Innocence Protection Act

The turn of the 21st century was an interesting period for discourse about crime and punishment in the United States. The goal was often "to ensure that innocent people are protected" from the throes of death row,[116] as the conversation centered on wrongful convictions, DNA, and capital punishment. A number of bills addressed a variety of issues within this general area,[117] but one is particularly relevant for the innocence movement.

Senator Patrick Leahy, a Vermont Democrat, in 2000 introduced the Innocence Protection Act (IPA), "a carefully crafted package of criminal justice reforms designed to protect the innocent and to ensure that if the death penalty is imposed, it is the result of informed and reasoned deliberation, not politics, luck, bias, or guesswork."[118] The bill was co-sponsored by Gordon Smith, an Oregon Republican; the bipartisan nature of the bill was emphasized time and time again.

The IPA had three key areas of reform. The first was to increase inmates' access to postconviction DNA testing and to set up standards and regulations for such testing. The second was designed to ensure that capital defendants were given access to adequate legal representation through recruitment and funding standards. The third was compensating the wrongly convicted who were exonerated. The initial bill also covered the death penalty alternative of life without parole and the right to an informed jury, and it tasked the Justice Department with preparing annual reports on the administration of the federal death penalty.

The Death Penalty Information Center helped prepare reports, provided background information, and assisted with media relations for the bill. The press conference for its announcement "was quite dramatic, standing room only, and the coverage of the bill was extensive."[119] The media was fairly receptive; one report described it as a "promising measure," and while it "stop[ped] short of abolishing the death penalty, . . . key provisions would lessen the chance of unfairness and deadly error."[120]

The introduction of the IPA was driven in large part by what Leahy called the "national crisis" over capital punishment.[121] It was later introduced in the House of Representatives by Ray LaHood, a Republican from Illinois, and William Delahunt, a Massachusetts Democrat. Henry Hyde, the chairman of the House Judiciary Committee, liked the bill, describing it as a "very reasonable treatment of a very difficult and delicate issue."[122] Yet despite the timeliness of its proposal, the bill's bipartisan nature, and support from Bill Clinton, Al Gore, and Janet Reno, the IPA was not passed in its first year.[123] Still, DPIC described it as "the most prominent legislative proposal in Congress on the death penalty in 2000" and made it a priority for the year ahead.[124]

Over the next several years, as exonerations piled up and the national death penalty debate raged on, the IPA kept cropping up. The goal, according to Leahy, remained "simple, but profoundly important: to reduce the risk of mistaken executions."[125] Several variations on the bill were introduced. Senator Orrin Hatch, for example, a Republican from Utah and chairman of the Senate Judiciary Committee, wrote a bill addressing DNA testing but left out provisions on competent counsel. In an attempt to bridge the gap between sides, Senator Dianne Feinstein introduced the Criminal Justice Integrity and Innocence Protection Act, which covered both DNA testing and competent counsel.[126]

Innocence, DNA, and the death penalty continued to be topics of debate for several years. Most critics of the IPA objected not to its underlying goal but to its reach and specific provisions within the bill. When the IPA contained provisions relating to habeas corpus reform, some thought that went beyond the boundaries of what the bill should cover; some also objected to the ways in which the federal government could withhold funding from states.[127] When the Innocence Project became more heavily involved in the process in 2002 and 2003, one issue of contention was regarding where the bar should be set in order to obtain DNA testing.[128]

Ultimately, the Innocence Protection Act was passed in 2004 as part of the larger Justice for All Act, which covered a variety of issues related to victims' rights, DNA, and wrongful convictions. The IPA in particular contains provisions to provide standards for inmates' access to postconviction DNA testing, to ensure quality defense representation in capital cases, and to compensate exonerees. Kirk Bloodsworth became heavily involved in the reform effort, and one provision of the IPA was named after him: the "Kirk Bloodsworth Post-Conviction DNA Testing Grant Program" authorized $5 million over five years to help states pay for DNA tests.[129] The Justice for All Act went into law on October 30, 2004, and remains one of the innocence movement's greatest policy successes.

Beyond Capital Punishment

While the events in Illinois and the Innocence Protection Act largely dealt with a conversation about wrongful convictions and the death penalty, the effects went beyond the confines of capital punishment. In particular, the 1998 conference had a profound impact on what ultimately became the innocence movement. Seeing the wrongly convicted together, in person and in one location, not only put a sympathetic face on the potential dangers of the death penalty but also prompted a realization about flaws in the criminal justice system more generally. There was "a broad and continuing interest in the subject of innocence and the death penalty,"[130] but the renewed capital punishment debate was "also spurring greater scrutiny of the fairness of our entire justice system: the reliability of criminal convictions; the poor quality of public defense; the availability of DNA and other forensic science; racial discrimination; and the integrity of the prosecution function."[131]

The faces of the wrongly convicted provided clear and powerful examples of the flaws in the justice system, and the "gruesome problems" that had "been overlooked for so many years [were] starting to burst into public view."[132] The problems seen in the cases of the men and women who attended the 1998 conference were not restricted only to death penalty cases; issues like witness misidentification and poor lawyering, which led to many of the capital errors, were widespread. "There is no reason to limit the review to capital cases," wrote Cardozo law professor Peter Lushing. "Anything that can go wrong in a capital case can go wrong in any criminal case."[133]

This realization—that the criminal justice system was potentially riddled with problems—prompted widespread skepticism about the basic functioning of the justice process. As journalist Bob Herbert wrote, "If the criminal justice system has such a poor track record when it comes to capital cases, imagine what the situation is like in the cases with much less at stake. How many thousands of people have been wrongfully convicted? In how many instances have the real criminals been ignored by the authorities, and thus allowed to remain free and prey on others? How many innocent people have been maimed or killed in the name of the law?"[134] The events in Chicago spread the notion that the criminal justice system may be flawed in important, fundamental ways. Some of the reforms recommended by Ryan's commission extended beyond capital punishment. Reforms such as improving lineup procedures and recording interrogations are familiar to people in the innocence community and, as Rob Warden suggested, could potentially save thousands of wrongful convictions in non-capital cases.[135]

But the 1998 conference had a more direct impact on the development of innocence as a movement. It brought together people who shared the belief that wrongful convictions were common and worthy of attention. Rob Warden described the conference as "a turning point. It was key to the movement."[136] Barry Scheck similarly said it was "extremely important,"[137] as it brought together a number of people who were interested in wrongful conviction issues and who had started or were interested in starting innocence projects.

Perhaps the most important long-term development was the idea for a national network of organizations dedicated to innocence work. Among the events at the conference was a session on "new initiatives," one of which was an advocacy coalition, a national "Innocence Network" set up at law schools around the country, to work on wrongful conviction cases.[138] It was proposed by Scheck, who hoped to see innocence projects in every state and believed that such a network would uncover more cases, in turn raising awareness about the scope of errors in the justice system. "If we can get more people on the ground looking for evidence," Scheck told a reporter, "we can free a lot of innocent people."[139]

The conference was directly responsible for the foundation of several innocence organizations. Most notably, the Northwestern Center on Wrongful Convictions, founded by Rob Warden and Larry Marshall, "was an outgrowth of that conference."[140] Their approach was slightly different than that of the Innocence Project at Cardozo, in that they did not focus solely on DNA evidence. This should not be surprising, however; they had a fair amount of experience with capital murder cases, which rarely involved DNA, Warden said: "The vast majority of DNA exonerations occurred when there were sexual assaults. In our murder cases, only 10 or 12% involved sexual assault. So you could say that every time we've shown the fallibility of the evidence used in cases where there was DNA, there are nine other cases that rested on evidence in which there is not DNA available to exonerate the person. We had to go back and really look at these other cases."[141] Steve Drizin, a clinical professor, staff attorney, and former legal director of the Northwestern Center, suggested that this element of the conference—the coming together of like-minded folks that led to the foundation of innocence groups—was critical: "In my lifetime, that's the single most important event in the innocence movement, because from that conference not only sprung the . . . Center on Wrongful Convictions, but it also gave birth to a number of other innocence-related organizations around the country."[142]

Indeed, the importance of the 1998 conference to the innocence movement goes beyond the gathering in Chicago. Scheck and Neufeld, both of whom attended, had the vision for an organizational coalition early on, and the 1998 conference appears to be their first real clarion call for others to follow their lead. In the wake of that conference and the energy it generated, they began expanding the innocence advocacy network.

Building the Network

Scheck and Neufeld had already begun developing a network in the legal community, and recognizing the strength of their position as an organization and "the unique ability of the academy to change people's perceptions and understanding of the criminal justice system," they made "a very conscious and deliberate decision to try to spread this through law school clinical programs." Students quickly became hooked, and drawing on their excitement, Scheck and Neufeld "very self-consciously" built the network through the legal academy.[143]

Around the time of the 1998 conference, Scheck and Neufeld put out a call to law schools across the nation. The Innocence Project was having success, but they were inundated with both DNA and non-DNA cases that they could not handle. They also held a DNA training event in New York that was attended by law professors and students from around the country.[144]

To spur the growth of law school programs, Scheck and Neufeld set up a course called "Wrongful Convictions: Causes and Remedies." The course went through some of the key factors that contributed to wrongful convictions, such as eyewitness misidentifications and false confessions, with different experts addressing each topic. Scheck described the course to me: "We held 14 classes at Cardozo Law School. We brought in leading experts in each of the different issue areas to give lectures for an hour, hour and 15 minutes, whether it was Gary Wells on eyewitness misidentification, Michael Saks on pattern forensic evidence, Steve Bright on indigent defense or bad lawyers. Peter and I did one on DNA. Mark Olive did one on postconviction and the right of actual innocence. Bryan Stevenson did one on race and the criminal justice system. And on it goes."[145] This was shortly after Westlaw, a leading research service for lawyers, scholars, and law students, set up The West Education Network (TWEN), a way for law schools to share and distribute information. In effect, TWEN served as a virtual extension of the law school classroom. The syllabus for the "Wrongful Convictions" course was distributed over TWEN, and the course sessions were broadcast via video conference with other law schools, including Northwestern, Duke, Santa Clara, and Tennessee. It was live and allowed people to call in with questions.[146]

The course "was really a very good idea"[147] but perhaps somewhat ahead of its time; the technology for such a concept was very young, and it may not have been quite as effective as it otherwise could have. The lectures were recorded and physically mailed, along with the syllabus and other curriculum materials, to law schools around the United States. This allowed the schools to have a course with sound academic content and high-quality lectures and readings, all on a topic in which many law students were becoming interested. As Scheck pointed out, it also lent itself to including a field-work component, as the classes brought in lawyers from the community to work on cases with faculty and students.[148]

It was in this very active and conscious way that Scheck and Neufeld spread the idea of the clinical innocence project throughout the nation's law schools. It showed people in the legal academy that "this is a real course of study . . . that is interdisciplinary." Involving not just the law but the physical and social sciences added depth to a topic that captured the attention of young lawyers and law students and sparked a movement in clinical legal education. Building the network of advocates in such a fashion was vital to the movement, according to Scheck: "We did, very self-consciously, begin to build out all the projects in what became the Innocence Network through law schools. The advantage is that we got to change the perception of a whole generation of lawyers who became themselves defense lawyers, prosecutors, judges, influential individuals, and change perceptions within the academy of the system itself and the risk of executing and convicting innocent people."[149] In addition to the legal academy, Scheck and Neufeld continued to actively develop their network in the criminal defense community, in particular, the National Association of Criminal Defense Lawyers (NACDL). When they needed legal assistance, Scheck said they would go through the NACDL handbook to find lawyers in a given jurisdiction. "We would just call people up and say, 'Can you help us as local counsel? And by the way, for nothing,' because there was no money to finance any of this."[150] Scheck later served as president of the NACDL in 2004–2005.

The NACDL was supportive in a more concrete sense as well. At the NACDL Midwinter Meeting and Seminar in February 2000, there was a two-and-a-half-hour program on "how to start an innocence project," at which Scheck was a main speaker. A flyer for the meeting emphasized the value of innocence work, saying, "Nothing you have done or will ever do in your practice will be as rewarding as freeing an innocent person from death row or a lengthy prison sentence."[151]

By 2000, there were ten innocence projects around the country. A meeting was held in Chicago, which turned out to be the first of annual meetings that continue today.[152] At the end of that conference, there was a meeting for those who were "interested in . . . moving forward as a group of like-minded lawyers across the nation."[153] At the meeting, Scheck, Neufeld, and others discussed the need to get organized, and they began to consider the things they needed, such as governance and communication. Though the Innocence Network was not yet formalized, it was essentially born.

The Innocence Network

Theresa Newman from Duke and Kathleen "Cookie" Ridolfi from Santa Clara became the first co-chairs of the new coalition. The group did not have a formal status as an organization, nor did it initially have a mission statement or official criteria for membership. Over time, however, the group realized that they "needed . . . to tighten things down a little bit." They developed a mission statement, and in 2004 and 2005, a planning committee composed of project directors developed a structure and membership criteria.[154]

The criteria for and obligations of membership in the Innocence Network are laid out plainly; the crux is that organizations seeking to join must be "dedicated to providing pro bono legal and/or investigative services to individuals to prove their innocence of crimes for which they have been convicted."[155] Organizations that meet the basic criteria can be admitted as provisional members, and if they continue to meet the standards, they can be voted in as full members.

Importantly, organizations cannot automatically use the name "Innocence Project." They can get a license to use it if they become a member of the Network in good standing.[156] This restriction was intentional: Scheck and Neufeld trademarked the name "Innocence Project." Neufeld points out that the incentives for this decision were not financial, as "there is no financial gain." Rather, they thought their organization would "take off" and that others may want to follow suit. Thus, "to have some quality control—some—knowing that you can't obviously mandate that people do exactly what you do, but some quality control, by trademarking that name, we could make sure that the organizations that used it . . . follow some of our principles."[157]

Having standards for organizations that sought to join the Network was vital, as was having restrictions on who may use the name "Innocence Project." These things were done "by necessity."[158] As Christine Mumma, the director of the North Carolina Center on Actual Innocence, said, "If one innocence project screws up, it affects all of us."[159] If the name was available for anyone to use, the door would be open for it to be abused and tainted. For example, if an organization were to call itself an "Innocence Project" and charge clients for representation or fail to provide adequate services, the reputations of others who use the name would be compromised. Newman said it is particularly bad if such an organization were to "create havoc in district attorneys' offices," which may then look at another innocence organization and think, "We're not gonna work with you. You're just like those people!"[160]

In other words, the branding of the innocence movement is important, and thus the Innocence Project "protects the mark."[161] It stands by the fact that its postconviction DNA exonerations represent cases of individuals who are truly innocent, and those stories have created the narrative focus of the movement. "We stand by those," Scheck said, "and that has had a very important [effect on] protection of the brand. DNA exonerations have created a brand that we protect, . . . that carries over to the non-DNA cases. We're very self-conscious of that. Both the narratives and the branding are important."[162]

The Network also created guidelines for ethics and best practices, which is important not only for protecting the brand but also for legal purposes. "This is different from straight-up postconviction work,"

Newman said. "We still have a lot of legal issues, but when you have actual innocence, it's an entirely different thing."[163]

With membership criteria, a clear mission, and organizational standards, the Innocence Network was officially born, with Newman and Ridolfi as copresidents. The first 15 official members were admitted in November 2005, and the Network has expanded tremendously since then, adding new organizations every year.

The Innocence Project also made changes in 2004 that allowed the organization and the Network to expand beyond exoneration casework.

Focusing on Policy

From the outset, Scheck and Neufeld had a vision for the Innocence Project. They knew the value of DNA evidence in securing exonerations with a strong scientific basis for factual innocence, but they also recognized that each case was "a learning moment for the criminal justice system."[164] From this recognition flows policy reform; that is, if we understand how and why justice miscarried, changes can be implemented to help prevent such errors from occurring in the future.

By 2004, the Innocence Project had success as a clinical program at the Cardozo School of Law and was approaching ten staff members at the school, but Scheck and Neufeld wanted to expand, particularly into policy work and public education. In order to do so, they decided to make the Innocence Project an independent nonprofit organization.[165]

One of the first orders of business was to hire an executive director, and Scheck and Neufeld found the perfect fit in Madeline deLone. She had spent part of her career working on health-care issues in prisons and jails and was a prisoners' rights attorney and advocate. "While I liked it," deLone told me, "and in lots of ways it was very thrilling, and I loved the intellectual challenge of it, I loved the clients, and I loved the victories, I didn't love litigation as a way of spending my day and as a way of solving problems." She was looking for something "in a leadership role or in an administrative capacity." She heard about the Innocence Project, and some friends suggested she contact the organization. She did, and after meeting Scheck, Neufeld, and the small staff at the time, she "was really taken with [them]."[166] In March 2004, deLone became the first executive director of the Innocence Project as an independent nonprofit.[167]

Scheck described the importance of this period for the organization and the movement. "The key moment around all of this is when we hired Maddy deLone as our executive director and started coming up with strategic plans and operating as a nonprofit," he said. The organization's leadership made "a very conscious decision to make this a major nonprofit and an anchor organization for various groups that were in motion around social justice causes."[168] They recognized their unique position in terms of their utility for other social justice and civil rights organizations that worked in the criminal justice arena and thought that, as an independent organization, they could serve as a valuable resource for those groups in addition to working on their own issues.

In terms of tackling issues specific to wrongful convictions, the Innocence Project took a major leap into policy work in 2004. Scheck and Neufeld had essentially laid out a succinct policy agenda in the appendix to their book *Actual Innocence*. And while they had engaged in some policy-reform efforts, they decided to start their own policy division at the Innocence Project and found a director in Stephen Saloom.

Saloom had previously run a criminal justice policy group for the ACLU in Massachusetts and had worked as a contract lobbyist in Connecticut representing an array of progressive organizations such as the Connecticut Civil Liberties Union, the Coalition for Lesbian and Gay Civil Rights, and the Connecticut AIDS Action Council. With experience as a lobbyist in multiple states, Saloom took a job developing a policy network among the affiliates of the NACDL.

Shortly after starting the job, Saloom met the NACDL president-elect, Barry Scheck, and the two immediately connected. "He had a mind for this kind of stuff, obviously," Saloom said. "The Innocence Project was growing, and its potential was really starting to brim. . . . And we really connected."[169]

Thus, within the course of Saloom's first year at NACDL, he met Scheck and learned about the Innocence Project: "We were covering some of the same issues, [so] we would stay in touch with these folks." Saloom was invited to speak at the 2004 Innocence Network conference, where he met deLone in her new role as executive director. That summer, deLone contacted Saloom to discuss ideas when she was creating a job description for a policy director at the Innocence Project. Saloom described their telephone conversation: "So I spent some time with her on the phone, . . . and at a certain point, I said, 'Look, I have to apologize, because I'm just drawing on my own experiences here. I don't really have a lot of other reference points.' And she said something to the effect of, 'Well, you know, I wouldn't worry about it too much, because given what I've heard from you, if in fact you want to take this job, I don't really have to write this job description right now.' And so that worked out very well."[170]

On October 4, 2004, Saloom became the Innocence Project's first policy director. Saloom had learned the ins and outs of doing state policy work, and his experience certainly helped bolster the Innocence Project's policy mission and led to some of its early successes: "My unique experience as a state lobbyist in more than one state [is] very important here, because if you're a lobbyist in any given state, if you're effective at all, it's because you know the people in the building, and you know the culture of the building and the politics of the state. And with all of that in mind, you can be effective in that state legislature. And if you're effective in that state legislature, you're pretty well set."[171]

Saloom also understood the importance of having a network of policy advocates, and in 2005, he set up an innocence policy network. The network, which Saloom described as "fairly informal but . . . fairly high functioning," has one person from each Innocence Network project who serves as the policy point person, with whom the Innocence Project policy department works. The policy point person is "the person on the ground in each state. They know the legislators, they know the legal community, they speak out on the issues, and we [the Innocence Project policy department] help them. It's kind of that same remote support-center thing." Setting up such a network came from Saloom's prior experience, since he understood not just the importance of having a network of advocates but the relationships among them. "A state advocate doesn't need a national person to come into their state and tell them how it's done," he said. "A state advocate needs a national organization to say, 'How can I help you?'"[172] Thus, the Innocence Network has someone in most states to work on priority issues in the local area, and the Innocence Project, the largest Network member, offers support. Saloom also began holding a conference each year for just the policy people. It allowed a small group of people to get together "in one room, talking about, 'Where are we gonna go from here?'"[173] At these meetings, advocates discuss potential reforms and issues involved in getting them into practice, identify priority issues, and so forth.[174]

Unlike most of the smaller organizations, the Innocence Project tackles reform on a national scale and assists individual states on priority issues. At the time of my interviews, its policy priorities were eyewitness reform, recording interrogations, and forensic issues.[175]

The Innocence Project also pursues reform through litigation. It has a Strategic Litigation Unit composed of attorneys who, rather than focus on representing individuals, work on cases where they think they can change the law. For instance, some focus specifically on eyewitness identification cases, while others work on interrogation-reform cases. This unit complements the policy department and stays in regular communication with it.[176]

These developments—the formation of the Innocence Network, the branding of the work, and the growth into the policy arena—represent innocence for the first time becoming a real *movement*. There was now an established network of organizations dedicated to the issue, working together in promoting collective goals. In other words, this was the establishment of the innocence movement as we know it today.

The Innocence Movement Today

The Innocence Network is the core the of the innocence movement. In 2012, Georgia businessman Charlie Edmonson, who was a board member at the Georgia Innocence Project, gave the Innocence Network a grant, with which it hired a full-time staff. The Network Support Unit is housed at the Innocence Project's offices in New York and is directed by Meredith Kennedy.[177]

Despite the Network's hiring of full-time staff, it remains a loose affiliation, an "association of organizations," as Kennedy called it.[178] Since its initial introduction of 15 members in November 2005, the Innocence Network has grown to include approximately 70 organizations around the world, more than 50 of which are based in the United States. Today, most states, though not all, are covered by one or more organizations.

Every member organization is an independent entity, though there is an advisory board—"they're not a board of directors because the Network isn't a legal entity"—that essentially oversees the functioning of the Network, which might include decisions about membership criteria, members who are not meeting those criteria, revoking membership, policy positions, and the like. This advisory council meets twice per year, once in the fall for a longer, multiday meeting and once in the spring for a shorter meeting at the Innocence Network conference. There are also a number of standing committees, including ones focused on membership, international efforts, and ethics and best practices, as well as an amicus committee. Working groups are put together to handle specific tasks such as strategic planning.[179]

The organizations and advocates themselves, though, are the heart of the movement.[180] Although the organizational model established by the Innocence Project has been followed by many Network members, not all resemble the seminal group in every way. As of the end of 2014, more than 60% of the 68 member organizations were either affiliated only with a law school or were nonprofits affiliated with a law school. Others are nonprofits that are independent (16%) or affiliated with another educational institution (6%); for example, at least one clinical program is based out of a university social science department, and one is housed in a biology department.[181] Still other members are pro bono sections of law firms (3%) or affiliated with public defender offices (12%), including groups in Massachusetts, Connecticut, Delaware, Kentucky, and Ohio.[182] Even within the Network, the exact structure varies. North Carolina, for instance, has a unique setup, where a central organization— the North Carolina Center on Actual Innocence—handles intake for clinics at various law schools in the state.[183]

Innocence Network organizations also vary widely in size. In 2014, the total budget of all members was more than $32 million, but the ten largest organizations alone composed 60% of that total; the median budget was only $236,618. The New York–based Innocence Project is by far the largest organization—it was responsible for generating more than one-third of the nearly $28 million in revenue in 2014—followed by the Northern California Innocence Project and the Northwestern Center on Wrongful Convictions. The funding from these organizations comes from a variety of sources; more than 90% comes from grants, university contributions, individual donors, and special events.[184]

The size discrepancies exist in terms of staff numbers as well. As of October 2016, the Innocence Project lists 68 staff members on its website, including Scheck and Neufeld, and have litigation, policy, research, and social work departments. However, in 2014, fewer than ten Network organizations had more than five employees; the average number of staff was only four, the median was only two, and several members functioned with no full-time employees. The innocence movement therefore relies heavily on volunteers, who contributed more than 54,000 hours to Network organizations in 2014, and pro bono attorneys, who contributed more than 143,000 hours.[185]

Despite these differences, innocence advocates share a few key goals. Nearly all organizations do casework, investigating and litigating potential wrongful convictions. In addition, a number of them engage in policy advocacy and public education, and many provide reintegration services for exonerees returning home.

Freeing the Innocent

Innocence Network organizations receive nearly 20,000 requests per year for assistance. While approximately three-fourths of them are rejected, members other than the Innocence Project had a backlog of almost 130 cases each. It is not surprising, then, that the most common priority for Innocence Network organizations is to make progress on their cases. While most Network members are involved in casework, the vast majority are not limited only to DNA cases, as the Innocence Project is; in 2014, only five organizations were DNA only, five were non-DNA only, and the rest handled both.[186] Importantly, it is not just Network members that secure exonerations of innocent prisoners. Organizations such as Centurion Ministries—remember, the first nonprofit established in the United States dedicated to wrongful conviction work—also work on cases and secure exonerations but are not members of the Network. Even beyond such organizations, exonerations may be secured without the assistance of a formal innocence organization.

For these and other reasons, tracking wrongful convictions can be a dubious task; by definition, such errors are hidden from view, and thus tabulating rates of wrongful convictions and exonerations is virtually impossible to do with any certainty. A recent report published by the National Academy of Sciences, which is arguably the most scientific and empirically grounded estimate of wrongful convictions, suggests that a conservative estimate of wrongful convictions in death penalty cases is 4.1%,[187] and most estimates place the error rate in felonies at 1%–5%,[188] though these estimates have been disputed by other lawyers, scholars, and even Supreme Court justices.[189]

Despite the difficulty of estimating how many wrongful convictions occur, a variety of approaches can help us understand the scope of the innocent movement's successes. Perhaps the most widely cited figure in terms of number of exonerations is that offered by the Innocence Project. It tracks only DNA exonerations since 1989, which, as of October 2016, total 344. The first 250 DNA exonerations were analyzed systematically by law professor Brandon Garrett in a book that received critical acclaim.[190] Another popular source is the Death Penalty Information Center; its list, counting exonerations from death row since 1973, contains 156 cases.

Although a number of scholars and other writers have compiled their own sets of wrongful conviction cases, the lists maintained by the Innocence Project and the Death Penalty Information Center were, for most of the past 20 years, the most commonly cited exoneration lists. In 2012, however, a new project was launched as a collaboration between the University of Michigan Law School and the Northwestern University Center on Wrongful Convictions that became the largest depository of information on known exoneration cases.

Law professor Samuel Gross and colleagues published a seminal article in 2005 cataloguing and describing 340 DNA and non-DNA exonerations, which at the time was the largest collection of exonerations. However, it became clear very early that the list was "badly incomplete,"[191] and to overcome this would require a much more extensive project.

Around this same time, Rob Warden and Michael Radelet had the idea of publishing an encyclopedia of wrongful convictions.[192] They knew Gross and initially wanted him to write a review of the volume. They also thought it was important to have a database for people to access. The project was slow going, and by 2008, it was clear that their approach was not the most effective way to proceed. The era of the print encyclopedia was basically over; as Maurice Possley said, "As with any book, the day it is published, it is outdated."[193] Warden and colleagues decided to make it an online product that was easily accessible. Gross took on an increasingly prominent role in developing it and ultimately took the lead on the project. Warden had amassed a large paper file at Northwestern University, which was the starting point as their core of cases. In stages, they converted the paper files into the online database format.[194] Looking for assistance in finishing up the herculean task, they brought on Pulitzer Prize–winning journalist Maurice Possley.

Possley had covered criminal justice issues extensively while working at the *Chicago Tribune* and had focused on errors in particular, including an investigative series on prosecutorial misconduct. He left the *Tribune* in 2008 and in 2009 joined the Northern California Innocence Project to research prosecutorial misconduct in California. He left the project in the fall of 2011 when his funding ran out. Gross, whom Possley already knew, reached out to him about the registry and ultimately hired him to help write the remaining case summaries. While doing so, Possley found more exonerations and realized that in order "to keep this thing going, it needed a curator. If you want this to be a living, breathing entity, you need somebody who is essentially curating it."[195] The group needed a researcher to keep digging for cases and updating the database, and Possley was hired full-time in April 2012.

Launched in May 2012 with nearly 900 cases, the National Registry of Exonerations (NRE) was and is the largest and most up-to-date collection of exonerations. It works to keep track of all known cases since 1989, which currently total more than 1,800. Gross serves as the head of the project, Possley is a full-time researcher, and they generally have a research fellow to assist on case summaries and other projects.

Although the NRE does not purport to be an exhaustive collection of all wrongful convictions—the actual number is unknowable—it is the largest collection of exonerations and provides an invaluable resource to researchers, advocates, policy makers, and anyone else interested in wrongful convictions.

Reforming the System

For Scheck and Neufeld, from the outset, their innocence work was about more than just securing exonerations. Of course, freeing the innocent is at the heart of the work, and without those stories, the innocence movement would not exist. But the cases also represent powerful opportunities for reflection, analysis, and ultimately, change. Scheck described each case as "literally a learning moment for the criminal justice system," which feeds directly into policy reform. Thus, whenever a wrongful conviction is unearthed, it is important to examine what factors contributed to the conviction "and what kind of remedies [can be] put in place to prevent it from happening again, or to at least ameliorate the weaknesses of the system." This "fundamental dynamic" of the innocence movement is key and drives the policy-reform agenda.[196]

The policy successes have been described briefly already in this book and in detail elsewhere. In general, though, the priority areas tend to reflect the contributing factors that are seen most often, particularly in DNA exonerations. These include changing eyewitness identification procedures, recording interrogations, ensuring preservation of biological evidence, improving inmates' access to postconviction DNA testing, and oversight of forensic testing labs. On these and other issues, the Innocence Project offers model legislation policies that can be used by advocates and lawmakers in drafting and proposing new laws. The agenda has had some impact; well over half of the states have passed some type of innocence reform, and hundreds of individual agencies have implemented some type of change to their practices.

Another, equally important policy area that has been prioritized by the innocence movement has been the development of statutory compensation policies, laws that tie directly into a third goal of the movement.

Reintegrating Exonerees

Those who are engaged in wrongful conviction work know that the hard work does not end when someone is exonerated and freed from confinement. Like any institutionalized person, an exoneree may face a variety of struggles upon release.[197] Innocence organizations often work with exonerees to help them rebuild their lives. The Innocence Project has its own social work department; others do not have such a formal approach, but many groups work with their exonerees upon release to help them find housing, employment, and other necessities. There are also organizations dedicated specifically to post-exoneration issues; several Network members fall into this category, including at least two that were founded by exonerees themselves.[198]

An important element of the innocence policy agenda encourages states to assist exonerees through compensation statutes. These laws, which provide monetary and other reintegration assistance, currently exist in more than 30 states and the federal government, though those that exist vary widely and are limited in utility.[199]

The Benefits of a Network

Clearly, innocence advocates have had some success; more than 1,800 people have been exonerated, and policy reforms have been passed and are in the works across the nation. Perhaps most importantly, though, there seems to be some energy here. In legal and political circles and, to some extent, in the public sphere, there appears to be a recognition that the criminal justice system errs with enough frequency to warrant reform.

Of course, not all of the exonerations and policy reforms have been the work of Innocence Network members, but the presence of such a network is vital to creating and maintaining the energy of the movement. In addition to being influential in the legal academy and thus impacting up-and-coming lawyers, an established national network provides a number of benefits.

At the most basic level, the Network is an important resource for communication and education. Member projects keep in touch, the Network sends out a newsletter, and an annual conference—a massive undertaking to plan and organize—is held each spring to bring together advocates, exonerees, and others. The specific benefits of these things may differ between members. For those who are new to innocence work, the benefits might be mostly educational. As Theresa Newman pointed out, postconviction work is different when innocence is involved, and if a group is the only one in its area doing it, advocates may not have anyone nearby to turn to for assistance. Thus, having the Network provides the group with resources for engaging in the work. At each yearly conference, there are sessions on starting an innocence project, DNA basics, habeas litigation, and other topics that may be challenging for beginners.[200]

The importance of having a communication network and an annual meeting of like-minded folks is not only beneficial for newcomers, however. For nearly everyone doing this work, keeping up-to-date about what others are doing and having others to discuss legal issues, frustrations, and anything else with is immeasurably valuable. Sometimes, as former codirector of the Northwestern Center Jane Raley said, this amounts to technical issues or assistance with a case: "There is a lot of cooperation. For example, today, somebody was asking, 'Has anybody encountered this issue?' . . . And I was able to respond, 'This came up in one of my cases, this is the argument I used, and here's the case where the argument won.' And so it's a resource that we all have. There are exchanges all the time about experts. 'Who's the best?' 'Where should I have my DNA tested?' 'Has anyone worked with [this person]?' It's wonderful."[201]

Members also provide a useful resource if something comes up in a case and outside assistance is necessary, as law professor and codirector of the Northwestern Center's Women's Project, Judy Royal, described: "What we do sometimes, if we have a case where there's a codefendant, and we can't represent the codefendant because, for example, there might be, theoretically, a conflict situation, so they should have a separate attorney, . . . in that situation, what we typically do is contact another attorney, another innocence project, to represent the codefendant. And we would likely then work together on the common issues."[202]

So, although the Network is a loose affiliation and much of the collaboration is informal, its benefits to members are crucial. "It's a lot of networking and informal working together, more relationship building, because it's very specific, what we're doing," said Erika Applebaum, the former director of the Innocence Project of Minnesota. "And to know that my friend Lindsay in Arizona has the same or a similar type of case and I can call her and talk to her about it is really wonderful."[203]

But the benefit of having this communication network runs deeper than being able to find assistance with technical matters. Perhaps the most important benefit is the emotional support it provides, a point made by a number of people I spoke with, including Meredith Kennedy:

> I think the value [of the Innocence Network] is in everybody talking to each other. This work is really hard work. It is isolating work, it can be really isolating. There are high highs and low lows, and I think the burnout factor, particularly for attorneys that are litigating these cases but others too, is high. And being able to talk to someone else who's been through whatever it is that you're going through, whatever challenge it is that you're up against, whatever ridiculous ruling you've gotten, [an] incredibly frustrating point where you are in trying to find evidence or something like that, I think it saves a lot of people.[204]

Theresa Newman made a similar point:

> These are defeating. This kind of work is very difficult and frustrating, and when you know you have an innocent client and you can't get that person out, it's . . . a little bit soul crushing. So to be with other people who are doing the same work and to see the successes that we get collectively carries a lot of people forward to go back to the office the next day and keep trying. . . . It's difficult to keep going back. It's difficult to stay. I like to practice law level-headed and rational and honest and believing that the truth will prevail. It's difficult to maintain and to hold that line, but when you're together with people who are doing the same work, it's easier. So that's a big benefit.[205]

There is also some reputational gain in being associated with a national network of organizations dedicated to a specific cause. This ensures that organizations or advocates are not viewed as outliers or radicals and can help legitimize the movement's goals by reinforcing statements on legal issues or calls for policy reform. For instance, Aimee Maxwell, the former director of the Georgia Innocence Project, mentioned the importance of having the backing of a larger network when submitting an amicus brief, which the Network has done in more than 100 cases.[206]

Newman summed up the benefits of the Innocence Network succinctly: "Education, reputation, inspiration. I think those are the three that I would identify as the three principal benefits."[207] This speaks to something that is important for any movement. Regardless of the specific cause or mission, it is important to have shared goals and a shared purpose, and the innocence movement seemingly has these things. They create a collective identity that unites like-minded advocates in a quest for change and provides legitimacy for the movement and individuals' participation in it. As Maxwell said, "The importance of the Network isn't what they give me. It's just that we're all together on this."[208]

The Expanding Movement

Although the individuals and organizations that make up the Innocence Network largely drive the innocence movement, the advocacy network can and must change, adapt, and expand. Part of this may be Network members expanding in new directions. For example, the Northwestern Center has spawned two sister projects dedicated to particular issues: the Center on Wrongful Convictions of Youth, which focuses on key issues in juvenile justice, including wrongful convictions, and the Women's Project, which examines questionable convictions of female convicts.

The movement is expanding beyond the traditional innocence advocates, too, as practitioners join the fight. As described earlier, several Network members are based in public defender offices, but other practitioners and policy makers are also becoming involved, including those in law enforcement. Police agencies around the nation have been experimenting with reformed eyewitness identification and interrogation procedures, for example, and the International Association of Chiefs of Police held a summit on wrongful convictions and participated in a recent Innocence Network conference.[209] Prosecutors have also taken notice; although prosecutors may be among the most resistant to the innocence movement, the development of Conviction Integrity Units in district attorneys' offices shows some willingness to engage with this issue.

On a much larger scale, another recent development highlights the innocence movement's expansion into and bridging of areas, including the law enforcement, defense, and forensic communities. In 2009, the National Academy of Sciences released a report called *Strengthening Forensic Science in the United States: A Path Forward*. Among other issues, the report highlighted some limitations of and problems with microscopic hair analysis.[210] This report, combined with a series of exonerations between 2009 and 2012 that involved flawed forensic testimony by FBI hair examiners, led the FBI and Department of Justice to collaborate with the Innocence Project and the National Association of Criminal Defense Lawyers on a systematic review of cases involving microscopic hair comparisons. It was the largest postconviction study ever conducted by the FBI,[211] and some shocking results were released in April 2015. Focused on cases handled before 2000, the review found that 26 of the 28 FBI analysts "provided either testimony with erroneous statements or submitted laboratory reports with erroneous statements." Furthermore, in 257 of the first 268 trials reviewed—96%—erroneous statements were made by examiners, including at least 35 cases in which the defendant was sentenced to death.[212] While the findings of this historic study do not indicate that all of the defendants were innocent, these revelations have led to an extensive reevaluation of many cases, including those of George Perrot, who was convicted of raping a 78-year-old woman in Massachusetts in 1985, and Timothy Scott Bridges, who was sentenced to life in prison for the rape of an 83-year-old woman in North Carolina in 1983.[213] The investigation was followed closely in legal and academic circles and generated its share of coverage, both in specialized outlets such as *Forensic Magazine*[214] and in popular outlets such as the *Washington Post, Slate,* and even England's *Guardian.*[215] The investigation was expanded in early 2016.[216]

Clearly, the errors exposed by the innocence movement can generate an increased skepticism of the justice system from within, including judges. I. Beverly Lake, former chief justice of the North Carolina Supreme Court, was so inspired by exonerations in the state and concerned about the public's confidence in the justice system that he helped develop the North Carolina Actual Innocence Commission to examine wrongful convictions, identify potential reforms, and make policy recommendations.[217] Similarly, Jonathan Lippman, former chief judge of New York's highest court, the Court of Appeals, was a leader in commissioning the New York State Justice Task Force in 2009.[218]

Judicial acknowledgment of and grappling with innocence represents a major step forward for the innocence movement. While it has always been a concern for some jurists, perhaps the most aggressive take was that of Supreme Court Justice Stephen Breyer in his dissenting opinion in *Glossip v. Gross* in 2015. Joined by Justice Ruth Bader Ginsburg, the dissent argued that the death penalty's "serious unreliability" was one of the main reasons why it should be deemed unconstitutional. Breyer cited research that has "found convincing evidence that, in the past three decades, innocent people have been executed" and wrote that the "evidence that the death penalty has been wrongly imposed (whether or not it was carried out), is striking." The dissent used information from the National Registry of Exonerations and the National Academy of Sciences report authored by Sam Gross and colleagues to make the argument that errors happen frequently enough to determine that the death penalty is highly unreliable and thus "cruel" under the Eighth Amendment.[219]

There have, of course, been other interesting legal developments beyond judicial acknowledgment that wrongful convictions warrant some concern. One of the more interesting ones is the North Carolina Innocence Inquiry Commission (IIC). Established by the state's General Assembly in 2006 amid a rash of criticism, the IIC is an eight-member panel that investigates potential cases of actual innocence; it is selected by the chief justice of the North Carolina Supreme Court and the chief judge of the Court of Appeals. Cases with merit can eventually make it to an evaluation by a three-judge panel, which may officially declare someone innocent; the agency is the only one of its kind in the United States. As of October 2016, IIC investigations have led to the exoneration of ten people.[220]

In addition to appealing to legal practitioners and lawmakers, several recent initiatives have helped the innocence movement's message reach the public sphere at an unprecedented level. In 2013, journalist and *This American Life* producer Sarah Koenig was contacted by Rabia Chaudry, whose friend, Adnan Syed, was convicted in 1999 of murdering his ex-girlfriend. Chaudry thought Syed was innocent, and years before, Koenig had written about his defense attorney, who was disbarred in 2001. Chaudry asked Koenig to look into the case, and she agreed. Koenig began her investigation and made it the subject of a podcast called *Serial*, which debuted in September 2014 to critical acclaim. Anya Schultz of the *Daily Californian* described it as "rich and intriguing," likening the listening experience to "hearing Sherlock Holmes' diary." Schultz said the episodes left her with "an intense desire to know the truth of what happened," a sensation that was "captivating."[221] The show won a Peabody Award, a distinguished accomplishment for excellence in broadcasting and electronic media, and was quickly downloaded more than five million times, "far more than any other podcast in history."[222] *Serial* reached number one on the iTunes charts within weeks, and by February 2016, it had been downloaded more than 100 million times. The series sparked more extensive reinvestigation of Syed's case and has generated spin-off podcasts, media coverage, a *Saturday Night Live* skit, and plans for a television series.[223]

Another recent development in popular culture was the Netflix series *Making a Murderer*. The series was directed by Laura Ricciardi and Moira Demos, who were graduate film students at Columbia University in 2005 when they read about the case of Steven Avery. Avery had been convicted of a sexual assault and served 18 years in prison before being exonerated through DNA testing. Two years later, while pursuing a $36 million lawsuit against the county, Avery was arrested and charged with murder, though he always maintained his innocence. Ricciardi and Demos thought the case might serve as a good topic for a documentary and drove to Wisconsin for a preliminary hearing. The next year, they moved to Wisconsin to begin the decade-long process of developing the film series.[224] *Making a Murderer* debuted on Netflix in December 2015 to rave reviews. A *New York Times* review called it "immersive, compulsive and unpredictable."[225] *Forbes* writer Paul Tassi described the show's significance, saying it was "the first Netflix show that seems to have completely consumed its viewerbase from top to bottom. . . . The story of Steve Avery has seemed to hook pretty much everyone who has laid eyes on it."[226] The series's success, which came on the heels of *Serial*, was not just in its critical reception but also in its widespread popularity. While Netflix does not release statistics and there are not official ratings for the medium, one research company suggested that *Making a Murderer* rivaled *20/20* in terms of viewership.[227]

While these series are not without their critics—a number of people, including many officials, believe they were produced in a biased way, more as advocacy pieces than journalistic exposés or documentaries—it is clear that media such as *Serial* and *Making a Murderer*, which do not delve directly into proven wrongful convictions but highlight potential flaws in the justice system, are immensely popular and may have a widespread impact on public opinion toward the justice system. Tassi wrote that the discussion in the wake of *Making a Murderer* felt like a "truly national conversation";[228] in fact, a Change.org petition to free Steven Avery garnered more than 500,000 signatures.[229]

These developments, in terms of both popular culture and the involvement of legal practitioners in wrongful conviction issues, are only a few examples of new and interesting initiatives that have been sparked, in large part, by the innocence movement. And importantly, many of these developments are fairly recent—they are, in a sense, still in progress—and thus it is too early to determine how successful these efforts are and whether they will have a lasting impact. Still, they seem to be indicative of a trend. The openness of criminal justice and legal professionals and policy makers to the issue of wrongful conviction, and the popularity of questionable case stories, are clear indicators of the power of innocence to change perceptions and potentially impact criminal justice practices now and in the future.

* * *

Although the idea of wrongful convictions is an old one, it was not until the period described in this chapter—from the action surrounding innocence and the death penalty in the late 1990s and early 2000s to the formation of the Innocence Network—that innocence began to resemble the *movement* we now recognize and identify.

While the overlap between innocence and the death penalty revolved heavily around events in Illinois, the tonal shift in the death penalty debate was nationwide. Anti–death penalty groups and activists began using the death row exonerations as a key argument against the death penalty,[230] and there seemed to be a general sense that "the tide may be turning against unquestioning death penalty support."[231] The capital punishment conversation came to include innocence consistently and heavily during this period, which generated widespread interest, and wrongful conviction coverage began to bleed over into popular culture around this time as well. The movie *Hurricane*, about the wrongful conviction of Rubin Carter and starring Denzel Washington, was released in 1999 to critical acclaim and sparked some discussion of wrongful convictions. That same year, *A&E* ran a program on wrongful convictions and the death penalty, to which DPIC contributed.[232]

This period also saw innocence expand beyond casework in a concrete way. Before this, wrongful convictions had not yet had a major impact on policy or practice that could be felt beyond the immediate cases. Now, however, these cases and what they represent had been used to successfully impact the practice of capital punishment in a major death penalty state, led to a shift in the nature of death penalty discourse nationwide, and directly impacted federal lawmaking. Like any movement, the goal for innocence reformers was to have a broad impact, and in this era, that goal became a reality.

Perhaps most importantly for the innocence movement, the events in Illinois played a direct role in kick-starting the development of a national coalition of innocence organizations with shared interests and core values. The Innocence Network, as it is known today, is the structural core of the innocence movement, and its development was inspired by the 1998 conference. Since its inception, the Network has grown more than fourfold. The formalization of such a coalition marks a shift for innocence from an important, albeit underappreciated issue to a full-on legal-reform movement and has helped the innocence movement become a powerful force for progressive change in the criminal justice system.

PART II

Innocence as a Social Movement

4

"It Did Go against the Grain"

The Foundations of a Movement

History is rarely clean. Though in retrospect historical developments may seem inevitable, deeper analysis usually yields a more nuanced story. Such is the history of the innocence movement.

The movement is often dated to 1989, when DNA was first used to secure an exoneration in the United States. In many ways, this is a true story, but it represents the clean version of it. In reality, the story is more complex, more nuanced; a number of individuals, organizations, decisions, and events led to the rise of the innocence movement, and while DNA played a pivotal role, it did not spark the movement with the "inevitability" that is sometimes implied.[1]

There are several problems with limiting the explanation of the innocence movement solely to DNA and its power to secure exonerations. First, it leaves out the key foundational pieces that had begun shifting into place in the decade before 1989. It also fails to acknowledge that, even with DNA and its first exonerations, there was no *movement* until more than a decade later. And finally, it lacks context.

Considering the innocence movement narrative in light of these limitations begs for a deeper understanding. In this chapter, I focus on the foundations of the innocence movement—those things that were shifting into place before a movement actually developed. I begin with a discussion of the historical context in which the innocence movement began.

Political Turbulence and American Criminal Justice

In some ways, the past half century of criminal justice in the United States has been defined by change. The 1960s through the early 1970s, according to historian Samuel Walker, "was the most turbulent [period] in all of American criminal justice history" and is sometimes referred to as the "due process revolution," though the changes went beyond just due process.[2]

Many of the developments involved the Supreme Court's intervention in the criminal justice process. The Court placed restrictions on police officers, most notably in the cases of *Mapp v. Ohio* in 1961 and *Miranda v. Arizona* in 1966; the former dealt with restrictions on evidence found through illegal searches and seizures, the latter an attempt to protect a suspect's right against self-incrimination.[3] The Court also intervened in the trial process in *Gideon v. Wainwright*, when it ruled that every felony defendant has a Sixth Amendment right to an attorney at trial.[4]

A prisoners' rights movement also developed during this period, and activists began pursuing prison reform through litigation. The Supreme Court established that prisoners had basic constitutional rights, and prison reformers fought for and won rights to religious freedom and outside correspondence. Disciplinary procedures in prisons were reformed, and prisoner segregation was ended.[5] As with its involvement in police practices, the Court's reforms in prisons introduced accountability into the system, holding criminal justice officials to a higher standard; as Walker notes, these decisions "hastened the bureaucratization" in both police departments and correctional facilities.[6]

It was not just the day-to-day operations of the criminal justice system that underwent changes. The death penalty was under attack, and the Supreme Court again stepped in. In the early 1960s, civil rights attorneys began targeting the racial disparities in capital punishment, which broadened to a more general constitutional attack on the practice, an interesting development considering most early death penalty opposition had focused on morality and had attempted abolition through state and local legislatures.[7] The key ruling came in the 1972 case *Furman v. Georgia*, in which the Supreme Court ruled that the death penalty as practiced was arbitrary and capricious, striking down all existing capital punishment statutes.[8]

Many of the criminal justice developments of the era were tied to the broader civil rights movement. Skepticism of the government, authority figures, and sociocultural norms was widespread, and a new political consciousness was fostered in U.S. culture, particularly in the African American community; this consciousness worked its way into the criminal justice system. People became more aware of the extensive racial disparities in criminal justice, especially in the death penalty. The Supreme Court emphasized the importance of individual rights for all suspects and defendants, a focus that bled into cultural life more generally. More and more, social problems were defined in terms of individual rights, and this newfound "rights consciousness" changed the legal and political landscape.[9]

Race and crime became inextricably intertwined during this era. The civil rights movement raised public awareness about racial disparities, and by the mid-1960s, many poor, urban minority communities were seemingly at war with law enforcement, as riots erupted in cities across the country during the "long hot summers," year after year.[10] And if general social upheaval and dramatic changes in criminal justice practices were not enough, a crime wave swept the nation and became an important, salient topic in national politics.

In the post–World War II era, nearly all industrial countries experienced an increase in crime. In the United States, however, levels of violent crime were substantially higher than those abroad, and beginning in the early 1960s, crime levels in the United States began to increase significantly. According to FBI data, the violent crime rate in the United States increased from 160.9 per 100,000 citizens in 1960 to 363.5 in 1970 and to nearly 500 in 1975, a more-than-threefold increase.[11]

In the midst of this rise, President Lyndon Johnson appointed the President's Commission on Law Enforcement and Administration of Justice in 1965. The commission sponsored research on crime— including the development of the National Crime Victimization Survey (NCVS), which is now one of the main sources of information on crime and victimization in the country—and issued its final report, *The Challenge of Crime in a Free Society*, in 1967. The report followed most criminological thinking at the time, linking crime to social ills and lack of economic opportunities. This was the "heyday of rehabilitation"; the emphasis was on community-based treatment, and the number of individuals on probation and parole increased substantially. The federal role in criminal justice grew and spending increased dramatically. Still, the crime rate continued to climb, and violence in prisons reached a fever pitch. A string of prison riots, capped by the infamous Attica riot in New York in 1971, "was the final straw" for many people, "convincing them that something was fundamentally wrong with the entire criminal justice system."[12]

Crime rates were high, and people were scared; in the mid-1960s, only about one-third of Americans reported feeling afraid to walk alone at night near their homes, but this proportion increased to nearly half by the early 1980s.[13] The threat of victimization was real, or at least perceived to be very real, among the general public. Drug use also increased, race relations were on edge, and a harsh "tough on crime" attitude came to dominate criminological thinking. On the heels of the due process era, the nation swung hard toward crime control.[14]

A number of developments during this period are indicative of the punitive climate. A popular policy, in place at the federal level and more than 30 states by the mid-1980s, was preventive detention, which in part allowed judges to deny bail to defendants who were supposedly dangerous. The constitutionality of preventive detention was upheld by the Supreme Court in 1979,[15] a decision suggestive of the new Court, which had transitioned from the liberal Warren Court to a more conservative one under Warren Burger. The Court backed away from its active role in monitoring prison conditions[16] and created exceptions to checks on law enforcement, namely, the exclusionary rule[17] and *Miranda* requirements.[18]

The rehabilitative model, so popular in previous decades, came under fire, as conservative writers like James Q. Wilson and Ernest van den Haag propagated a message that "nothing works" and suggested that the answer was harsher punishment, including the use of the death penalty, to incapacitate and deter offenders.[19] A popular target of discontent was indeterminate sentencing—the practice of sentencing offenders without stating an exact period of time or specific release date. Liberals believed the practice to be discriminatory, while conservatives believed it was too often soft on crime. The response was to focus on career criminals and establish sentencing guidelines to limit judicial discretion. The United States Sentencing Commission was created by Congress in 1984, the federal sentencing guidelines took effect in 1987, and by the mid-1990s, the number of federal inmates nearly doubled.[20] A large proportion of this increase was from drug offenses, the most notorious of which was the penalty for crack cocaine; a conviction for possession of five grams with intent to distribute carried a five-year sentence, while that same sentence for powdered cocaine required 500 grams or more, a 100:1 ratio.[21] States also implemented strict mandatory-sentencing guidelines, including "three-strikes" laws, in the mid-1990s. First passed in California, three-strikes laws mandated long sentences for third-time felony offenders.[22]

This complete tonal shift away from rehabilitation and the punitive policies that resulted were part of the larger "wars" on crime and drugs. First declared in the 1960s, these wars were energized again in the 1980s and 1990s. President George H. W. Bush announced a new war on drugs in 1989, while the war on crime centered on urban violence under President Clinton in the 1990s.[23]

The punitive climate in the United States and the resulting reforms in criminal sentencing led to a massive increase in the correctional population across the country. The number of prison and jail inmates more than doubled from 1980 to 1990, and by 2000, there were nearly two million inmates in the United States.[24] Crime was firmly part of the social, cultural, and political landscape; the public was concerned, and its protection became "the dominant theme of penal policy."[25] Political capital was gained by appearing tough on crime, and politicians used rhetoric laced with discipline, punishment, and public safety to maintain that appearance.

Another aspect of this "punitive turn," as sociologist David Garland calls it,[26] was the return of the death penalty. The Supreme Court upheld the constitutionality of new death penalty laws in 1976 in *Gregg v. Georgia*, and in 1977, Gary Gilmore became the first prisoner executed in ten years. Initially, there were few executions that followed—only five in the next five years. That number jumped to more than 20 in 1984 alone and to more than 50 in 1995. Furthermore, the number of inmates on death row increased from less than 700 in 1980 to more than 3,000 in 1995, ensuring that the execution pipeline remained full.[27]

By the mid-1990s, the era of punishment was in full swing. There were well over a million people in prisons and jails across the country, the death penalty machine was well oiled, and the United States had in place some of the harshest sentencing laws in history. There was little indication that the punitive turn would abate, as politicians called for still-harsher punishments.[28] Interestingly, crime was mostly a bipartisan issue; as Walker notes, the divide between conservative and liberal crime policy had vanished, as prominent Democrats called for more prisons and longer sentences.[29] Punishment, in the name of preserving law and order, was the edict of the era.

With such a criminal justice field—dominated by rhetoric of punishment, discipline, and fear, with strong racial undertones—concern for suspects, defendants, and inmates fell by the wayside. During this period, particularly in the 1980s and 1990s, rehabilitation was heavily criticized, the individual rights of suspects and prisoners were deemphasized, and appearing "soft" on crime was an easy way to lose an election. This climate thus begs an interesting question: where does innocence fit in this larger criminal justice picture?

If one were to take stock of the vast literature on the modern era of criminal justice and the punitive turn, the impression may be that innocence does not fit in this picture. Although many scholars have examined and attempted to explain the era of punishment, virtually none of their coverage includes innocence.

Political scientist Stuart Scheingold, writing in the 1980s, viewed the criminal law as the product of value conflict among competing groups in society, reflective of the interests of those that are most powerful. Punitive responses to crime, he argued, are a part of U.S. culture, where the myth of increasing stranger violence and the cultural emphasis on individualism produce a public view that punitive policies are necessary and desirable responses to criminal behavior. This belief makes the American public vulnerable to symbolic messages from politicians, particularly during times of social upheaval.[30] More recently, Garland has attributed the punitive shift to a set of social and cultural changes that he describes as "the coming of late modernity."[31] He argues that an increase in the political salience of crime and criminal justice issues, changes in the ways crime has been represented, and other social shifts led to the development of a crime-control culture, which developed from society's collective experience of and adaptations to crime.

Other writers have emphasized the importance of the social and cultural roots of modern criminal justice political discourse,[32] moral panics,[33] and the interactions of these anxieties with decreased confidence of the public in policy experts, which led to the use of crime as a major political issue.[34] Still others have focused more explicitly on the racial elements of criminal justice practices.[35] These are all linked to media depictions of criminal justice.[36]

All of these explanations help us understand how and why the United States entered the age of mass criminalization and imprisonment, but in none of these examinations of the modern criminal justice system is innocence even on the radar. How, then, was innocence able to find a niche during this turbulent period?

The implication from the innocence literature seems fairly simple: DNA. Wrongful conviction scholarship often implies that this is the explanation for the rise of the innocence movement. Although this explanation is incomplete, DNA certainly played a vital role.

The "Magic Bullet" of DNA

Although dozens of wrongful convictions had been uncovered prior to the late 1980s, they were often met with skepticism or downright dismissal. Despite evidence that suggested a person was innocent, talk of criminal justice errors was rarely met with true concern; the response tended to suggest that the person was not innocent but got off on a technicality or had done something else to warrant conviction and punishment. At the very least, if it was accepted that an error had occurred, it was seen as exceptionally rare and did not justify systemic reform. DNA provided a way to get past this dismissive response.[37]

Peter Neufeld, who worked on exonerations in the pre-DNA era, stressed how important DNA was: "The difference between what we did . . . in the Coakley case and [the] post-Coakley era was, number one, it was anecdotal, number two, you would not be able to have a kind of gold standard of innocence." DNA, however, provided evidence of innocence that was more or less "scientifically irrefutable,"[38] according to Neufeld: "You know, there have been a lot of people who have written books, who've done studies prior to DNA testing, on the ghosts of the unjustly convicted. But the problem is that they can never argue with sufficient certainty to a hostile audience that these people were, indeed, innocent. . . . But with these DNA exonerations, there is no debate anymore. There is a consensus, or much more than a consensus, in fact, an almost unanimity that these people were stone-cold innocent, but nevertheless were convicted of something that they didn't do."[39] Paul Casteleiro, who also worked on pre-DNA exonerations, agreed: "DNA made the argument that it doesn't occur or [that] it only occurs in the rarest of situations—[it] put the lie to that. That's what DNA did." He said that while people always knew that wrongful convictions occurred, "DNA put the meat on the bones" in a way that "wasn't theoretical; it wasn't dependent on the word of different people. It really created some good, objective evidence."[40] Maddy deLone similarly emphasized this point: "All of a sudden, there was this absolute identity-prover, . . . and it was really with the ability to prove it in a way that could not be disputed that sort of captured people."[41]

DNA, then, took proof of innocence "to a different level."[42] But it also allowed people to see what had gone wrong. As Casteleiro noted, "It told you how some of these wrongful convictions were occurring. It told you that people were misidentified, clearly, and you can't get around that, . . . and that false confessions do occur."[43] Similarly, Maurice Possley said, "DNA gave us a certainty we didn't have before, and with that certainty, we were able to go back and see, 'Why did this happen?' . . . And with that, you can go back and see, well, the science was bad or the witness lied."[44] Thus, DNA enabled advocates not only to uncover errors using powerful science but also to understand how and why errors occurred, which is a crucial step toward developing corrective reforms.

Importantly, DNA also had an important implication beyond the cases in which it was utilized. It showed definitively that people were wrongly convicted, Rob Warden said, "and that, in turn, gave credence to the non-DNA cases where there was persuasive evidence of wrongful convictions."[45] Similarly, Casteleiro said that DNA "kind of gave legitimacy to people that do believe . . . that false convictions do occur."[46] Thus, as Possley put it, DNA "not only empowered people to get involved but justified it. This was going to be able to prove something definitively."[47] The result was that people inside the system might become more willing to look at all cases, even those that did not involve DNA evidence. This is an important point made by a number of the individuals with whom I spoke, including deLone:

> I think DNA, while it's only going to be available in, depending on who you believe, 5 to 10% of violent felonies, . . . all the things we see that went wrong here, all the kinds of evidence that were accepted by juries as evidence of guilt, you find in other cases where you don't have DNA at the center. But now you can start saying, "Okay, fine, so you had three

eyewitnesses, and you have somebody it turns out was incentivized, and you had somebody who confessed, but look at the inconsistencies in what in fact [was at] at the crime scene and what he said." You can deconstruct the cases, and you can say, "That's just like X, Y, and Z DNA exonerations." So the DNA cases created a little pathway through which people could start to really bring forth all of these other exonerations.

The importance of DNA to the innocence movement cannot be overstated, and its importance is certainly not lost on the advocates who are involved in the movement; time and time again in our conversations, it was emphasized. DeLone summed it up succinctly when she said, "I don't know that without DNA we would have any of this."[48]

Commentaries generally point to the first DNA exonerations in 1989 as the key starting point for the movement, and there is some truth to this. Although it is impossible to know with any certainty, it is entirely possible, or even likely, that without DNA, the innocence movement would not have gotten off the ground, and if it did, it would almost certainly look quite different.

It would be fair to suggest, then, as Possley did, that the innocence movement "sort of evolved out of DNA."[49] The new scientific technology can thus be seen as a spark for the creation of a movement. As Barry Scheck told me, "technological innovations" may serve as a "springboard" for a movement: "I do think that's important with respect to the innocence movement because it was this most reliable of technologies, DNA testing, and its transference to the forensic arena that's had a tectonic impact on the litigation and on people's perception of the system as a whole."[50] While all of this is true, I would offer slightly different language than is often used. In social scientific parlance, saying that the innocence movement "evolved out of DNA" seems to suggest that DNA was the "cause" of the movement's emergence, which is not quite accurate. Rather, DNA served as a key foundational piece on which the innocence movement was built. More specifically, it was the DNA *exoneration* that was important.

This is an important distinction. The development of DNA technology in and of itself is significant, but in terms of its leading to the rise of the innocence movement, it was merely an opportunity. And as with any opportunity, it needed to be recognized, framed, and seized in order for it to help generate a movement. This key point is often lost when scholars point to DNA as the sole reason for the rise of the innocence movement.

DNA was not initially seen as a tool for seeking justice through the righting of wrongful convictions. Despite the fact that in its first use in a criminal investigation, the "Blooding" case in England, it exonerated an innocent suspect, much more attention went to its identification of the guilty party. Similarly, when it suggested that David Vasquez was innocent in Virginia in 1989, the focus was on capturing the true perpetrator.

This is not surprising; when DNA first made its way into the U.S. legal system, the punitive turn was in full effect, and the technology was aimed squarely at law enforcement as a tool to solve crimes and catch guilty criminals. The companies that conducted DNA tests, Cellmark and Lifecodes, made their connections through advertisements in law enforcement journals and professional meetings. This emphasis is also seen in their advertising, in which DNA fingerprinting technology was presented as a definitive way to link offenders to a crime scene. In one 1988 advertisement, for instance, Cellmark claimed that "criminals leave more conclusive evidence than ever before" and that DNA fingerprinting "may be the difference between conviction and acquittal." It went on to say that it could obtain "conclusive results in only one test," even "from samples that are months or even years old."[51]

The initial promotion of DNA technology as a law enforcement tool provides support for Zalman's social constructionist perspective: the way we understand DNA exonerations is a construction that has been shaped by a variety of factors,[52] rather than representing some inevitable universal truth. To take one step further back, what matters is the framing of DNA. That is, the understanding of DNA as a tool for seeking justice through exonerations was not an inevitable outcome but was shaped by a number of factors. The question then becomes, what were those factors?

I have described many of those elements throughout the narrative thus far, but they can be put together to provide a more complex and dynamic understanding of the innocence movement's foundations.

The Foundation of a Movement

Three classic aspects of social movement theory can help us better understand how the foundation of the innocence movement shifted into place. Political opportunity research emphasizes the changes that occur that make the target system more vulnerable or receptive to change. DNA certainly provided an opportunity to demonstrate with near certainty that the criminal justice system erred, but it had to be framed properly. In other words, the important part is not just that DNA exonerations occurred but that DNA was widely understood as a way to seek justice through exoneration. This matter of framing or issue construction is another area of social movement scholarship, covering the ways in which mutual understandings or meanings are created that make collective action worthwhile or legitimate. The third strand of social movement theory can help us understand how this framing occurred. Research on mobilizing structures focuses on the ways in which people engage in collective action, encouraging us to examine the key people and organizations involved. All of these areas work together, and all were important for the innocence movement.

DNA technology provided the opportunity to find flaws in the criminal justice system, thus rendering it vulnerable to reform efforts. Collective *action*, however, requires organization. Specifically, mobilization scholars stress the importance of social movement organizations (SMOs), which have goals in line with a movement's preferences and attempt to implement those goals.[53] Importantly, an organization had already been established years before DNA technology.

Organizational Foundation

Centurion Ministries was not founded with broad, reform-minded goals; as Jim McCloskey told me, the organization's development "wasn't any great scheme or plan" of his: "when each door opened, we went through that door."[54] It does, however, deserve credit for helping to establish an organizational foundation for the innocence movement. Despite its relatively small size and narrow scope, Centurion was founded years before anyone else was doing wrongful conviction work in an organized fashion. Starting such a group was a risky move given the legal climate and skepticism of people in the 1980s to the idea of wrongful convictions. Yet McCloskey and Kate Germond made it work and showed that it was possible to sustain a successful nonprofit organization in the area of wrongful convictions for an extended period of time.

Of course, the innocence movement is about more than just casework, which is Centurion's focus. This contrasts sharply with the Innocence Project and sets the organizations apart as independent and unique entities.

The Innocence Project was founded as a clinic and focused on casework, but its founders, Barry Scheck and Peter Neufeld, saw the potential in this area of work and set up their organization to expand. They developed an organizational model that could be replicated at other law schools around the country and made a point to encourage the development of such clinics. Today, their model is commonly followed to some degree by nearly all innocence projects.

Although Centurion Ministries and the Innocence Project are quite different organizations, they are both important to the early days of the innocence movement. As noted earlier, Scheck and Neufeld were aware of Centurion prior to the formation of the Innocence Project and had regular communication with Centurion in the time leading up to and immediately following the founding of their organization. One exoneree even remarked to me that without Germond and Centurion, the Innocence Project would not exist as it does today. Whether or not this is entirely true—as noted, Scheck and Neufeld recognized their opportunity early on and developed a much different organization—Centurion certainly deserves credit for establishing wrongful convictions as a viable area for nonprofit work. Thus, Centurion and the Innocence Project are responsible for laying down the organizational foundation for what ultimately became the innocence movement.

Lawyering for a Cause, Leading a Movement

A movement can only be as strong as its leaders. Fortunately for the innocence movement, the early days brought two visionary leaders in Barry Scheck and Peter Neufeld. Early on, they recognized the opportunity that DNA presented and were willing to take advantage of it. DNA could do more than just free individuals. "It's a real learning moment,"

Scheck said. "We should seize it, in the criminal justice community, in the legal academic community."[55]

It is not surprising that Scheck and Neufeld emerged to pick up the torch for innocence. Engaged in political activism from a young age, both saw law as a way to achieve something that extends far beyond the courtroom. "I never got involved in the law from the traditional perspective of wanting to be a courtroom lawyer," Neufeld once said. "That was not interesting. But it was, rather, seeing the law as a vehicle for social change."[56] In other words, both Neufeld and Scheck are quintessential cause lawyers, dedicated to using law and legal tactics to institute broader change and "seek a more just world."[57]

Some scholars have dated the origins of cause lawyering as far back as the era of slavery, when legal activists worked to reform slave laws, while others root it in the legal actions of the early labor movement.[58] The first significant emergence of cause lawyering occurred during the New Deal period of the 1930s, when the expansion of the federal government provided opportunities for young lawyers to help implement regulations and defend them from constitutional challenges.[59] Decades later, when the civil rights movement gained momentum in the 1950s and 1960s, lawyers like Thurgood Marshall gained prominence as they used legal strategies to advocate for the rights of minorities and motivated scores of law students to fight for progressive social change.[60]

The 1960s era of activism spawned numerous legal-reform organizations and public-interest law firms. This culture created a generation of young lawyers and students with a real sense of activist duty, and many pursued careers in law as a way to take part in promoting important social reform. Neufeld and Scheck are of that generation. In one interview, Neufeld acknowledged the importance of the era when talking about what gave him his sense of the big picture: "The '60s, obviously, played a large part of that because there was a sense of empowerment that you personally, by taking action, could make a difference. And so whatever work we got involved in, we thought, 'Well, God, this is how we can make a difference.' Whether it's one small trial or a painting or a mural, it was going to be, hopefully, powerful and have that kind of significant impact. So that was the '60s. There's no question about that."[61] Scheck expressed a similar sentiment, describing the monumental importance of the civil rights movement to an up-and-coming generation of potential lawyers:

> I grew up in an era where one saw that in the civil rights movement,
> law was an instrument of social change and was essential to winning the
> rights of African Americans in the South and across the country, to get
> the vote, to participate in public services in this country. It's the great
> movement of our time. You think back to what's been accomplished in
> this country within our lifetimes in terms of civil rights. . . . It's really
> extraordinary to think about. And lawyers had a lot to do with it. In fact,
> we were all probably oversold on the extent to which law could be an in-
> strument of social change. By the time I graduated from law school, there
> was a whole generation of us that kind of felt like, "Oh, we'll be able to do
> that. We're people's lawyers."[62]

This sense that Scheck, Neufeld, and a bevy of other young lawyers
had—that law can have a major impact on important social issues—
carried into their professional careers. The Bronx Legal Aid office, where
Neufeld and Scheck worked and met in the 1970s, was an underfunded
group of young, politically active lawyers who had protested the war
and campaigned for civil rights. "A lot of the people that I worked with
in that public defender's office in the South Bronx were all just like me,"
Scheck said. "They were all politically motivated people. They wanted to
be people's lawyers. . . . It was a great group."[63]

The activist spirit remained with Scheck and Neufeld, and given their
backgrounds and experiences, it makes sense that by the mid- to late
1980s, when they became involved in the DNA battles in court, they recognized the tremendous opportunity in front of them. They had served
as public defenders and had professionally come of age; Neufeld had
some experience with science in court, and Scheck was by then a clinical professor at Cardozo, a "stimulating environment" where he could
choose issues that he thought were important and that was "a good place
to stay intellectually alive."[64] It is not surprising, then, that they worked
hard to seize the incredible opportunity they saw in front of them to
generate legal and social reform.

Everyone I spoke with recognizes that it was Scheck and Neufeld's
work, their vision, and their willingness to take on the leadership role
that led to the growth of the movement. Kate Germond, for example,
gives them immense credit for informing the public about the issue: "In
terms of making the world aware of wrongful convictions, certainly the

use of DNA testing and then the advent of the Innocence Project and then, you know, basically heralding themselves—and again, it's not a negative—really made the public begin to be aware of, 'Holy shit, there's something broken here.'"[65]

This is already one layer beyond the limited assertion that DNA exonerations simply occurred and sparked a movement. Serendipitous as it was, it just so happened that when DNA entered the courtroom, two cause lawyers were at the point in their careers to recognize and seize the opportunity and that an organizational foundation could be developed to support a broader movement. However, it was not just within these organizations and within the law that individuals spurred the growth of the innocence movement.

Identifying the "Problem" of Wrongful Convictions

A movement needs not just people and organization; at the core of any movement is its cause, the *problem* it seeks to address. Innocence advocates did not necessarily have this in the early days.

As early as the work of Edwin Borchard in the 1930s, scholars, journalists, and other writers occasionally compiled and described cases that they believed were wrongful convictions. However, even by the 1980s, skepticism and disbelief accompanied coverage of wrongful convictions. The criminal justice system was resistant to accusations of factual error, and those who worked on this issue outside of the law, both in journalism and in academia, faced as much of this resistance as those within the system. Wrongful conviction work was often viewed as a waste of time, according to Rob Warden, one of the earliest journalists to work in this area: "There was a time, back in 1983, when I first wrote a story about someone who I thought had been wrongfully convicted and sentenced to death for a crime he hadn't committed, [that] the mainstream media and even the legal profession said, 'Come on.' Nobody believed it. Everyone believed we had the best criminal justice system in the world—and we may—but that wrongful convictions didn't occur. And if one did on occasion, it was such a rare anomaly that we certainly didn't need to make any changes in the system."[66] Ron Huff met with a similar reaction when he and his colleagues began research on the topic in the mid-1980s: "People thought, 'Why am I wasting my time with this?'" He suggested that wrongful convictions were seen as a "trivial issue" and any errors as rare, relatively unimportant aberrations.[67]

Those who worked in the system seem to have had little sense of the scope of wrongful convictions. Maddy deLone, who worked in jails and prisons at the time, said that very few inmates she met claimed they were innocent, so she "really didn't think about it."[68] Her focus was on how people were treated regardless of guilt or innocence. Even those who were doing wrongful conviction work were not necessarily sure of the scope of the errors. Kate Germond, who has "always been very cynical about America and how we treat people," believed that the criminal justice system might not be fair to the poor and to people of color but said, "the surprise was *how* broken it is."[69]

The lawyers who worked on some of the early cases, for their part, certainly believed that wrongful convictions occur but did not generally think about the extent of the issue. Paul Casteleiro said that he "always thought there were a good number of these cases out there" after becoming a lawyer but did not necessarily think about an error rate.[70] Even Peter Neufeld did not realize how widespread errors may be in his early days as an attorney: "I always thought, my whole life I've been practicing law, especially as a criminal defense attorney, that 98%, 99% of the people convicted by juries and judges must be guilty."[71] If defense attorneys working on cases of actual innocence had a difficult time grasping the scope of errors, it is understandable that others—the prosecutorial and law enforcement communities and the public at large—would struggle with it and be wary of accusations of error.

Part of this is a matter of perspective, according to Rob Warden: "I think it's like, lawyers only saw their one case—they didn't see the bigger picture. You'd find lawyers who knew about what had happened to a client but they felt it was isolated." The crusading journalists who worked early on to uncover cases of wrongful conviction and write about them, despite a media environment that was not always friendly, helped spread the word that there may be more of these cases than most people would believe. According to Warden, "if it hadn't been for great investigative journalists and wonderful people like Jim Dwyer in New York and Maurice Possley and Steve Mills in Chicago, the innocence movement wouldn't have gotten off the ground."[72]

Academic research also played a role in describing the potential scope of wrongful convictions in the early years. Previous writings dating back to Borchard had collected and described cases of wrongful conviction, highlighting problems with eyewitnesses, confessions, and other forms of evidence. In psychological research, work in the early 1900s had found problems with witness testimony,[73] and by the 1980s, psychologists, led by Elizabeth Loftus and Gary Wells, had developed a fairly in-depth understanding of eyewitness identification.[74] This work, however, focused on one particular issue that happens to be related to wrongful convictions in a significant way, rather than the broader scope of the matter.

The research conducted in the mid- to late 1980s took a different approach and was on a different scale. Huff and colleagues conducted a survey of judges, attorneys, and police chiefs—an intentionally conservative sample, according to Huff[75]—to gauge their estimate of the prevalence of wrongful convictions, the first survey of its kind. The estimates ranged from "never" to as high as 10%, and the authors drew the conclusion that a safe, conservative assumption for an error rate is 0.5%–1%. They are clear in pointing out, however, that even if this is correct and the system is accurate more than 99% of the time, it would still produce thousands of wrongful convictions each year.[76] This was a rather startling proposition at the time, when convictions and imprisonment rates were rising.

The Bedau-Radelet study, published in 1987, compiled more than 350 cases of possible wrongful convictions in capital and non-capital cases, by far the largest collection of its kind.[77] The authors' case database was expanded to more than 400 cases by 1992.[78] This was yet another shocking number, and together, these two studies went beyond any of the work that had come before. Despite the fact that the specific numbers may be shaky—the rate of wrongful convictions is unknowable, and so any estimate of the sort would be—they gave a sense of the potential scope of wrongful convictions in a way previous scholarship had not. And importantly, the Bedau-Radelet study in particular received a fair amount of attention.

The journalistic exposés of wrongful conviction cases in popular news outlets and the broader examinations of criminal justice errors in academic research helped begin to shift the nature of the conversation about wrongful convictions. Whereas early cases were sometimes seen as horrible injustices, they were thought to be individual, isolated occurrences, rather than part of a broader problem. As noted earlier, Warden suggested that part of the reason might be that attorneys were caught up in their own cases and sometimes missed the bigger picture, a classic case of missing the forest for the trees. "They didn't know it was part of a bigger thing," he said, "so journalists sort of put it together for them."[79]

This is an important shift in the conversation. To have people recognize individual cases of wrongful conviction as tragedies is one thing, but if they are seen as anomalies, it is hardly cause for widespread concern. However, if people could be convinced that such errors are not isolated but are systemic—in short, that there is a *problem* of wrongful convictions—then the case for innocence as a major reform issue is strengthened.

Framing DNA

The 1996 National Institute of Justice report *Convicted by Juries, Exonerated by Science* begins with a message from Attorney General Janet Reno. She writes, "The development of DNA technology furthers the search for truth by helping police and prosecutors in the fight against violent crime. Through the use of DNA evidence, prosecutors are often able to conclusively establish the guilt of a defendant." She continues to say that DNA "offers prosecutors important new tools for the identification and apprehension of some of the most violent perpetrators, particularly in cases of sexual assault."[80]

It would have been easy to stop there; after all, when DNA first entered the criminal justice world, it did so as a law enforcement tool, useful primarily in capturing guilty offenders. In England, when DNA cleared scores of innocent men before identifying the culprit in the "Blooding," the focus seems to have been on capturing the guilty and protecting the public. During Colin Pitchfork's sentencing in the case, the judge said, "Had it not been for genetic fingerprinting, you might still be at liberty," a quote that Aronson suggests "had a great deal of impact around the world and was reprinted widely."[81] Sir Alec Jeffreys also seemed to place the most emphasis on capturing the guilty in that case, saying that he felt relief because Pitchfork "was a serial murderer and would kill again"[82] and that "DNA testing helped to save lives."[83] Even when DNA testing came to the United States, the companies selling the technique did so by appealing to the law enforcement goal of solving crimes. Cellmark advertised its testing as a tool to identify guilty criminals, focusing on the front end of the process rather than postconviction testing.[84] Its major competition, Lifecodes, sold its tests in a similar fashion, even going so far as to claim that its test carried no chance of a false positive, an idea that "would come to be widely repeated by almost every proponent of the use of DNA evidence in the legal system."[85]

By the mid-1990s, however, the framing of DNA was changing. It was not just a tool for law enforcement, and Reno, in her message, did not stop at saying that the technology was a powerful way to determine guilt. "At the same time," she writes, "DNA aids the search for truth by exonerating the innocent. The criminal justice system is not infallible, and this report documents cases in which the search for truth took a tortuous path."[86] This is an important change in the conversation and challenges the "air of inevitability"[87] that accompanies the assertion that DNA exonerations alone are the explanation for the innocence movement's emergence. Its emergence was due to a confluence of factors—the organizational foundation laid by Centurion Ministries and the Innocence Project, the vision of movement leaders Barry Scheck and Peter Neufeld, and the coverage of wrongful convictions by journalists and academics—that all had a profound effect on reframing DNA as a tool not only to capture the guilty but also to exonerate the innocent. This understanding of DNA, its framing as a tool for seeking justice through postconviction exonerations, is at the core of the innocence movement and served as its key foundation as it developed in later years.

Innocence in the Punitive Turn

That innocence first began to gain traction from the 1980s through the mid-1990s may seem like something of a paradox when considering the environment at the time. Much of this occurred in the midst of the punitive turn, when the United States was on a historic swing toward crime control. Virtually all emphasis in criminal justice—socially, culturally, politically, and legally—was on punishment and retribution in the name of public safety.[88]

Frank Baumgartner and colleagues took note of this emphasis, saying that it was a period when "social and political trends [were] not particularly favorable to the innocence movement."[89] A high crime rate was a part of the obstacle, according to Peter Neufeld, who said that getting criminal justice reform efforts off the ground during the punitive era was difficult "because there was such a huge concern with the crime rate." People were afraid of crime, and "what moves people the most [is] not love; it's fear."[90] This was a major hurdle for reformers, as Barry Scheck pointed out, saying that even when those who were working in the system knew that changes were necessary, they were unable to accomplish them "because there [was] just so much demagoguery going on. 'Let's get three-strikes laws, let's get a death penalty here, let's ratchet up the punishments, let's run against crime,' because politically, that's popular, particularly in an era when crime is rising. But it may not be effective law enforcement at all. There is not a lot of room for rational debate in the area of criminal justice."[91]

Yet innocence advocates managed to find some room in the conversation. And while it may at first seem counterintuitive, it is possible that the punitive turn actually played a role in the emergence of innocence. There are a couple of potential reasons for this.

Part of the equation is basic market demand. The increasingly severe sentences that were being meted out during this era increased the potential harm of wrongful convictions and gave prisoners more reason to search for a way out. "As sentences got more severe, and repeat offender laws, things like three-strikes laws, caused people to get locked up for longer terms, you had more people who were looking to seek help," Maurice Possley said. "If you look at the cases [of wrongful conviction that we know about], it's skewed towards people with longer sentences, because those are the cases that get attention."[92] Longer sentences give advocates more incentive and time to go back, dig in, and reinvestigate cases.

The massive growth of the inmate population that resulted from the new approaches to law enforcement and criminal sentencing also served to strengthen one aspect of the innocence argument and provided a defense against a major critique. Estimates of a wrongful conviction rate have generally been under 5%, usually hovering around the 1% mark. This low error rate has been used by critics who believe that the possibility of a wrongful conviction is too remote to warrant major changes in policy and practice. However, as the number of inmates increased substantially, that relatively low error rate became a powerful argument when translated into actual numbers. By 1990, there were more than a million inmates in the United States; by 1995, there were over a million and a half. Thus, even if the error rate was only around 1%, there were more than 15,000 innocent people in prisons and jails by the mid-1990s.

This point is not lost on those who were involved in innocence work in the early days.[93] DeLone, who was working in jails at the time, said that as the inmate population approached one million, she and others on the inside thought that the growth would surely abate. "But instead, no," she said. "As we approach a million, we enact more and more three-strikes laws, more and more mandatory, more and more life without possibility [of parole. It] goes on and on." While many who were convicted were sent to prison, many others ended up on parole or probation, where they would often violate conditions and be sent back in prison. "The whole thing was a formula for the expansion of the system," deLone said, and all of a sudden, even if the error rate is only 2% or 3%, "that's a lot of people."[94]

The emphasis on punishment throughout the 1980s and 1990s may also have impacted the innocence message on a psychological level. James Q. Wilson famously wrote in 1975, "Wicked people exist. Nothing avails except to set them apart from innocent people," a sentiment that became popular among conservative thinkers on crime and punishment.[95] The stronger the belief in this notion, however, the more important accuracy in identifying and punishing individuals becomes, a point brought up by Stephen Saloom: "I mean, arguably, the reason that states like Texas, for example, have been so good on wrongful conviction reform is because those who want to be tough on crime also want to seem like they're being fair at the same time." It is possible, he said, that "the harsher the punishments, the more you want to keep the innocent out, because really you're trying to scapegoat [offenders]." Saloom continued: "When you have a punishment-crazy society, it seems like there is really a significant element of scapegoating in that. That's really appealing to a certain segment of the population, . . . [and] you wouldn't want to be caught up because you're really trying to scapegoat this other segment of the population. So I don't find it so counterintuitive, and arguably . . . it makes the situation even more ripe for people who are concerned about [wrongful convictions]."[96] What Saloom described is a larger psychological process that accompanies the firm belief in harsh punishments for offenders. It is entirely possible that this had some influence on innocence advocates. As Maurice Possley pointed out, while the desire is to get everyone who is innocent out regardless of sentence length, "the sense of urgency is different" when the sentences become more severe.[97] Richard Dieter suggested that the threat of execution can have a particularly strong effect. In the late 1980s and early 1990s, "executions were no longer theoretical; they were real," he said, and as executions become more common and dates are set, "it really focuses everyone's attention."[98]

Saloom said a similar process can sometimes be seen with the victims in wrongful conviction cases, who may harbor extremely negative feelings toward the person convicted. Then they find out the person was innocent and may be "horrified . . . at the personal feelings they had for that individual" before knowing he or she was innocent. "It gets very complicated," he said, "and very involved, and I think there's obviously a huge, larger, macro-psychological element to punishing people hard and possibly wanting to make even more sure that innocent people are not subjected to that same punishment."[99]

There is a neat logic to this line of thinking; it seems to be a very human process. If a society wishes to be firm, it must be fair, and in criminal justice, perhaps nothing is more important to fairness than accuracy. In other words, if one is concerned about high levels of crime and believes that the way to combat crime is through harsh punishment, it is vital to ensure that those who are punished are truly guilty. As Wilson said, the "wicked" would need to be separated from the "innocent," and conflating those two groups by erroneously convicting innocents accomplishes little. At the very least, the public, which wants to be protected, and would-be offenders, who need to be deterred, must believe that the system is capturing and punishing true offenders, and in an era when DNA added scientific near-certainty to the notion of actual innocence, it became more important to get correct outcomes, thus strengthening innocence advocates' core message.

* * *

The roots of the innocence movement were laid in the midst of a historic punitive turn in U.S. criminal justice. These developments, however, have not generally been considered by scholars. In this chapter, I have aimed to provide a more nuanced understanding of the movement's foundations that goes beyond simply pointing to the first DNA exonerations in 1989.

This is not to undermine the importance of DNA technology to the innocence movement in any way. The "magical black box"[100] of DNA provided a standard of evidence that established actual innocence with a new, unprecedented degree of certainty and allowed advocates to uncover truths about the criminal justice system that had historically remained elusive. As Peter Neufeld once put it, "When you hold DNA up to the mirror and that mirror is the criminal justice system, the DNA points out all the cracks in that mirror in a way we've never seen before."[101]

DNA exonerations thus played an important role in the innocence movement; as Stephen Saloom said, "I'm not sure anybody would have believed that wrongful convictions really happen or known what to do to stop them if not for DNA."[102] They did not, however, occur in a vacuum. Perhaps it was simply fortuitous that DNA technology developed when it did, a matter of what Rob Warden might call "serendipitous happenstance."[103] But filtering it through a theoretical lens allows us to organize and make sense of the moving parts in a way that has not yet been done.

A movement may be set in motion by some type of innovation that makes the target system more vulnerable to change. With regard to the innocence movement, the advent of DNA technology was surely the innovation that rendered the criminal justice system susceptible to reform. An opportunity, however, is not guaranteed to be seized and turned into something larger; what is important is not just the change that occurs but the interpretation of the change that challenges the legitimacy of the system. Regardless of how big an event or change may seem upon reflection, it "only becomes an 'opportunity' when defined as such by a group of actors sufficiently organized to act on this shared definition." The "causal force" of political opportunities, then, comes from the interaction between the structural changes that occur and the changes in the perception of the system that are sparked.[104]

By thinking about DNA as an opportunity in this way, and considering the other factors surrounding it, we can better understand how the foundations of the innocence movement were laid in the 1980s and 1990s. That is, DNA might best be viewed as a necessary factor—indeed, the key factor—for the movement's emergence but as an insufficient one on its own. We must look to the people involved and the environment in which DNA emerged to better understand why it was able to have the effect that it did.

DNA entered the legal system at a time when an organizational foundation for innocence work was already being laid by Centurion Ministries. Around the same time, two cause lawyers happened to become involved in courtroom battles over DNA, quickly recognized the opportunity for reform, and were willing to become leaders in a new area of law and justice. With this recognition, they developed an organizational model that could be replicated and set out to ensure that it was. This was also a time when journalists and academics were beginning to identify the problem of wrongful convictions, thinking and writing about the potential scope of errors in the justice system. These factors combined to ensure that DNA was framed not only as a tool for law enforcement to solve and prosecute crimes, as it was initially viewed, but also as a post-conviction tool to identify errors and uncover problems in the criminal justice system.

All of these things coalesced in an era of strict law-and-order politics, which may at first seem counterintuitive. It is possible, however, that the age of punishment actually played a part in the early development of the innocence movement's message. Increasingly severe sentences not only raised the potential cost of wrongful convictions but also increased demand from inmates for assistance and provided a greater opportunity to reinvestigate cases and discover errors. Furthermore, the substantial growth of the system bolstered the message that, even if the error rate was relatively small, a vast number of people were wrongly convicted, thus adding to the notion of wrongful convictions as a widespread problem. The severity of criminal sanctions of the era may also have bolstered the desire for accuracy, as strict punishment in the name of law, order, and public safety is useless if administered on the innocent. In other words, the correctional excesses of the punitive era may have been at least partially responsible for helping generate momentum for the innocence movement's core messages.

This understanding of the innocence movement's foundations is vital if we are to have a true sense of its history, but it is not the entire story. It is important to remember that, even by the mid- to late 1990s, there was still no *movement*. But the foundation was in place for its emergence in the years to come.

5

"It's Just Justice . . . Real Justice"

The Emergence of a Movement

As the turn of the 21st century approached, innocence was in an interesting place. Scores of individuals had been freed, the legal world was becoming aware of wrongful convictions, and Barry Scheck and Peter Neufeld were widely known as powerful legal advocates. Yet innocence was not at the forefront of criminal justice discourse and was not yet a priority for policy and practical reform.

This is a major issue with the notion that DNA was the sole reason for the rise of the innocence movement; nearly a decade after the first DNA exonerations, there was still no *movement*. There was, however, a foundation. By the late 1990s, the leaders were there, an organizational foundation and model were in place, and the advocates had a cause; but the movement had not yet taken shape as a force for progressive change.

The three areas of social movement theory discussed in the previous chapter—political opportunities, mobilization, and framing—can be integrated in a political process model, which suggests that opportunities, organizational strength, and cognitive liberation are all important elements of a social movement's emergence and development. The political process model also explicitly acknowledges the importance of broad socioeconomic and cultural processes in shaping a movement.

Opportunities are not just static or singular events but instead may be cumulative processes that shift and change over time. For the innocence movement, the key opportunity was the ability to use postconviction DNA testing to establish innocence with near-infallible certainty. And while much innocence scholarship has focused on estimating the prevalence of wrongful convictions and finding trends and patterns among known cases, each individual exoneration is a fascinating story. Covering a range of human emotions, each presents a compelling narrative to absorb. DNA allowed advocates to build up a data set of cases relatively quickly, which allowed them to think about reforms in a new way. As Brandon Garrett's work shows, systematically analyzing this data set yields fascinating and important insights into the criminal justice process and thus highlights what can be done to improve the system.[1] But it was more than just a data set to spark reform ideas; it was a collection of great stories. With DNA, Neufeld said, they "would be able to build up a group of cases, . . . a group of powerful narratives—which is how things really change; people love a powerful story—all of which involve cases where there was no doubt that the person was innocent."[2]

The Power of Exonerations

The emphasis on narratives is an important one, as the innocence movement is essentially driven by the stories of erroneous conviction. This is not to be underestimated; a story can be an incredibly powerful force. Psychologist Tom Trabasso suggests that "the narrative is powerful because it spans the realm of human mental and social existence." It is a key form of communication—indeed, "the dominant form of written discourse"—for people of any age and experience, from children to adults. Narratives allow people to make sense of things, "to make human experience meaningful and coherent."[3] We use them to interpret day-to-day experiences, relate those experiences to others, and create cohesive themes in the world around us.

Storytelling has always been an important theme in law. Some psychological research suggests that jurors use narrative structures to interpret evidence and make decisions.[4] There has even been a "law and literature movement" that uses literature to gain legal insights and understand various approaches to law.[5] Even in the area of cause lawyering, narratives have shown to be powerful forces when lawyers work for reform.[6]

Innocence advocates recognized the power of narratives from the outset. Centurion Ministries, the Innocence Project, and others use the press to tell the stories of their victories and gain support for their cause. Scheck described his first exoneration, the McLaughlin case, as "a formative experience," in part because he realized just how powerful the stories could be: "It was not just the lawyering and the research and the social science around eyewitness misidentification, but it was the power of the press." Now, Scheck said, they "always want to get [press attention] every time that there's an exoneration." With the belief that each exoneration is "a learning moment" for the system, telling the story of the wrongful conviction and how it happened is an important aspect of the innocence movement:

> That is a fundamental dynamic that underlies the system because it is a very powerful influence. Going all the way back to the initial campaigning, whether it's the Court of Last Resort or the campaigning in other countries, people understand and identify with the innocents who are wrongly convicted. There's an emotional power in it. It's the individual story. You know, it's always been said that the Holocaust, for example, is unknowable, but if you know the story of Anne Frank, as an individual, you can understand it better. And that's always been true of the innocence movement. It is the exonerees and what they go through and how they bear witness to what happened that provides an important spiritual power to this entire effort.[7]

The narratives of the innocence movement's individual victories are vital to the success of the movement as a whole. "Of course, the exonerations help," Aimee Maxwell said. "And seeing the exonerees, . . . how do you say no to them?"[8] Understanding the power that these stories wield and taking advantage of it is one of the greatest contributions of the early advocates, according to Stephen Saloom: "I think the genius of Barry and Peter and the other people involved in creating this innocence movement is that they understood that, if these things happen in isolation, randomly, quietly, none of this might happen. And if it would, it would happen very, very, very slowly. But given the power dynamic in the criminal justice system, it probably wouldn't have seen the light of day."[9] The set of cases, of stories, generated by and at the disposal of the innocence movement is useful both individually and collectively. Joseph Stalin reportedly said that the death of one is a tragedy, while the death of one million is a statistic.[10] Echoing a similar sentiment, Mother Teresa said, "If I look at the mass I will never act. If I look at the one, I will."[11] In both of these quotations, the sentiment is similar: a single tragic, emotional story can carry immense power and even spur one to act, but a large collection becomes a statistic, a simple number or figure that is easily overlooked. This dynamic underlies the power of the narrative, which enables individuals to relate to and make real meaning out of the stories they see or hear. Such narrative power has been crucial to the innocence movement. Stories of exoneration are compelling and emotional and can spur individuals—advocates, lawyers, students, policy makers, practitioners, and members of the public—to care about the issue and act.

Individual narratives, however, are not necessarily great to serve as a basis for policy reform, so having a collection or data set of them is crucial if that is the goal. Thus, the innocence movement's narratives are important on both levels. The individual stories can be used to garner sympathy and support among individuals and organizations, while the collection of cases as a whole yields valuable lessons about the types of reforms necessary to improve the justice system.

In this way, exonerations can be thought of as a movement opportunity. While wrongful convictions have always occurred, DNA created, or at least altered, the opportunity structure by making cases more believable and thus more appealing and by allowing a large number of them to be amassed in a relatively brief time span. They also added credence to the non-DNA exonerations, and when put together, a large database of cases exists to support the notion that wrongful convictions are not entirely aberrational but are, in fact, fundamental systemic problems. In other words, exonerations provide a compelling way to show that the criminal justice system is flawed, thus rendering it susceptible to reform and legitimizing such efforts.

A Matter of Timing

Some of the most powerful narratives the innocence movement has are the death penalty cases. This was particularly true in the earlier years, throughout the 1990s, when DNA was still relatively young and there was not yet a large database of exonerations. The narratives in capital cases were particularly energizing, as the threat of death, as Maurice Possley put it, "brings a certain element, finality, to a case that determinate sentences, even life without parole, don't have."[12]

Death penalty exonerations created more public attention for wrongful convictions than virtually any others. This makes sense, as it essentially meant two sets of people were focusing on the same cases: those from the innocence community, such as the Innocence Project, viewed them as egregious instances of erroneous convictions, and anti–death penalty advocates, who may or may not be concerned with wrongful convictions generally, used the cases as prime examples of why capital punishment should be abolished.

Though much has been written about innocence and the death penalty, it is often described as a one-way street. That is, it is well established that the discovery of wrongful convictions in both capital and non-capital cases has bolstered the anti–death penalty movement and transformed the nature of the debate. The flipside of that, however, is rarely acknowledged: that were it not for the death penalty, the innocence movement may not have gotten off the ground as it did in the late 1990s. As Maddy deLone said, "the issues surrounding wrongful conviction are not as emotional as the issues around the death penalty. The ultimate penalty of death . . . raises the ante."[13] Therefore, the fact that many of the early exonerations came in capital cases is a key reason why the innocence movement was able to gain steam and garner support.

This support is due, in part, to the effort and energy that death penalty abolitionists put into drawing attention to exonerations. It is not surprising that they would do this given the state of the anti–death penalty movement at that time. Since the Supreme Court reinstated the death penalty in 1976, the abolitionist movement had mostly suffered casualties. Death sentences and executions increased in the late 1980s and throughout the 1990s, states were adding capital punishment laws rather than repealing them, and traditional arguments against the death penalty seemed to be losing some impact. As *New York Times* reporter Don Terry wrote in 1998, "In the 22 years since the nation resumed executions, the anti–death penalty movement has been battered, bloodied, and ignored."[14]

Anti–death penalty advocates at the time needed a new issue, a new way of approaching their cause, and innocence provided it. In some ways, it provided a counterpoint to the emotional pull of death penalty support. An argument for the death penalty, according to Michael Radelet, can be neatly summed up. There is a deterrence argument—"I just want to do something about high crime"—and a straightforward emotional pull. On the other hand, Radelet said he thinks that many people were against the death penalty in their hearts but had trouble articulating it. The anti–death penalty argument is "more subtle, more nuanced, more empirical" and thus can be difficult to make clear. Innocence was a clear way to justify opposition, as it "simplified the anti–death penalty argument and gave people a hook to hang their coat on."[15]

Radelet even suggested that the attention his research with Hugo Bedau received had less to do with the quality of the work—"It wasn't rocket science," he said—and more to do with the timing of its release. "I wonder, if we had published five years earlier, if it would have had the same receptivity," he told me, suggesting that 1987 may have been just the right time for it to have maximum impact because "everyone was so gung-ho on the death penalty."[16]

The importance of this timing should be considered in the history of the innocence movement. Given the mutual benefits of the innocence and anti–death penalty movements, the state of the latter can be considered an important opportunity for the growth of the former. That is, the anti–death penalty movement was in a difficult spot and needed a new argument or direction. Therefore, when exonerations began piling up—particularly after DNA was used to exonerate Kirk Bloodsworth—opponents of capital punishment put massive amounts of time and effort into ensuring they were noticed. The spate of death penalty exonerations throughout the 1990s, in turn, bolstered the public profile of the innocence movement.

Of course, the opportunities I have described may not have amounted to anything were it not for the organization of the innocence movement; after all, opportunities are only one aspect of the potential for a movement. There also needs to be some type of organizational structure in place to take advantage of those opportunities. Part of this is leadership; put simply, a movement needs leaders. For the innocence movement, Barry Scheck, Peter Neufeld, and others emerged as leaders early on, as discussed in chapter 4. There also needs to be an infrastructure in place, essentially a communication network, for working together and sharing ideas. The organizational and advocacy pipeline must also remain filled, making motivation for movement participation essential. All of these are important if a movement is to develop, be sustained, and grow.

Projects and Networks

The innocence movement has a strong organizational component that greatly contributes to its success. The oldest innocence organization, Centurion Ministries, is now more than 30 years old, and the one that leads the movement charge, the Innocence Project, has been around for more than 20. Having such a strong organizational base is vital. In particular, having a large, forward-thinking organization like the Innocence Project as the face of the movement can be a benefit to all in the movement.

Even in the early days, when the Innocence Project was a small outfit at Cardozo Law School, it managed to achieve tremendous success, and this ramped up when it became an independent nonprofit organization: "One of our early nonprofit advisers told us, . . . 'You guys punch above your weight.' . . . In terms of 'earned media,' as they call it, media that you get just by being a subject of news when you do something, we had enormous earned media and public recognition. So it often seemed as if we had a much larger infrastructure than we did in the first instance, because our cases were everywhere and they got a lot of public attention. And that made a big difference."[17] The other organizations the Innocence Project inspired—those described in chapter 3—have nobly followed in the footsteps of the Innocence Project in many ways. Given the difficult nature of innocence work and the small size of many of the organizations, the amount of success the movement has achieved is remarkable. Part of that success is the hard work the organizations put in at the case level, of course, but it also speaks to their reputation as organizations and the reputation of the innocence community in general. Aimee Maxwell described the importance of her organization's reputation in having success with the Georgia legislature: "One of the key things that I think is really important in what we do is we have a really great reputation. I go to the legislature, I don't lie, I don't fudge; this is what it is. You can trust me when I say something. I can back it up."[18]

The innocence community has strong ties to the criminal defense community, with which its issues often overlap, and with the forensic science community, which ensures that the movement has at its disposal empirical, scientific support.

Still, the biggest strength of the innocence movement in terms of resources is the people involved, and perhaps no group is more important than students.

Law Students

The Innocence Project began as a clinic at Cardozo Law School, and many others followed suit. Today, while the organizations that compose the Innocence Network are diverse, the clinical law school program is still an important piece of the innocence movement's fabric. "In the beginning, it was basically the Center on Wrongful Convictions and the Innocence Project in New York," the Northwestern Center's Jane Raley said. "And now there are all sorts of innocence projects all across the country, and many of them, like ours, are part of a law school program, which is wonderful because the greatest resource we have [is] our students. In fact, we couldn't take as many cases as we do without the assistance of our students."[19] More than 90% of Innocence Network members that do legal work relied on student support in 2014, including screening and investigation of cases, representing clients, and helping with post-exoneration work.[20]

The importance of law students to the innocence movement goes beyond basic person power, however. The decision to spread the innocence clinic throughout law schools was a conscious effort, as Scheck and Neufeld saw that "law students . . . responded very powerfully to each exoneration." Law students often carry with them a sense of idealism, "one of the key driving forces in the innocence movement," and Scheck and Neufeld recognized this. As noted earlier, spreading the movement in this way allowed them "to change the perception of a whole generation of lawyers" who would go on to become practitioners and policy makers. "It was a powerful, powerful force," Scheck said. "Each person that was exonerated appeals to people's sense of idealism as to how this system ought to work."[21]

Influencing scores of young lawyers, making them aware and passionate about wrongful conviction work, is an outcome of the decision to spread the movement through the legal academy. This ensures that the advocacy pipeline remains full, as the innocence-clinic model essentially allows for the reproduction of movement advocates. Maddy deLone said that the growth of the movement has made a career in wrongful conviction work possible now more than ever:

> As there are more and more projects around the country and the projects around the country are growing so that there are now staff attorney positions, we're seeing former students from one clinical program being hired as a staff attorney in the next. So now, thinking of yourself as a person who could spend your legal life being [involved in] an innocence effort or [as] a Network project attorney is a possibility, whereas, ten years ago, there were a few places, and most of them were a couple of people. You couldn't imagine, you couldn't say, "Well, what I want to do is work at an innocence effort for the rest of my life." You wouldn't; that would have been silly. But we're seeing that now. We're seeing former students from one project being project directors in other places. We're seeing some cross-pollination of projects across the country.[22]

There are, of course, practical challenges to creating advocates through law school clinics. Ryan Costello, who worked with the Life After Innocence clinic as a law student at Loyola University in Chicago, said his goal was to continue doing innocence work, which he believes to be true of many students, but that opportunities to work for innocence organizations are extremely limited. A similar observation was made by Laura Nirider, the director of the Northwestern Center on Wrongful Convictions of Youth.[23]

While not all students who pass through an innocence project will go on to work for one, the experience is still formative and informs their thinking moving forward, and many stay involved in innocence work in some way. For instance, Shannon Leitner, who worked with the Michigan Innocence Clinic as a student and then as a research fellow for the National Registry of Exonerations, did not necessarily desire to do innocence work full-time but wanted to keep a couple of pro bono cases on her plate while pursuing a career in a law firm.[24] Costello said something similar of students in his clinic, who he said may not work solely on wrongful convictions but remain "tangentially involved."[25]

DeLone said the Innocence Project has seen the same with a number of their students who, regardless of their professional direction, remain involved:

Often, the students who end up with law firms will look and reach out and try to get pro bono cases working with us. So we have a number of examples of people who, ten years later, are still helping their law firms stay involved with our work. Some of our former students—and I know it's true for projects across the country—go to work as public defenders, or they work as prosecutors, or they work for judges. And I think they help . . . keep the message going and help think about a different way to practice criminal law on all sides of the equation. So that's been terrific to see.[26]

Thus, even if students do not explicitly remain involved in wrongful conviction work, those who are impacted by innocence clinics as students "becom[e] part of the fabric of the criminal law system, . . . and that changes the understanding, the receptivity, the voice for the issues in the country."[27]

This aspect of the innocence movement is indicative of another important element of it. Conventional wisdom suggests that individuals who are passionate about a particular issue will become involved in a movement dedicated to the cause. However, as sociologist Ziad Munson has shown, preconceived beliefs about an issue may not be the cause of activism. Rather, as he demonstrated in his study of the pro-life movement, dedication to an issue may be a consequence of activism. That is, a variety of factors may lead an individual to participate in movement activities, and only after participating will he or she develop strong beliefs and commitment to that particular issue.[28]

This pattern seems to be true of participants in the innocence movement. Neither Ryan Costello nor Shannon Leitner went to law school to focus on innocence work, and it was only after hearing exonerees' stories, meeting them, and becoming involved in the clinic that they developed a commitment to the issue. In fact, Costello said he "was completely ignorant of this line of work," but after meeting a couple of exonerees through a friend in his first year of law school, he decided to get involved in the clinic.[29] Similarly, Laura Nirider knew virtually nothing about the issue but enrolled in the clinical course at Northwestern University and ended up making a career in the innocence field.[30]

This post-involvement commitment is also true of more established participants such as Rob Warden. "I am so glad that I sort of fell into it, pretty much by accident, actually," he said. "I didn't set out in life to do this. I set out in life to become a journalist. I didn't set out in life to become a reformer."[31] Similarly, Steve Drizin said that innocence was not on his radar when he became a lawyer. He focused on juvenile justice law and had dabbled in innocence work; but a string of cases led him to work more closely with the Northwestern Center, and he has made it a primary focus since.[32] Christine Mumma, a leader on innocence issues in North Carolina, came from the corporate world and was not drawn to innocence as a social justice outlet but saw an opportunity to solve problems in the system.[33]

The development of a deep passion for innocence issues only after participating in wrongful conviction work is true for virtually all of the movement participants I spoke with and is important to understanding the movement. It is often not a preconceived dedication or concern about wrongful convictions that drives participants to become involved in this line of work. Rather, people's social and professional networks lead them to it for other reasons, and the dedication and passion for the issue results from participation.

Part of the allure for innocence movement participants—what helps lure them in, builds commitment, and keeps them connected—is a strong emotional pull. And the emotional element should not be forgotten, as it is important for the survival and growth of the innocence movement.

Emotions and the Innocence Movement

For an advocacy network to remain strong, there must be something keeping individuals attached and engaged with the cause. Doug McAdam uses the term "solidary incentives" to refer to the things that "provide the motive force for participation" in movements.[34] For the innocence movement, the emotional attachment that advocates feel to the cause and to their clients is perhaps the key factor in keeping them involved despite the trying nature of the work.

A strand of social movement scholarship focuses on the role and importance of emotions to movements.[35] Not only might emotions motivate people to participate in movements, but they can create solidarity and a sense of togetherness among participants. This is especially important for the innocence movement. The powerful narratives of the exonerees create an emotional pull that attracts supporters and potential advocates. And perhaps even more importantly, emotions keep innocence advocates involved by creating the solidary incentives that drive action.

Innocence work can be incredibly daunting. Defeats come often and take a variety of shapes. Perhaps the worst is pouring time and energy into a case, only to find out that the person was truly guilty of the crime. Centurion Ministries suffered one such instance in the case of Roger Coleman. After working on the case for several years, Jim McCloskey truly believed in Coleman's innocence. Coleman was executed in 1992, believed by some to be an innocent man. In 2006, however, DNA testing confirmed that Coleman was, in fact, the perpetrator.

McCloskey said in his press release after the tests that it was "a bitter pill to swallow." He and Centurion did not run from the case, however, but confronted it head-on. "Those of us who seek the truth in criminal justice cases," McCloskey wrote, "must never be afraid of finding it. . . . The Truth can be very elusive, and even illusory. Our search for facts can delude us into thinking that what we have found is gold, only to discover that it is in fact fool's gold. But once the gold of absolute truth is revealed, we must embrace it, and be thankful that we have finally uncovered it."[36]

The case was difficult for McCloskey, and he spent a week at a religious retreat, though he "came out of that with no answers at all." He moved on by jumping into other cases and trying to help the next person.[37]

Even if a case does turn out to be a true wrongful conviction, securing an exoneration is rarely a straightforward process. There may be a string of small defeats throughout a case; Aimee Maxwell said they may lose more often than they win, "and the biggest loss is we can't find the evidence."[38] The cases can sometimes drag on for years. "These cases take forever," said Paul Casteleiro, who had one case that had been on his plate for more than a decade when we spoke. He described an innocence case as "a very frustrating endeavor" and said, "If you're not committed, you wouldn't do it."[39]

Overcoming this frustration is sometimes just a matter of persistence, as Maxwell described: "I'm in Georgia. Nobody wants to change anything in Georgia. And lots of people say no, lots of people don't want to deal with it, and you can't let them get in your way." She described a recent trip she had made to the parole board arguing for DNA testing in a death penalty case as one of the worst moments of her life: "It's just—it's shocking. But," she said, gesturing toward exoneree Clarence Harrison, who sat with us during our conversation, "how do you give up?"[40]

Even with the most zealous and persistent advocates, however, time is limited. Rob Warden described a case in which a client, Anthony McKinney, died in prison: "We have such persuasive evidence that he was wrongfully convicted and that he was innocent, and we had it going back five years. Even after we were granted a hearing, it was delayed and stretched over five years. He died in prison and now it's basically moot. We can't do anything on his behalf now."[41] Even a successful case, one that ends in exoneration, can be emotionally trying. Of course, the experience of helping exonerate someone is powerful: "There are very few experiences equivalent to seeing someone walk out of prison," Maurice Possley said, "knowing that you played a role . . . in showing they were innocent. I equate it to seeing your child being born."[42] Casteleiro said that the "feeling of winning is a great feeling" and that those who are involved in the case experience "exhilaration for having accomplished something."[43]

Still, righting a wrongful conviction is not pure bliss. "A lot of the times, there is not joy for the person walking out," said Casteleiro. "There is bitterness, anger." He said that those who worked on the case may have to temper their emotions to some extent and remember that the exoneree has "been traumatized by this process. . . . It's a much more complex thing. There is joy, yes, in the event. But what has occurred, there is no joy in."[44]

Shannon Leitner said that this realization can take its toll: "Something I always struggle with [is that] a lot of these cases are incredibly sad and incredibly moving, and oftentimes even the best outcome is not that fantastic. I worked a bit on the exoneration of David Lee Gavitt, who spent 26 years wrongfully incarcerated. And you know, it's an amazing story, but at the same rate, he still lost 26 years of his life."[45] Given how difficult the work is and how little financial incentive there is for most young lawyers to become involved in this area of law, it may seem surprising that anyone would dedicate his or her career to wrongful convictions; but there is a remarkably strong emotion in the work, and that emotion is one of the key driving forces of the innocence movement. Naturally, wrongful convictions elicit an emotional, visceral reaction. "Any decent person recoils at the horror of an innocent person being put in jail for the rest of his or her life or facing execution," Scheck said in one interview. "And that's what we're talking about in these cases: the worst nightmare one can imagine."[46]

When I asked the people I interviewed why they keep doing this work, the answer given by nearly everyone was an emotional one. The work is rewarding on multiple levels. The first is on a very personal, individual, human level; these advocates are doing something to improve the lives of people and families. In describing the exoneration of one of Centurion's clients, Daryl Burton, McCloskey told a reporter, "It was a feeling of pure joy and satisfaction, and you feel redeemed and vindicated, as does the exonerated person. . . . You're giving new life to a person."[47]

Leitner, who spent time in the Peace Corps, said she finds more fulfillment in having an impact on individual lives rather than focusing on broader issues. The focus on individuals is one of the things that drew her to law: "Part of what I realized in the Peace Corps is I really struggle with the meta-level. . . . I am a person that feels much more success when you have individual, one-on-one things. . . . I feel a lot more fulfillment when I can help an individual client."[48]

In one interview, Peter Neufeld described the joy that can come from impacting the lives of an individual when he talked about the case of Tony Snyder in Virginia. After the governor agreed to a pardon, Neufeld flew into Richmond, where he told Snyder's mother to meet him at the airport. When he got off the small plane, she was "literally bounding down the tarmac" and picked up Neufeld in a "bear hug," a moment he will never forget. "That feeling," he said, "that sense at that moment is probably one of the best feelings I've ever had in my life, knowing that you could give that woman so much comfort and so much pleasure. And that's the kind of feeling that I'll probably carry with me to the grave."[49]

Alan Maimon, an investigator with Centurion Ministries, similarly discussed how meaningful it is to impact not just an individual but his or her family as well. He described a case he was working on for a man who has been in prison for 30 years. The man's daughter, who was four years old when he was convicted, was engaged to be married for a number of years but would not get married until her dad was free to walk her down the aisle. Maimon got to know the daughter and said, "When you see not only the way it's impacted an individual's life, an individual whose liberty has been taken from them for . . . years, but you see the impact it's had on their family and on their community, there's no lack of motivation. There's no fear of burnout because we see every day how it's impacting people."[50]

McCloskey said that the emotional element "absolutely is" what draws people to the work, including volunteers. He said that Centurion does not have to worry about recruiting volunteers because "they come to us," and they often stay for an extended period, sometimes years on end. They are "moved and inspired by the work and want to be a part of it. It gives them a sense of purpose and mission in life."[51]

Working on an exoneration case is a powerful thing for people and can be the beginning of a lifelong relationship between the advocates and their client. The exonerees themselves are at the heart of this emotional connection. "I learn from them," McCloskey once said, "about forgiveness, humility, courage, and grace."[52] Kate Germond, whose office is adorned with photos of exonerees and others, told a reporter, "There's always a time when my heart is big. It is usually afterward when I sit down and look at the photos, and tears are streaming down my face. I'm seeing these beautiful, strong people who were suffering horrible things because of this betrayal done to them by the criminal justice system."[53]

In addition to helping individuals, the focus on the system is another moving aspect of this work. Innocence work is clearly fulfilling at the case level, but many people in the movement also find it rewarding on a broader, reform-minded level: being part of something that can lead to legal, social, or political change. Warden said it was great "seeing that we are getting some reforms and we're moving in the right direction and having a genuine impact on the criminal justice system. Not very many people really do have that kind of impact on any aspect of society, and so I've found it very rewarding."[54]

For Neufeld, igniting change is a major incentive for the work. "It's not always a question of innocence or guilt," he said, but thinking beyond the immediate impact of the case in terms of altering people's "outlook on justice, on racism, on the drug wars, on sexism, on all kinds of issues. It's terrific to be a vital part of that."[55] For example, he once talked about how the case of Abner Louima, a Haitian man who was severely mistreated by police in New York City, was used to challenge police brutality and accountability on a bigger scale: "To break that open and to bring that suit forward . . . and to do it in a novel way, not just to hold the city accountable but to go after a police union . . . and hold them accountable, and make that the first case in the country to hold a police union accountable for brutality, which will then be utilized, hopefully, around the country in all kinds of communities is, in itself, very rewarding."[56]

Innocence work seems to be inherently rewarding on multiple levels, but celebrating victories is important to remain invested and motivated. Karen Newirth, an attorney in the Innocence Project's Strategic Litigation Unit, described the wins as "exceptionally thrilling."[57] At both Centurion Ministries and the Innocence Project, the walls are lined with photos of exonerees. At Centurion, the conference room is home to framed newspaper articles about each of the organization's exonerations. These mementos are important, serving as reminders about what the innocence movement is and why the people in the movement keep doing this work; when I asked Germond what keeps her motivated, she said simply, "The faces of these folks we free."[58] As Jim McCloskey put it, sitting in his office and pointing at the photos around the room, "This is the story."[59]

Just as celebrating individual victories is important, so is keeping some perspective on the movement's successes as a whole. When I met with Aimee Maxwell, there had been 311 DNA exonerations, which "doesn't sound like a huge number." But, she pointed out, these represent 311 instances "where we identified them, found the evidence, and were able to make it through the system. That's huge. And do you know how amazing it is to find the evidence after 20 years? Holy crap! It is literally a needle in a haystack." She mentioned the Calvin Johnson case, during which the investigators pulled a box of evidence out of a dumpster. "It is quite miraculous, actually," Maxwell said. "It is truly a miracle, and I don't mean that in a—" She paused for a moment, before finishing: "Well, actually, I mean it in every possible way—truly a miracle when we find the evidence."[60]

Reminding oneself about successes and incremental victories is important. Scheck, once asked about resistance to change and why that has prevented the movement from achieving more in a shorter amount of time, disagreed with the sentiment. "I have to look back at it another way," he said. "We've achieved a lot." Given how rare DNA is—it is present in less than one-fourth of criminal cases—the headway made is impressive, Scheck said: "We have a whole program and whole agenda of reform, and it has reframed criminal justice issues in very important ways. So we're making an enormous amount of progress on that front."[61] Similarly, Newirth said that when thinking about the collection of successes the movement has achieved, "it really feels like we're going in the right direction."[62]

For innocence advocates, recognizing successes and victories, even ones that seem relatively small or incremental, can help maintain the emotional connections to their work. Those emotional connections, both on the individual case level and on the larger reform level, provide the "solidary incentives" that keep advocates going and help hold the movement together.

The Innocence Message

If opportunities and organization provide the "structural potential" for a movement, "cognitive liberation" attaches meaning to the situation to facilitate action. If something is seen as a problem, the system may lose legitimacy and increase the demand for change.[63]

With regard to the innocence movement, the notion of cognitive liberation is tricky. It is tied very closely to the opportunity structure described earlier: the collection of wrongful conviction cases provides the lens through which problems in the criminal justice system can be identified. Put simply, people must recognize wrongful convictions as a big-enough problem to necessitate systemic reform.

Ideally for the innocence movement, that message will reach the masses or at least seem as if it is reaching the masses. According to Stephen Saloom, "It's legislators' perception of their voting constituents' perception that . . . has significant influence on criminal justice policy making."[64] Wrongful convictions, though, are likely not at the forefront of the public's collective consciousness; issues about crime and justice generally do not have the political clout they did in previous decades, when they were influential in local, state, and federal elections.

Within criminal justice and legal circles, however, innocence is a powerful argument. In the early days, the reaction to wrongful convictions was supreme skepticism, according to Saloom: "A lot of criminal justice practitioners said, 'Ah, it's a flash in the pan. It might happen once in a while. It's a gimmick, whatever it is.' And they tried to stonewall it and not heed the lessons and not consider what we might be able to learn from these wrongful convictions. But over time, they've come around."[65]

Today, the discovery of wrongful convictions and knowledge about how they occurred appears to have caught on enough to spur changes to practice and policy and, in some cases, to discourse more generally. Part of the reason for this is the basic nature of wrongful convictions. At the most fundamental level, nobody wants to see an innocent person punished for a crime he or she did not commit. Innocence advocates recognize this and have taken advantage of the appeal of their message, as Saloom described:

> We've long recognized . . . it took a little while for the other parts of the criminal justice system to come along, but especially now, we recognize that no one in the criminal justice system wants these problems to happen. So we regard . . . the courtroom adversaries as allies in these policy fights. Everybody, we believe, police, prosecutors, judges, all want to see an accurate criminal justice system that is just and not an inaccurate criminal justice system that creates injustices. . . . So we come to our allies across the system, our colleagues across the system, often to partner up with them. So it's good, and we enjoy that. It's a nice way to do work.

The broad appeal of the movement's message makes "talking about wrongful convictions . . . completely different than talking about the rest of the criminal justice system," according to Saloom. "They're guilty. We're talking about innocent people here!"[66]

Innocence is an issue that carries moral weight for anyone; regardless of affiliations or beliefs, it can invoke powerful feelings in people. Neufeld said that this simple fact separates innocence from other movements for legal reform: "We were talking about helping people who were stone-cold innocent, and everybody—doesn't matter what their political background is—feels it's a terrible wrong to put an innocent man in prison. So even the most law-and-order people felt it's just terribly tragic when an innocent person goes to prison. So therefore we could appeal to all people, no matter what their political background was, in a way that any other criminal justice reform effort in the prior three decades could not."[67] This fact gave innocence advocates the "moral high ground, if you will,"[68] and made the message appealing for the public and people within the system. "I mean, law enforcement, prosecutors, everyone wants to get it right," Erika Applebaum said. "No one wants an innocent person behind bars, and they definitely don't want to be a part of it."[69] Aimee Maxwell summed this idea up concisely: "What we do is not Republican, it's not Democrat. It's just justice—I mean, real justice."[70]

In addition to the general moral accessibility of the innocence movement's message, it can be packaged and framed in such a way as to appeal to particular groups, adding an interesting element of political messaging to the movement. Folks in the defense community are naturally aligned with many aspects of the innocence movement, and the due process–oriented nature of the issues generally appeals to liberals. But other framings may appeal to conservatives, libertarians, and those who are concerned with crime control. As Saloom said, "A conservative person doesn't want to see the government take away a person's liberty when they shouldn't,"[71] a sentiment that may be equally true for libertarians.

Innocence advocates also utilize a crime-control frame, which suggests that wrongful convictions can pose a major threat to public safety. As Saloom and others pointed out, "Nobody except the real perpetrator wants to see an innocent person convicted of a crime."[72] Indeed, a number of wrongful convictions have led to a continuation of heinous crimes by the true perpetrator.[73] This framing of wrongful convictions has helped the issue find some appeal despite the fact that it really began to brew in an era of law-and-order politics and when the national political scene was not particularly welcome to progressive reformers and legal activists.[74] Even those who did the earliest work sensed this. Ron Huff, for instance, thought early on that if he and his colleagues wanted to build a coalition, they had to hook people focused on law and order. He said he made a point to always remind people that a wrongful conviction means that a guilty person is on the loose.[75] This "true-perpetrator angle" is essentially the "Republican pitch" for wrongful conviction re-

form, though Christine Mumma said this frame has really become utilized in recent years.[76]

This message can be a powerful force as DNA exonerations pile up.
As wrongful convictions garnered increased attention, advocates realized that they had "to get people where their self-interest is, or they're
not going to be motivated."[77] And importantly, DNA provided a unique
opportunity to show definitively that wrongful convictions were a public
safety matter; in 140 of the first 333 exonerations tracked by the Innocence Project, DNA not only freed an innocent person but identified the
real criminal. As Neufeld pointed out,

> When we identify the real perpetrator, we would go back and look at his
> background, and we would be able to prove that in the interstice between
> the time of our client being wrongly charged and then convicted, and the
> 15 years later when our client is exonerated and we're able to identify the
> real perpetrator, that the real perpetrator committed a number of other
> violent crimes. And had the police and prosecutors used more robust
> techniques to investigate and prosecute, as opposed to the techniques that
> allowed the innocent person to be convicted, then perhaps they would
> have actually identified, arrested, the real perpetrator and prevented all
> those other serious violent crimes that happened in the interim.[78]

In a sense, then, the innocence message is about "just good law enforcement," according to Scheck,[79] and advocates recognized the importance
of getting this message out to the law enforcement community and to
the public, stressing that by "increasing the efficacy of law enforcement
and prosecution, we not only reduce the likelihood of miscarriages
of justice, but we'll enhance the efficiency and certainty of the system
and reduce crime consequently." By presenting an argument that is in
people's "self-interest," innocence advocates were able to appeal to those
across the ideological spectrum and even get "a positive response from
some people in law enforcement."[80]

Both the moral accessibility of the innocence message and its framing
as a public safety issue were crucial to movement's emergence. Neufeld
suggested that it was in large part "because of those two aspects, defining aspects about the wrongful conviction movement, [that] we were
able to get traction at a time when our precedents had failed."[81] This

versatility in framing makes the innocence movement broadly appealing. "We really are a mainstream movement," Scheck said. "That's where
the importance of this really lies, in being able to cross party lines and
generate reasoned discussion, debate, and analysis of what's wrong with
our criminal justice system and what we can do to solve it."[82]

Environmental Context

In addition to opportunities, organizational strength, and cognitive liberation, a political process approach recognizes the importance of the
broader environment in shaping movement development and activity.
In chapter 4, I discussed how the punitive turn may have impacted the
foundations of the innocence movement. This period of law-and-order
politics stretched past the turn of the century, but the downward trend
in crime rates may have helped open the door for innocence and other
progressive criminal justice reform.

The punitive turn was sparked, to some degree, by a major increase
in crime; beginning in the mid-1960s, property crimes increased fairly
steadily for at least a decade, while violent crimes did so for nearly 30
years. The punitive turn was characterized by the developments that
accompanied this trend: sensational media coverage of crime and violence, punitive rhetoric among criminal justice officials and politicians,
public fear of crime, mass incarceration, and so forth. While these outcomes continued beyond the turn of the century—imprisonment numbers continued to grow at an incredible rate until late in the first decade
of the 21st century—the crime trend itself faced an entirely different fate.

In the early 1990s, the increasing crime trend reversed rather dramatically. From 1991 through 2000, property crime decreased by nearly
a third to its lowest level in three decades. Similarly, violent crimes decreased every year beginning in 1993, reaching their lowest levels since
the late 1960s.[83] While the reasons for these remarkable and unexpected
declines are murky at best,[84] the crime decline in the United States was
very real and is a contextual factor worth consideration in any examination of criminal justice reform of the era. As I described earlier, Neufeld
suggested that working on progressive criminal justice reform in previous decades was so difficult in part because of the high crime rates. As
crime rates dropped, the door may have been left open for progressive

reform, such as that promoted by the innocence movement, which was not concerned exclusively with reducing crime and violence. When I spoke with Neufeld about these larger trends and about the innocence movement seemingly going against the grain in some ways, he said, "In the '90s. Not any longer, because the pendulum has shifted on those is-sues [as] crime rates began to precipitously drop."[85]

Another environmental factor worth consideration is the economy. The nature of the innocence movement may keep it somewhat insu-lated from major economic shifts, which can be the death knell for other reform efforts. For innocence, however, economic prosperity may be slightly less important, as the reforms generally do not require legis-latures or agencies to come up with large amounts of capital. "I don't think they go together necessarily," Aimee Maxwell said. "We're not asking them for money usually. And what we're asking them is actually helping."[86]

In fact, the economic downturn at the end of the first decade of the 21st century may have benefited the work of the innocence move-ment and other nonpunitive criminal justice reforms. As budget crises emerged in counties and states throughout the country, the desire to reduce the prison population grew, and alternatives to incarceration became more necessary.[87] The innocence movement's messaging—get the innocent out of prison and rethink the criminal justice process—is rather palatable given the economic situation and may even benefit wrongful conviction work, according to Maxwell: "You know, we were going down the path of damn near putting everybody in prison," she said, "and now we're having to pull back. And of course, thanks to the really crappy economy, we're having to get people out of prison." She added with a laugh, "I mean, I've told all my clients, 'You guys are the only ones benefiting from this economy, but yay!'"[88]

*　*　*

Innocence emerged as a movement in the late 1990s and early 2000s after the foundations were laid in the decades prior. The development of the movement was the result of a variety of factors, discussed in this chapter through a political process framework.

The individual and collective power of the exonerations that piled up presented an opportunity for reform, and it just so happened that the anti–death penalty movement was at a point in its history that it needed a new issue to latch onto. These opportunities were recognized and seized by advocates, and pragmatic and charismatic leaders like Scheck and Neufeld worked to develop a strong organizational network that not only was poised for success in exonerating clients and achieving policy reform but also could be sustained and expanded by influencing young lawyers-in-training. This development occurred alongside the fairly wide recognition that wrongful convictions were a big-enough problem to warrant support. The broad moral and political appeal of the innocence message helped spread this notion and also helped insulate the movement from some of the larger shifts in the criminal justice world, though the reduced crime rate very well may have helped increase the palatability of innocence and other progressive criminal justice reform.

The discussion presented in the previous chapters sheds light on the innocence movement and its development that goes beyond the somewhat-true but limited assertion that DNA was the sole spark that caused the innocence movement. Thinking about it more concretely as a movement not only establishes an important and interesting theoretical grounding but also provides more historical context than is commonly present.

Innocence has clearly become a force for change in the criminal justice world and can certainly be thought of as a movement of sorts. But one interesting question remains: is innocence really a social movement, and can it be characterized as a "new civil rights movement?"

6

The "New Civil Rights"?

Reaching beyond Innocence

The Innocence Network's annual conference is held each spring. The location varies, thematic sessions change, and speakers come and go; but each year, there is a moment during the conference that brings everyone together in a celebration of lives seemingly lost but regained.

Attendees gather in a large ballroom, seated at round tables that hold six or eight people. All types mingle; advocates, exonerees, scholars, journalists, and lawyers sit together, eat, drink, and enjoy each other's company. It is a mostly joyous occasion, a reunion of sorts, where friends and colleagues get together for a laugh. But the vibe changes when the lights go out and the large projector kicks on.

The new ones go first. A short video clip is shown about each exoneree who has been freed since the previous year's conference. Amid sighs, gasps, tears, and applause, each person walks up and stands on a stage at the front of the large room. Once the first-timers are there, every other exoneree in attendance is brought up one by one until the stage is crammed with men and women who, without the help of the advocates in the room, could very well be dead or in prison. Music plays as attendees cheer and cry; the exonerees share hugs, high-fives, laughs, and tears as they celebrate the lives they regained. There is an unpredictability to the session; the 2014 one ended with a sing-along of "Lean on Me," led by Illinois exoneree Antoine Day.

For me, in attendance as a researcher but something of an outsider to the innocence community, the moment was incredibly powerful, emotional, almost cathartic. And it was upon witnessing this scene that, for the very first time, I saw innocence as a movement.

What is a social movement? The answer to this question is murky, at best. There is no universal definition of a social movement. Many have been offered, often focusing on different aspects of collective behavior.

Some writers define social movements on the basis of what they look like, the people and groups involved or the tactics employed. Others base their definitions on the object that the behavior seeks to change.[1] For some scholars, social movements are defined by informal protest tactics; to others, social movements are about power, often involving the struggle for political representation.

These definitions are fairly specific, but several researchers have defined social movements in more general terms, "as nothing more than the preference structures directed toward social change"[2] or "a sustained and self-conscious challenge to authorities or cultural codes by a field of actors (organizations and advocacy networks)."[3]

None of these definitions is any more "right" than any other. And while some people may suggest that the innocence movement does not fit a particular academic definition of a social movement, it makes little sense to paint such a narrow definitional picture. At the most basic level, the innocence movement is driven by an established network of advocacy organizations dedicated to changing the criminal justice system. As a collective body, the group has been doing this for more than a decade, and several organizations go back much further. More than 1,800 innocent prisoners have been freed, reforms have been implemented at all levels of policy and practice across the country, and innocence has altered the thinking and discourse about some important elements of criminal justice in the United States. In other words, it is clear when we look at innocence in the United States that *something* has and is happening. But what is that something, on a more normative level? Is it a true social movement? And how is it viewed by the people involved in it?

The Innocence *Revelation*

The rise of innocence as a major factor in the U.S. justice system has been described in a number of ways. Law professor Richard Rosen has commented that the current "age of innocence" marks "an exciting new period of American criminal justice."[4] Keith Findley described it as "the most dramatic development in the criminal justice world since the Warren Court's Due Process Revolution of the 1960s."[5] More dramatically, Lawrence Marshall, Daniel Medwed, and others have written of the "innocence revolution" in the United States.[6]

Perhaps the most interesting description of the innocence movement is one that extends its scope beyond criminal justice, harking back to the quintessential social movement in modern U.S. history. Some innocence advocates have suggested that wrongful convictions have sparked a "new civil rights movement,"[7] and law professor Daniel Medwed has suggested that innocence may be "the civil rights movement of the twenty-first century."[8]

Such rhetoric is powerful and transformative; it suggests something much larger than a set of exonerations and some policy reforms. Standing in the large room at the Innocence Network conference with hundreds of exonerees, their supporters, and other advocates, one can indeed sense this. While difficult to describe, it simply feels as if the meaning of this work stretches beyond the individual exonerations and reaches toward something much greater.

Marvin Zalman describes the movement as the actions of a group of people "who, since the mid-1990s, have worked to free innocent prisoners and rectify perceived causes of miscarriages of justice in the United States." This movement, he argues, is driven by "innocence consciousness," or the idea that enough people are wrongly convicted to justify efforts to exonerate them and promote systemic reforms.[9] This idea provides a sound jumping-off point for a general discussion of what the innocence movement is and what it is not.

To paint in very broad strokes, the innocence movement is marked by the acknowledgment that the criminal justice system can and does err and by the importance of heeding the lessons that flow from that acknowledgment. That is, it is marked by a shift from the long-standing belief in the high accuracy, even near-infallibility, of the justice system, toward the acceptance that it is an imperfect system that does sometimes arrest, convict, and punish innocents.[10] Thus, the innocence movement may be more accurately described as a *revelation* rather than a *revolution*. It is an idea, or an ideal, about the basic function of the criminal justice system, and anyone who supports and advances that ideal may be characterized as a part of the movement.

Those who work in the movement have different opinions on what, exactly, the innocence movement is and the extent to which it is a true movement. Stephen Saloom, for example, believes that "any person who takes any action" toward preventing, identifying, or remedying wrongful convictions is part of the innocence movement: "I think if there's a supporter out there or somebody who makes a political decision based on wrongful conviction issues or, frankly, who at a dinner party with the parents of the other three-year-olds from the day-care center is talking about this and saying it's important, . . . it seems to me that every single person who cares about preventing wrongful convictions, keeping wrongful convictions from happening, and making sure that justice happens in the wake of a wrongful conviction is part of this movement."[11] There are degrees, of course, as some people "have the privilege of being able to dedicate their careers" to the movement. But Saloom firmly believes that "every single piece matters." He notes that any person who talks about this issue may encourage someone who is in a position to influence a policy or a case to act. "You just never [know]," he said. "There's a chaos-theory type of element to it or a randomness to it. . . . I would think any movement wants to embrace anybody who shares those ideals and encourage their participation in the movement."[12]

Maddy deLone offered similar thoughts and emphasized that the importance of factual innocence has slipped from the front and center of the justice system: "It's never been, sort of, focused on in thinking about the criminal justice system," she said. "Do we convict the guilty? Do we exonerate the innocent? Do we not arrest the innocent? There is a presumption of innocence, which has been lost." The innocence movement, then, is "a group of people, be they journalists, lawyers, students, activists, formerly incarcerated people, or anybody, family members, who are trying to make sure that innocence is a force in criminal justice that people care about." She brought up the famous Blackstone ratio, that it "is better that ten guilty men go free than that one innocent suffer," but suggested we have gotten away from that idea: "People say it, but I think the movement, if it's anything, is an effort to restore us to those basic principles."[13]

Such a cause, "to put innocence back on the table and make it a force that we care about," is certainly a noble one. To accomplish this task, the innocence movement relies heavily on science, and DNA is a vital element. According to Barry Scheck, "DNA just became a way to reframe the issue in a fashion that the criminal justice community would understand and react to positively."[14] But it is not just the use of DNA to prove innocence that is important. As deLone told me, the work is driven generally by science and logic, which includes not only forensic science but also the social sciences—psychology, sociology, and so forth.[15]

This reliance on scientific reason is, according to some commentators, a key differentiator between the innocence movement and the criminal justice reform efforts that preceded it. Previous ones, such as the Warren Court's "rights revolution," were based on "value judgments," while "the innocence revolution is born of science and fact."[16]

To put this all together in broad terms, the innocence movement has sparked a revelation that the criminal justice system makes mistakes with some regularity—"there are far more innocent people than anybody ever really believed,"[17] as Scheck has pointed out—and is defined by a desire to reemphasize the importance of factual innocence in the criminal justice system. But does that make innocence a true social movement?

Innocence, Civil Rights, and Social Movements

The framing of innocence as a social movement can take a variety of shapes. Those who are involved in innocence work have different views on the extent to which it is a social movement and offer a number of reasons for their perspectives. The first person to describe it as a movement to the Innocence Network was sociologist and former Arizona Innocence Project director Robert Schehr, who brought it up during an early Network board meeting. The initial reaction from others was to focus instead on more concrete issues, but as the Network grew and they began to work on issues together, such as writing amicus briefs, "it really felt more like a movement."[18] Indeed, in some of my informal conversations with exonerees and advocates, they suggested to me that the national organization of innocence advocacy is enough to warrant calling it a social movement.

Karen Newirth talked about the Innocence Network conference and how it evokes feelings of a social movement, with "a huge number of people who are committed to the same work and the same outcomes. . . . Certainly, the innocence movement feels like a real social movement with shared goals and beliefs and a shared agenda and shared tools."[19] Ron Huff also thinks of innocence as a social movement and said that if you think of it in conjunction with the anti–death penalty movement, it is one of the "three big civil, human rights movements" along with gay rights and immigration reform.[20]

Some who work in the innocence field are somewhat indifferent about the extent to which it is a movement. Staff at Centurion Ministries, for instance, seem more concerned with their casework than with debating whether innocence constitutes a social or civil rights movement. "I'm not saying it could not possibly be that," Jim McCloskey said, "but it's not part of our thought process. That's not what inspires me. That's not what I connect to." He said he is motivated by freeing innocent prisoners and bringing them home to their families, though he is happy if others think of Centurion's work as part of a broader movement.[21] Kate Germond echoed those sentiments: "I think with us, we just put our heads down and do the work. We're not peeking over the hedge. . . . Jim and I are sort of the foot soldiers, you know? We get up, we're not thinking much beyond the battle, and that's just the way I think we're hardwired."[22]

Erika Applebaum, the former director of the Minnesota Innocence Project, said something similar. She said she is "more of a nose to the grindstone" type and is more focused on the day-to-day business.[23] Like McCloskey and Germond, she sees innocence as something of a movement but is not motivated or driven by that fact.

Others are more ambivalent about calling innocence a movement, disagreeing about the extent to which it resembles a true social movement. Richard Dieter, for instance, expressed trepidation about calling innocence a movement and about lumping it together with the anti–death penalty movement, which "has been your typical movement." He described the two as "parallel phenomena," and while he expressed the importance of innocence work and the lessons learned from it, he hesitates to call it a movement, which "sounds like something with protests and organizing and people demanding change."[24]

Michael Radelet also said he does not think of innocence as a social movement, which are generally organized by people who have something at stake. For example, he said, many activists in the gay rights movement are part of the LGBTQ community, and in the civil rights movement, the majority of leaders were people of color. "They all have something at stake," Radelet told me, which makes innocence as well as the anti–death penalty movement something different.[25] This sentiment was echoed by law professors Abbe Smith and Laura Nirider, both of whom emphasized that social movements are generally led from the ground up rather than being driven by legal professionals.[26]

Others see it as a movement of sorts but not necessarily a major social movement. Journalist Jim Dwyer described it as an "intellectual movement. It has to do with intellectual inquiry. How you know what you know? . . . I wouldn't say I see it as a social movement."[27]

Samuel Gross has an interesting perspective on the matter. For a long time, he told me, he "absolutely disliked and resisted" the idea of calling innocence a social movement. Having been to Mississippi in the 1960s, he thinks of a movement as "much more broadly based than something dominated by lawyers. . . . Feminism is a movement, gay rights is a movement. I did not think of innocence as a movement." But over time, as innocence picked up support and began to include more than just lawyers, he said he now "tolerate[s] it." And while he thinks of it as a movement now, "it's not a mass movement and not a major social movement."[28]

The skepticism toward calling innocence a social movement seems to be largely rooted in the fact that it is not, on the surface at least, focused on fundamental social issues. Peter Neufeld has pointed out that the importance of wrongful conviction work stretches beyond the innocence of clients. In selecting cases, advocates look for those "where there are significant issues beyond the narrow parameters of the client's case. . . . We're looking for those instances where we can use it to educate, to engage in legal reform, social reform, new legislation."[29]

But what about the civil rights framing of the innocence movement in particular? Neufeld said in one interview that he "think[s] of our innocence cases as civil rights cases as much as they are criminal defense cases." They are not just about the courtroom, he said, but deal with issues like racism, poverty, unequal access to resources, mental health, and "other sensitive issues in America" that "play out in criminal justice." And there is, he pointed out, a network of organizations working on legislation and education. "They're all doing social injustice reform. That's what I call a civil rights movement."[30]

Naturally, using civil rights language to talk about the innocence movement immediately triggers thoughts about mid-20th-century racial oppression, but to those who do, it is not just about race. In one interview, Scheck said they "look at it as a kind of civil rights movement to reframe criminal justice issues."[31] And Neufeld told me that civil rights cannot be limited only to racial issues:

> "Civil rights movement" has not been limited to dealing with racial oppression. The first civil rights movement dealt with racial oppression. However, that term was then borrowed by the women's movement, by the gay rights movement. They all considered themselves civil rights movements. So in that respect, this movement to prevent wrongful convictions and improve the criminal justice system so it uses more science and more reliable methods to investigate and adjudicate cases is a civil rights movement, because it will free people from prison who are wrongly convicted and it will improve the whole criminal justice system to make it . . . more reliable and ultimately more just. So in one sense, that makes it a civil rights movement.[32]

Though the phrase "civil rights" may not be restricted solely to racial equality, using it immediately racializes the conversation as people reflect on *the* American civil rights movement, and this can breed criticism. In several informal conversations, people suggested that using such rhetoric was pretentious and ego driven; a couple of people even suggested that such framing is financially motivated, as Scheck and Neufeld have a civil rights law firm in New York City and thus have a direct stake in the understanding of innocence movement issues as civil rights matters.[33]

While not everyone took such a harsh approach, the civil rights language can lead to skepticism when it triggers notions of racial oppression and the day-to-day living experiences of entire groups of people. Jeremy Travis, the former director of the National Institute of Justice, for instance, said he sees innocence as a movement but does not necessarily think it should be characterized as a civil rights movement. "I hold the civil rights movement in very high regard," he said. "People will often say, 'Well, this is a new civil rights issue.' People say that about education. People say that about a variety of things. I'm not quite sure how this [innocence] is a civil rights movement. It is a movement, no question, that has gained a lot of momentum, . . . but I'd characterize it somewhat differently."[34]

Paul Casteleiro hinted at this perspective as well when asked if he sees innocence as a civil rights movement. "It's quite obviously a civil rights issue," Casteleiro said, "because it involves the rights we all have. But I don't see it as a civil rights movement. It doesn't involve basic living rights [like] drinking water from the same fountain or going to the same schools." As a movement, he sees innocence more narrowly as a justice system issue, about "making people accountable," rather than about civil rights.[35] Similarly, Christine Mumma said she sees it as being about "continuous improvement" in the justice system but does not really consider it a civil rights movement.[36]

But is there any connection between major civil rights movements and the innocence movement? There is, of course, an obvious connection between race, class, and wrongful convictions. The exoneree stage at the Network conference contains all types of people, but unsurprisingly, there is a clear overrepresentation of people of color, much like there is in the criminal justice system more generally. This fact seemingly adds to the civil rights framing of the innocence movement. "Absolutely, I think it is . . . a civil rights issue," Germond said, "because our clients, most of them are of color, and if they're not of color, they were poor. There are very few exceptions."[37] Similarly, Maurice Possley said he thinks of innocence as a social movement "in a sense that people are being wrongfully convicted, and it typically happens among the poor. Yeah, there's a racial component, but it is largely economic: people who don't have a lot of resources who end up wrongfully convicted."[38]

The racial and socioeconomic component of the work is a key aspect of the civil rights discourse used to describe it. That topic came up in my conversation with Peter Neufeld: "There is no question that, as we talk about the causes of wrongful conviction and the remedies, our own data, both anecdotal and empirical, indicates that one of the greatest causes of wrongful conviction is racism in this country." He described the disturbing trend in black-on-white sexual assault cases, whereby the proportion of exonerations in such cases is several times larger than their proportion in general. Neufeld also pointed to research that links race to the other contributing factors of wrongful convictions, including poor defense representation and prosecutorial misconduct. "So clearly," he said, "race is a driving force."[39]

A problem arises with framing the innocence movement in terms of civil rights, however. While wrongful conviction cases touch on issues that go far beyond the criminal justice system—race and class but, even more broadly, culture and power—the innocence movement's agenda does not appear poised to address such broad issues. The innocence reform agenda has been focused on vitally important but relatively narrow criminal justice factors that lead to wrongful convictions, such as errors made by eyewitnesses and interrogations that lead to false confessions. Common reform priorities include adjusting identification procedures, recording custodial interrogations, and ensuring oversight of forensic labs, but innocence advocates are far less involved in sweeping discussions about race, class, and gender. Until that happens, the framing of innocence as a "new civil rights movement" may be difficult to sell to a wider audience.

For example, when I asked Steve Drizin, who is intimately involved in the innocence movement, if he sees the movement as a new civil rights movement, he offered a unique insight:

> No, and I take offense when we cast ourselves as a civil rights movement. The simple fact of the matter is that the innocence movement, for it to become a civil rights movement, is going to have to broaden its scope to have an impact on the entire criminal justice system, and as of now, innocence is a very small piece of the criminal justice pie. And the movement is led largely from the top down by white, privileged lawyers, on behalf of a mostly minority population. And to me, that's not a civil rights movement. Until the movement is broadened so that it becomes not an innocence movement but a reliability movement, so that the reforms aimed at increasing the accuracy of the criminal justice system are not only to the benefit of innocents but also perhaps to the benefit of people who may be guilty, the innocence movement can't, to my mind, lay claim to being a civil rights movement. There are much bigger problems in the criminal justice system than the innocence issue—length of sentences, the nature and conditions of incarceration, racial bias. To me, these are much bigger problems that sometimes get obscured when there's too much focus on innocence.

Drizin went on to say that he thinks one of the "strokes of brilliance" in founding the Northwestern Center was not calling it an "innocence project," because to him, "that has always meant something more than just the exoneration of innocents."[40]

Similarly, Nick O'Connell, the son of exoneree Frank O'Connell and former development director for Centurion Ministries, indicated similar trepidation. While he understands the framing of innocence as a social or civil rights movement and agrees with it to an extent, he also expressed concern that the current policy agenda may not necessarily solve the problem. To do so may require the much more difficult task of promoting broader cultural change and implementing accountability into the criminal justice system.[41]

So where does this leave the innocence movement?

One would be hard-pressed to make a convincing argument that innocence, on its own, is a movement on the same level as the American civil rights movement, but it is undeniably related to important and fundamental social issues. In saying this, I mean not to disparage the innocence movement or to downplay its importance—far from it; wrongful convictions have had a major impact on the criminal justice system, as the issue has a certain appeal and salience that many others lack. Instead, my goal is to evaluate the framing of the movement and, by doing so, to develop a better sense of what it is and what it is not. This in turn can help us understand where the true transformative power of the innocence movement lies.

The idea that innocence is not, on its own, a civil rights movement is not a radical one. In fact, in analyzing the ideas of those who suggest it is, this conclusion is logical. When I asked Scheck what is meant when he and others say that innocence is a "new civil rights movement," he said simply, "We mean it precisely": "When you start looking at the criminal justice system from the perspective of all the forces that can result in a miscarriage of justice and an innocent person being convicted, it's not simply that people deserve due process of law, although that's an important value. But we really need to change concretely the accuracy of the system."[42] This last part, the "need to change concretely the accuracy of the system," is similar to what Drizin said. As Drizin pointed out, however, the innocence movement has yet to make broad systemic reform—in other words, reform *not* focused on innocence—a major element of its reform agenda, as there are much bigger issues in the criminal justice system than actual innocence. And when Scheck continued, he described some of these other problems that are in need of reform, in particular, "the deplorable state of many prisons and jails" and the incredibly high rates of imprisonment, especially of racial minorities.[43]

These are incredibly important issues in the contemporary United States and are ones to which innocence can speak and potentially have a major impact. As Lisa Kern Griffin has written, stories of injustice, such as those shared by the innocence movement, demonstrate to the public that their perception of the justice system may be inaccurate. Traditional popular culture—*Law and Order, CSI,* and the like—have perpetuated the notion that most cases have neat resolutions; the police seek the truth and catch the bad guys, who are found guilty and punished. However, tales of injustice, including those seen recently in the news media and through series like *Serial* and *Making a Murderer,* signify a shift in "popular culture's portrayal of the criminal justice system" and encourage the public to see the common lack of resolution in cases and thus think more critically about the process and its injustices.[44]

Several people I spoke with described the ways in which wrongful convictions are useful for promoting important changes in criminal justice beyond the narrow confines of innocence. One such area, discussed by Aimee Maxwell, is prison conditions: "I think it's more of a civil rights movement in the idea of really taking a look at justice, . . . because our guys come out with stories of what horror they went through in prison. They are innocent people who've had to go through that horror. Is that horror necessary to make people better people when they come out? No, of course not. I think they can talk about the horror of prison and the problems in the criminal justice system in a way that people listen."[45] Maxwell described a recent story she read about a man who was incarcerated at a young age and raped in prison, and she suggested that a similar story with an innocent person can spark a desire for change: "When an innocent person is saying, 'I went through all of this hell, in addition to just going into prison,' I think people are going to start to think, 'Maybe this isn't the way we want to be.'" In other words, innocence makes that issue of prison reform more relatable, more salient, and ultimately more appealing. It also undermines retribution as the fallback option for critics, who might otherwise suggest that offenders deserve what happens to them in prison. "Well, if they're innocent," Maxwell said, "how do you shake your finger and say, 'You deserve what you get'?"[46]

Maddy deLone expressed a very similar idea, suggesting that innocence changes the nature of the conversation about criminal justice reform: "I certainly know from my own experience of working with people who committed the crimes they said they committed—they still should never have been treated the way they were treated when they were inside—that when they get out, they are not listened to or heard in the same way. They are just as human as the exoneree. They are no more or less honest . . . as a birthright, you know? But there's something about the innocent person that allows people to hear the stories in a different way."[47] Reforms involving issues like prisoners' rights can be difficult to achieve, but inserting innocence into the picture makes them more approachable and more palatable. Importantly, it is not just limited to prisoners' rights. In some ways, criminal justice has become a modern battleground for civil rights issues. A number of recent events—the police shooting of an unarmed black teenager in Ferguson, Missouri, and the resulting social unrest; the killing of Eric Garner in Staten Island, New York; the shooting of two New York Police Department officers that followed; and many others—have sparked conversations about fundamental issues like race, authority, and the relationship between citizens and the state.[48] And more generally, over the past several decades, criminal justice has been closely tied to key social issues. Debates over the war on drugs and mass incarceration, for example, are intimately related to conversations about race, class, families, and neighborhoods.

These are only a few examples, but they serve to show that criminal justice is an interesting window into wider issues, as the Innocence Project's director of policy Rebecca Brown pointed out: "I think criminal justice, in a lot of ways, is really a very good lens through which to look at larger social problems. . . . I mean, the truth is criminal justice will always tell you a good amount about what is wrong with your society, about what is wrong with your culture, and I think that it couldn't be more obvious in our culture." Thus, the work being done to bring attention to the problems in the criminal justice system, "to the insanity of the system, is absolutely a social movement."[49]

Judy Royal, from the Northwestern Center, offered similar thoughts. She pointed out that the organization's goal has never been restricted to "helping individuals" but includes "reforming the criminal justice system," which is laced with racism and classism. Thus, it is not just about wrongful convictions; the problems in the system, from unfair arrest practices to post-release employment, are all "part of society's ills. It is all connected."[50]

Innocence can therefore be a vital piece of the broader criminal, civil, and social justice discourse because it is a relatively easy way to "wedge into that conversation."[51] It can be a "great tool to get people who aren't really thinking about criminal justice issues or race or the less clear-cut or palatable issues," because it "has a pure status [and] can point to problems in the system."[52]

Innocence is a valuable resource for people working on key social and civil rights reform and "is leveraged" by those working on other issues, Neufeld told me:

> From the very, very beginning, in my own mind, I saw a nexus between wrongful convictions and race, and there's no question that our movement has demonstrated that it's true, providing more evidence of that. And if you want to use our work just as it was used by people in the death penalty movement to turn people against the death penalty, so too will those people in the civil rights movement, the NAACP or other organizations that are . . . fighting against mass incarceration and over-criminalization. They see that as a civil rights issue because most of the people being prosecuted and most of the people being incarcerated are disproportionately black or Hispanic. And certainly, they too can use in the future, and will use, our work, just as the death penalty [activists] did.[53]

Given how the innocence movement has demonstrated the fallibility of the fact-finding process, Neufeld questions how the system can focus on improving reliability with such an emphasis on locking up large numbers of people. Thus, he suggested that social and civil rights reformers "will be able to use our data, use the power of our narratives, to critique over-criminalization and mass incarceration, just as people for the last 15 years have used it to change public attitudes about the death penalty." He also mentioned how, internationally, the lessons learned about the U.S. justice system through the innocence movement are being used to improve the systems in other countries. Thus, the work of innocence advocates is tremendously valuable for a variety of other reform issues, and Neufeld hopes the work that innocence advocates do "can be exploited by lots of different civil rights and human rights movements."[54]

What Neufeld and others essentially are describing is not innocence as its own civil rights movement but as a key issue that can be a powerful piece of the much larger civil rights conversation. In other words, it is not quite accurate to characterize innocence, in and of itself, as "a new civil rights movement," as some people do. It is, rather, a legal-reform movement that can serve as a relatively small but intensely powerful piece of other modern civil rights struggles.

A number of interviewees essentially said this more directly. Rob Warden described the innocence movement as "an extension of the civil rights movement" and tied it in with other important criminal justice issues, including disproportionate minority contact with the justice system, the impact of justice system involvement on families, and overly harsh punishment.[55] Similarly, Ryan Costello suggested that "working on racial issues within the incarceration system is like the new civil rights movement. . . . How our administrative systems, particularly the prisons and parole systems work, that's a huge civil rights issue," and "exoneration is one subset of that."[56]

Innocence, then, is not its own civil rights movement but an important support column for one, as Meredith Kennedy said: "I don't know that I'd say it's the 'next civil rights movement,' but . . . it is a movement. I see it happening globally. I mean, the issues aren't all exactly the same. It's not like there's a platform that is, sort of, three bullet points that everyone is subscribing to and pushing. But absolutely, I think criminal justice reform, it's the larger bucket. I think that's a social movement, and I think innocence is a key leg of that table."[57]

This point was made by a number of those with whom I spoke, including Alan Maimon, an investigator for Centurion Ministries, who said he thinks innocence is "certainly part of a larger social movement": "I think that's beyond dispute."[58] Similarly, both Emily West, the former research director for the Innocence Project, and Shannon Leitner, when asked if they thought of innocence as a social or civil rights movement, described it as just one piece of a much larger pie. "I'm not sure that the movement is limited only to innocence," Leitner said. "It almost feels like innocence is part of a broader movement."[59]

*   *   *

I began this chapter by describing my experience at the Innocence Network conferences and how, upon seeing the exoneree stage, I for the first time got the feeling that innocence was a movement. I stand by that assertion. Clearly, the innocence movement is a force for change.

The hard work of lawyers, journalists, and investigators has changed the lives of thousands of people—innocent men and women who sat in prison for crimes they did not commit, their families and friends, and others affected by these miscarriages of justice. Many of these individuals were resurrected from the depths of human experience, and their lives, as well as those of their loved ones, will forever be changed because of it.

The innocence movement has also changed perceptions. At the most basic level, wrongful convictions raise questions about justice and fairness and how well our system achieves them. It has made people realize, in a very concrete way, that the system, much like the human beings who design and administer it, is fallible. Such a realization is powerful and has been the catalyst for changes to policy and practice across the United States.

The innocence movement is clearly an important legal-reform movement and can safely be called a social movement, but those carry very different connotations than declaring it a "new civil rights movement." That, I argue, it is not.

Any time something is declared a "civil rights movement," the imagery generated is that of the racial oppression that came to a head in the 1950s and 1960s. The civil rights movement was a battle for basic day-to-day equality for millions of people. It developed and was spread, in large part, through black communities and institutions.[60] Although activists were not exclusively African Americans, a large segment of the movement was made up of constituents who had a direct stake in it and who risked their lives for change.

Although the term "civil rights movement" may not be restricted solely to racial equality, other movements that share that phrase more closely resemble the original one. Perhaps the most notable example, the gay rights movement, is led in large part by the millions of gay and lesbian individuals fighting for equality.[61] And although lawyers and legal tactics can and have played important roles in civil rights movements,[62] they were never the heart of it; that consisted of the constituents themselves who made up the majority of the movement bases.

The innocence movement does not resemble these other civil rights movements. That does not mean, however, that it is not extremely valuable or important or that it cannot or should not be a part of the civil rights conversation. As noted earlier, many modern civil rights issues play out prominently in the criminal justice system. Law, police, courts, prisons, and prisoner reentry are all tied intimately to contemporary discussions of race, class, gender, mental health, and other social issues; they generate questions and encourage debate about individuals, communities, and the power of the state.

To repeat a point made earlier, the criminal justice system is a fascinating lens through which to view the social world and provides a telling window into our culture. Wrongful convictions provide perhaps the most compelling window into that system and the processes that play out within it. All of the factors that impact what we see in criminal justice also affect wrongful convictions; race, class, gender, politics, and moral emotions all impact the extent to which people receive justice.

Herein lies the issue with framing innocence as its own "new civil rights movement": the innocence movement's reform agenda has, for very good reason, focused mainly on altering police and prosecutorial practices, ensuring reliable forensic methods, and securing post-release compensation for exonerees. These are all important goals, and people in the wrongful conviction community should continue to pursue them, but they are very technical. Law professor Adele Bernhard agreed that innocence advocates probably could go further in discussing the broader issues, though the way to go about addressing this particular limitation is unclear. Still, it is worth thinking about, she said: "Let's take a step back and think about how the values of society at large permeate those organizations—the training, the hiring, the supervision—and [start] thinking about it from that perspective instead of focusing way down on the details of actual procedures."[63]

One potential path forward in this area is that taken by the sister projects of the Northwestern Center. Laura Nirider told me that the Center on Wrongful Convictions of Youth, for instance, is active in building relationships with outside organizations and tackling issues beyond innocence. For instance, its staff members write and join in amicus briefs on cases that speak to issues about due process rights and juvenile confinement, even if the clients are guilty.[64]

Regardless, when viewed through a broad lens that steps away from the legal and into the social, wrongful convictions are not about eyewitness misidentifications, false confessions, and overzealous prosecution. Such issues, while crucial to the legal process, are relatively small. Deep down, these cases are about social inequalities, power struggles, and culture. They are indicative of bigger struggles with race and class and gender. And while innocence advocates are most certainly aware of this fact, the innocence movement has yet to become heavily involved in broader social reform efforts. Instead, the reform agenda emphasizes important but very narrowly defined legal and criminal justice practices, rather than more fundamental social reform. There may be good reasons for this emphasis—such broad change is ambiguous and difficult to define, let alone actually achieve, and thus innocence advocates may be best served by focusing on incremental but attainable change—but until the innocence movement is proactive in building real, working alliances with people in the established civil rights community and becoming more actively engaged in broader social reform efforts, many people will remain skeptical of innocence laying claim to being a "new civil rights movement."

When I met with Nick O'Connell, he reminded me of a quote by famed lawyer and social justice activist Bryan Stevenson that is pertinent to this discussion about criminal justice, civil rights, and social reform. "The opposite of poverty is not wealth," Stevenson said. "I don't believe that. I actually think, in too many places, the opposite of poverty is justice."[65]

So perhaps it is not vital that the innocence movement become more active in fundamental civil rights or social reform efforts. After all, every one of these advocates, whether for innocence, racial equality, gay rights, or other matters, is ultimately seeking what he or she perceives to be justice.

Conclusion

The Challenges Ahead and the Future of Innocence

At a glance, the innocence movement seems fairly healthy. Every year, more of the wrongly convicted are freed, new policies are proposed and adopted around the country, and more organizations are started to advance the movement's goals. The 2016 Innocence Network conference had more than 550 registered attendees, the most since its inception. Overall, the movement is in a good place for the near-term. This does not mean, however, that it can now coast ahead as a self-sustaining force for change. Like any form of collective action, the innocence movement faces a number of obstacles that must be overcome in order to grow. These can range from concrete matters such as fund-raising to much larger political and cultural challenges. This chapter discusses a few of the difficulties facing the innocence movement in the years ahead, and while far from exhaustive, these represent some of the issues that came up during my conversations with movement participants and that will be faced in the near- and long-term future.

The Limits of Reform

Throughout the preceding chapters, I have outlined the various successes of the innocence movement: the men and women who have been freed from the shackles of unjust punishment, the successful policy reforms, and the growing awareness of wrongful convictions, among others. These accomplishments are noteworthy and ought to be celebrated; but the challenges that remain are numerous, and the many faults in the justice system are far from rectified.

The successful policy reforms themselves, while significant, are often limited in scope. The federal Innocence Protection Act was an important symbolic policy in that it represents wrongful conviction on the national legislative agenda, but as Zalman has said, it was "watered-down" from its original inception and ultimately limited in its reach.[1] And at the state level, while more than 40 states have passed some type of reform to help prevent wrongful convictions, many still have not, and those policies that have been passed vary wildly in quality. For example, in the area of eyewitness misidentification, a leading contributing factor to wrongful convictions, scientific research points to a series of reforms that may improve the accuracy of identifications, but as of late 2016, fewer than 20 states have addressed this issue, and among those that have, the scope of their reforms varies. Some states, such as North Carolina and New Jersey, cover all of the major areas identified by psychologists, while others, such as Massachusetts and Oregon, do not actually mandate any changes to police practices. The same is true in other areas; regarding false confessions, where the recording of interrogations is suggested to protect both suspects and officers, approximately half of the states have done something, but some have only expressed a preference for recording while others mandate it only in specific types of cases.[2]

Another important policy area is the aftermath of wrongful convictions. This issue has been acknowledged legislatively at the federal level, where there is a compensation statute in place and a law stipulating that exonerees' awards are not subject to tax. More than half of the states also have compensation statutes in place; however, they too are often limited in important ways. Exonerees and their families face a myriad of struggles upon release and, even with compensation statutes, often receive less assistance than presumably guilty parolees and probationers. The statutes in place have key shortcomings, including in their financial policies, health services, and provisions for other vital needs of exonerees.[3] Reintegration is an area of focus for some groups like the Innocence Project, which has a social work division to assist exonerees, and Centurion Ministries, whose employees work to develop a lifelong relationship with their clients, but many organizations are unable to dedicate the resources necessary to really make headway in this area, leaving exonerees to fend for themselves in many ways.

In addition to the concrete limitations of legislative reforms, there are important limitations in the law regarding wrongful convictions. The concept of "actual innocence" is still not well recognized by the courts, and having them do so is difficult given the structure of the U.S. adversarial system, in which the appeals process is focused on legal and procedural errors, rather than factual ones. This appellate structure makes it difficult to secure exonerations and arguably deemphasizes the presumption of innocence, which is supposed to be a core component of a due process–oriented adversarial system such as that in the United States. While a few isolated states have recognized claims for postconviction relief based on actual innocence, most have not differentiated these from other claims, and potentially innocent inmates still face many roadblocks when seeking relief and exoneration.[4]

There has also been a distinct lack of movement with regard to accountability for practitioners—police, prosecutors, and defense attorneys—who were involved in errors of justice. Police and prosecutors are largely protected by civil immunity and generally are not held responsible for their roles in producing wrongful convictions.[5] Similarly, standards for defense attorneys, particularly appointed counsel, are often minimal, and a lack of resources and incentives fails to motivate zealous defense advocacy.

None of these limitations are to take away from the accomplishments of innocence advocates in reforming the justice system, but the job of improving the system is far from complete, and furthering a reform agenda in criminal justice is a daunting task. Enacting change in the justice system is difficult due, in part, to the continued resistance to the notion of wrongful convictions. Innocence advocates face resistance at every level of their work. At the case level, they often face resistance from law enforcement when they seek to reinvestigate a case or test a new piece of evidence, though that is not always the case, as Barry Scheck pointed out: "When you walk in the door with DNA evidence that exonerates somebody, you find that police and prosecutors resist it, even if they didn't try the case in the first place. We found a lot of that, although in many instances we have prosecutors and police that come forward and say, 'Look, we want to do the right thing. I'm a minister of justice, that's my job. I want to correct my mistakes.'"[6] Advocates also face resistance when they try to implement policy changes in criminal justice agencies or through legislative efforts. Even if reforms are evidence-based, "there are absolute roadblocks to overcome in terms of perceptions of what these changes will provoke," according to Rebecca Brown. For example, she said there are "concerns that if we change the way we do eyewitness identification reforms, prosecutors are suddenly going to have a number of witnesses who say they're not certain."[7] Similarly, Peter Neufeld said police departments are hesitant to change their eyewitness practices because "they're so worried that they might lose one particular case because a real guilty person might not be apprehended."[8]

Scheck once described this resistance, saying that law enforcement officials sometimes think that admitting their mistakes will lead juries to become more skeptical, though this may not necessarily be a well-founded fear in his view: "They feel like it undermines the legitimacy of their efforts. I don't think it does. I think it actually, in the final analysis, enhances it. But that's what they worry about, that it's going to affect the jury in the next case."[9]

These concerns on the part of law enforcement are very practical ones that may be overcome with extensive evaluation research conducted by neutral parties. There is, of course, the potential for such research to reinforce those concerns if researchers find downsides to proposed reforms; as seen with the recent debate in psychology over eyewitness reforms, many changes may reduce mistaken identifications but may also reduce accurate ones, and this is an important aspect of the policy debate.[10]

Beyond these practical concerns are other sources of resistance that run deeper. At some level, the resistance may simply reflect the human tendency to resist admitting mistakes, "especially important mistakes," as Scheck said.[11] Nick O'Connell discussed this issue when talking about his father's case and the refusal of the police to admit their errors. He said that rather than make any concessions, the human tendency is to become defensive: "Even in the end, when confronted with it, when they get their hand caught in the cookie jar, their position is [to] dig in their heels and just say, 'Nope. No, we're right, we're right.' And they just take this pro forma position of fight, fight, fight."[12]

Scheck said the resistance in individual cases is due to a "confluence of forces." It is particularly difficult when the crime was especially heinous, due in large part to considerations about the community and the victims: "Within a community, you have the victims or the families of the victims, and they've been told for years, 'This is a terrible person. This is an animal, a beast that committed this terrible crime.' Prosecutors and police are very reluctant to go back to the victims, understandably, and say, 'Oh, we made a terrible error. I'm going to have to revive this horrible thing that you lived through and make you live through it again.'"[13] It is particularly difficult in sexual assault cases in which victims have mistakenly identified someone, because the victims are "doubly violated." Not only were they the victim of a horrendous crime, but they also have to "relive the experience and come to terms with the idea that, by mistake, they may have had a hand in putting an innocent person in prison. That's a hard thing to accept."[14]

Not only might people within the system be hesitant to admit mistakes, but those on the outside may hesitate to accept that the system erred. O'Connell discussed the interesting phenomenon whereby people tend to be skeptical of government institutions and practices yet place extreme trust in the criminal justice system despite the fact that the United States has the highest incarceration rate in the world. "You hear people frequently talk about the inefficiencies of government organizations," O'Connell said, "but yet, all of a sudden, we want to say, 'Well, I don't trust the Post Office with my mail, but, hey, when we're talking about life-or-death scenarios, they never get it wrong.'" And when it surfaces that the system may have gotten it wrong, he said, people often deflect, deny, and excuse: "You're looking around at people who are smart, caring people in all other walks of life and everything that they do, but on this one, it's either over their head or they don't have the time to figure it out." Alternatively, he said, people get caught up in the viewpoint in which "the whole notion of innocent until proven guilty is just a farce." That is, there is often a widespread assumption that if one is caught up in the system, he or she must have done something to warrant it. "I can't tell you how many times people would say that to Dad when they realized he was innocent. 'Well, what did you do?' Even once they realized he was innocent, they still go, 'What did you do?'—the implication being, well, a cop would never either just make a mistake or intentionally do something like that, ever."[15]

Even if people do admit that mistakes are made, they may be resistant to change that is dictated to them. Even reforms that may seem obvious and have long-term benefits face resistance. For example, one of the leading proposals to help alleviate the problems associated with false confessions is to record custodial interrogations. Doing so would provide an objective record of what happened, which protects both the suspect and the interrogators. However, Neufeld told me, advocates have faced resistance: "Why not do it? Well, the police officers are very resistant to it. They just don't want to have their hands tied. But what happened is, in Minnesota, there was tremendous resistance to it initially. But guess what? After it's been in existence a few years, now the cops love it."[16]

This resistance may be rooted in perceived alliances. Despite the fact that the innocence movement promotes ideas that have fairly wide appeal, there is still some element of choosing sides and allegiances. While innocence advocates see allies across the system and in general will not use the term "opponents," there is definitely an element of such a mentality,[17] and where it does exist, it is generally in reference to the law enforcement community. To the extent that the mentality of being on a particular side exists, it is mutual. As Brown told me, innocence advocates are generally lumped together with the defense community: "I think just getting people on board is sometimes just very difficult, because we are certainly conflated with the defense community. . . . I mean, we are defending people in a postconviction setting, [but] I still think that's separate and apart from what a criminal justice platform might look like from the National Association of Criminal Defense Lawyers. That said, there certainly are issues we see very much eye to eye on, and I think there's always going to be, probably, some level of distrust [from the prosecutorial community] when a platform comes from [the innocence] community."[18] O'Connell suggested that, when one tries to go up against law enforcement, it becomes analogous to sports teams, where a "competitive spirit" can develop, which leads to a divisive "us versus them" mentality and, ultimately, to a situation where "it's all gas and no brakes."[19]

Clearly, the resistance faced by the innocence movement can come from a number of sources. Paul Casteleiro suggested that, as much as the movement has accomplished, it likely has not changed perceptions within the law enforcement community in a major way.[20] There may also be an element of what O'Connell called "careerism." That is, people within the system are incentivized to not be seen making mistakes. Whether due to community preferences, political pressures, or other forces, law enforcement officials are incentivized to solve cases and win convictions. This often justifies what has been called noble-cause corruption, or the idea that the ends justify the means.[21] Furthermore, professional advancement comes from perceived successes; as an example, O'Connell pointed to the number of judges who come up through prosecutors' offices after winning convictions in major cases.[22]

There is also a political element to the perceived alliances of the innocence movement. For example, though the core of the movement's message is fairly bipartisan, reform is different depending on the politics of a given state. In North Carolina, for example, Christine Mumma said that prior to the Republican majority, innocence advocates "had to work hard but could get reform passed." Since the Republican majority, "it's more about holding on" to the things they have already achieved.[23]

Working with organizations and on causes outside the innocence movement can also breed notions of unholy alliances. For some innocence advocates in North Carolina, for instance, one of their primary goals is to keep themselves "far away from the death penalty." Working on death penalty issues would likely be political suicide given the politics and culture of the state. "When anything touches on the death penalty, we're done," Mumma said, in large part because in that state advocates positioned innocence firmly as a public safety, anticrime issue.[24] There is thus a fascinating element of political framing in the innocence movement's overcoming resistance.

Despite the specific sources of resistance, there seems to be an element of *institutional protectionism* involved. In discussing the wrongful conviction of the Central Park Five, Jim Dwyer used this phrase to describe the resistance of police and prosecutors to admitting that they made errors that led to the erroneous convictions of five teenagers. Those involved had much at stake, and their apparently solving the case was seen as a major public and political success. Thus, they had incentives to deny any errors and ended up getting "stuck with a mistake."[25] Such a pattern seems to be true throughout the system, from individual cases through legislative policy making, and continues to be a hurdle for innocence advocates to clear.

Even if this resistance is overcome, on a larger scale, the legislative agenda simply may not emphasize an issue like wrongful conviction but may focus on what are perceived as broader issues such as the economy or immigration reform. Policy makers can focus on only so much at any given time, and innocence may not be near the top of the legislative totem pole. However, given the resurgence in civil rights discourse and its connection with criminal justice, as discussed in chapter 6, it will be interesting to see whether innocence advocates can work their specific issues into the larger political picture in the coming years. Doing so will require advocates to overcome major resource limitations. These include some obvious ones; financial resources are always limited, and there are far more innocent people in prison than could ever be freed by innocence projects. But if the movement is to be sustained and continue to expand its influence on the criminal justice system at large, it must also maintain a stable of advocates and increase its mindshare among the public, both of which are challenges going forward.

The Advocacy Pipeline

I noted earlier that the innocence movement is driven in large part by the students who become involved in clinics while in law school. In this way, the movement has a unique opportunity to get people involved, cultivate their passion and dedication to wrongful conviction work, and essentially develop its own advocates. However, it is not a foregone conclusion that the innocence movement will continue to develop members at such a high rate.

Many of those who have become involved in innocence work—most notably Scheck and Neufeld but also others like Casteleiro—became involved in law because they wanted to do good, to be people's lawyers; in short, they are cause lawyers. However, they were of a generation that was influenced by the times. Having grown up in the era of the civil rights movement and the draft and the Vietnam War, they turned to law as a way to change the world. Given this fact, I asked several interviewees if they sensed that current law students, who are presumably the leaders of progressive legal reform in the future, have a different sense of activism or passion for social reform.

Unanimously, those with whom I spoke said they think that sense of activism is still present. Adele Bernhard said that when she was in law school, it seemed like there were a lot of social activists. "There is probably a smaller cadre of social activists in the law schools [today]," she said, "but they're still there."[26]

Activism also changes over the generations, so while young people still have a sense of activism, it is different than it was in earlier decades. Theresa Newman said that students and other young people today "have a strain of activism" but that it is not necessarily nurtured as it used to be. She said that, while she was young at the time, she remembers John F. Kennedy calling for young people "to do things," to become involved in the Peace Corps, and wishes leaders today would nurture the passion and activism of young people in a similar fashion: "I think if Obama had said, 'I want all you people to do x hours of community service per year, and we're gonna keep a registry,' I think people would have done it. . . . I thought with Obama, the youth were moved again, and I'm disappointed that he didn't ask them to do anything. He had them fired up and ready to go." Newman said she thinks younger generations still have a strong desire to do good and just need the opportunity to do it. "They want to be involved in something that they feel is more important than themselves, and they just need to figure out what that is."[27] Becoming involved in something like an innocence clinic can help spark their activist spirit.

Similarly, Scheck said that the sense of activism is not gone; "it's just different." While there is no clear issue like the draft for young people to band together and get up in arms about, many issues, particularly in the criminal justice system, "appeal to the activism of young people who are idealistic." Rather than being driven by protests, though, "it spreads virally now with social media." So while the nature of activism may be different from when he was growing up, it is far from gone: "I mean, my God, why would anybody today who is young and idealistic think that the great social justice movements are behind us? They're all ahead of us!"[28]

Neufeld also said that there are "extraordinarily large numbers of law students . . . that want to do work that involves social justice, economic justice, political justice, and racial justice." Private law firms often contact the Innocence Project because their young associates want to be involved in its cases pro bono. "They want to use us as a selling point," he said. Neufeld also pointed out that many up-and-coming lawyers, from top law schools and with great credentials, look for jobs with organizations like the Innocence Project and as public defenders. Thus, "there are plenty of people coming out of law schools today who have very much an activist perspective and want to do good work. . . . There's a ton of people who want to do this stuff."[29]

Even with many individuals who are interested in doing wrongful conviction work, it is not guaranteed that the innocence movement will continue to find top-tier talent to carry the torch. One reason is the economic barrier to pursuing careers in public-interest work. As several interviewees pointed out, the economics of law used to be very different. Scheck went to law school at the University of California–Berkeley partly because "the tuition at one of the top-ten law schools in the country was only $435 a semester," an amount that he "was able to make playing poker."[30] He was able to graduate without debt and pursue his passions. Casteleiro similarly said that lawyers of his generation left school without debt: "We came out and could do whatever we wanted to do."[31]

The economics of law have changed dramatically, however. Students regularly finish law school with tens, sometimes hundreds, of thousands of dollars of debt; according to the American Bar Association, for 2013 law school graduates, the average debt taken on by those graduating from public and private schools was over $80,000 and $120,000, respectively.[32] Such large amounts of debt create a major barrier to pursuing public-interest work. As Casteleiro said, the "biggest problem today is economics." He said that many students today "come out with mortgages, basically," and so "their opportunity to do pure public-interest law is limited."[33] Newman expressed a similar sentiment: "When you graduate from law school with $200,000 in debt, it's really hard to go out and say, 'I'm gonna change the world.' . . . You really need to pay down that debt. . . . These are very different times from the '60s."[34]

Drizin similarly said that many of the students he sees "have that sense of wanting to work to do good, to do public-interest work, to work for the common good," but that "it's a harder road for many of them to pursue because of mounting law school debt": "But I still see a passion and desire on the part of many students to do it."[35]

It is not just a matter of debt, however; the salaries for public-interest work have not increased in proportion to other areas of the legal profession. "What I do see and what really is different than when I went to law school almost 40 years ago is that the disparity in pay is huge," Bernhard said. While public-interest lawyers still generally made less than corporate lawyers back then, the difference "wasn't as great" as it is today. "Everything has escalated at the top end," while for those who work in public defense offices, things have stayed more stagnant. "There's no way that can't have an effect on people . . . unless you have another way of surviving [financially]."[36]

Scheck described this as "one of the real dilemmas" in law, pointing out that while corporate law salaries "have mushroomed," public-interest law salaries, "whether it's being a prosecutor or defense lawyer or legal services lawyers or any kind of public lawyer, have stayed very, very low." At the same time, the cost of going to law school has increased dramatically, and young lawyers are still encouraged to go into public law and work on social justice issues. "That's what we like to tell people when we give graduation talks. And they are looking at these huge debts. It's almost hypocritical, in a way. But that's created a real problem."[37]

There are efforts to try to get around this problem. One partial solution is loan forgiveness for doing public-interest work, an idea that both the federal government and law schools have discussed. Such programs could potentially serve as a "counter-push" to keep young lawyers interested in public-interest work.[38]

Jane Raley also said that her organization encourages its students to find other ways to do public-interest work while still dealing with their economic realities:

> We say, "Well, if you really are interested in this kind of work, when you do go out there to your big law firm job, live small so you have money to leave when you want to leave, when you've paid off your student loan." And then the other thing I like to tell students is, "Doing this kind of work does not have to be an all-or-nothing proposition. You can go work at your firm, but come back with us. You can do volunteer work, or you can take a pro bono case that we can't take for reasons of a conflict."[39]

Raley also said that former students remain involved in public outreach, fund-raising, and other initiatives to stay connected with the work even if they are unable to do it full-time.

Still, the relatively limited opportunities for public-interest work and the economic realities of pursuing it may remain a challenge for the innocence movement and other progressive legal-reform efforts as they struggle to maintain the advocacy pipeline required to sustain a movement.

Fatigue, Apathy, and Naiveté

The innocence movement has been unique in that it has generally been able to achieve some success without major public support or outcry. While most people would likely support the goals of the innocence movement, it is far from the forefront of the public political consciousness. The issues that dominate modern political discourse tend to focus on the economy, foreign affairs, or hot-button social issues; when criminal justice does come up, it is often in the context of policing and neighborhoods, heinous crimes, sex offenders, and other more visceral, emotional issues.

Innocence, on the other hand, is simply not on the minds of most people. Despite the publicity that many cases have received, Paul Casteleiro expressed reservation about the extent to which the public thinks about wrongful convictions: "I'm still not sure that anybody cares," he said. "I have my doubts that they really do."[40] Similarly, Jim McCloskey suggested that much of the public "is still naïve, as I was 30 years ago."[41]

While the lack of public outcry has not stopped the innocence movement from making headway in the legal world, more may be important if the movement is to continue growing and developing and particularly if it wants to expand beyond the narrow confines of police agencies and lawyers' offices toward large-scale policy reform. As Stephen Saloom said, getting the public to perceive a problem is a key to getting legislatures to act: "So that's why I'm always very concerned about getting public attention to these issues."[42] Aimee Maxwell similarly described the importance of getting attention on wrongful convictions: "The stories need to get to the general public. They need to get to the wealthy policy makers, and they need to upset the wealthy policy makers. That's when change happens."[43]

One of the problems with gaining attention for the issue, as Erika Applebaum noted, is that innocence does not hit people in the same personal way as other issues: "I think enough people don't see it as a problem, that it doesn't affect enough people. . . . People feel the injustice of it when they see it, but I don't think it's something in front of their face like their health insurance. They just don't see it affecting them. And it's not puppies and kittens and children that are hungry. . . . Right now, I don't think people know enough about it."[44] Thus, the media has an important role to play in the innocence movement's continued growth. However, there seems to be an issue of media fatigue. Maurice Possley said that when he first started covering wrongful convictions, editors were interested because wrongful convictions "were considered novelties in some ways." However, as they become more and more common, fatigue starts to set in. "They were considered bigger news stories than they are today," Possley said, though "they still get some news."[45]

Possley is not alone in this observation. As several interviewees noted, many of the early exonerations were front-page news. Now, Mc-Closkey said, many "only get a short snippet in the *New York Times*." He described a recent false confession case from Illinois that received only a short blurb that was buried toward the back of the paper.[46]

Judy Royal suggested that, for people working in the innocence movement, it can sometimes be difficult to deal with problems of fatigue because they are surrounded by people "who live and breathe" wrongful convictions: "It's so interesting and so compelling to you, and you feel so passionately about it, that you have a tendency to be talking about it at the drop of a hat, whether [people] want to hear about it or not." While innocence advocates are always trying to spread the word and educate people, the more powerful connection may be between "publicity and people's interest," and in this area, she wonders if they are reaching a point of diminishing returns: "One thing I wonder about is whether there's a little bit of fatigue about this issue. The [Northwestern] Center has exonerated so many people in recent years that I wonder if it's like, 'Oh yeah, another innocent person who was in jail for 20 years and exonerated. Ho hum.' I mean, obviously, that's not how we feel about it, but we wonder if the general public feels that way about it."[47] Maintaining public interest and concern is thus a major hurdle for the innocence movement going forward. Publicity on its own may not be enough, as Applebaum pointed out: "When something is on TV like *60 Minutes* or *Frontline*, people are so shocked. . . . but I think they still see it as a very small problem." One of the ways to continue to generate interest, then, is through more mainstream popular culture and social media. "That's how you get people," Applebaum said. "Unfortunately, nowadays, that's how people are paying attention to things. . . . Something flashes across the screen, or someone posts something on Facebook. I hate to say that social media has that much importance, but I think that's how people are paying attention to this stuff."[48]

In terms of mainstream popular culture, wrongful convictions, or at least some of the issues associated with wrongful convictions, have reached an incredible level of popularity in recent years. As I discussed earlier, series like the podcast *Serial* and the Netflix documentary *Making a Murderer* reached tens of millions of people and generated a cultural phenomenon around cases of questionable convictions. While it is still too early to know if these will have any lasting impact, it is entirely possible. As Duke law professor and former federal prosecutor Lisa Kern Griffin has suggested, series like these "bring[] the failures of due process into focus: careless police work, flawed forensics, forceful interrogations, unreliable witnesses and the woeful condition of state-funded criminal defense." She suggested that the coverage of the justice system has shifted, now encouraging a better understanding of the complexities and potential shortcomings of the legal process. Given the stories of police abuse and malpractice and the popularity of podcasts and shows dealing with miscarriages of justice, Griffin writes, "The moment is ripe for reform, culturally and politically."[49]

Innocence advocates, for their part, appear to be acutely aware of the importance on new forms of media, including social media. Several advocates and organizations run active e-mail campaigns and maintain an active presence on websites; as of October 2016, the Innocence Project has over 67,000 followers on Twitter and nearly 240,000 "likes" on Facebook. These media are new ways to share stories of exonerations, discuss policy successes and initiatives, and, ultimately, gain supporters and seek donations. And it appears that social media will continue to be an area of focus for innocence advocates, as the past few Innocence Network conferences have included sessions on how to use social media to advance movement goals, raise money, and more.

Critiques and Concerns

The innocence movement's message has very broad appeal; people on both sides of the ideological spectrum and throughout the criminal justice system generally support the idea of protecting innocent people from erroneous arrest, conviction, and punishment. But not everyone is fully on board with the movement's work. Relatively few people have been outspoken critics of the innocence movement, and those who have develop their critiques from very different perspectives.

The Myth of Innocence

Perhaps the most persistent critique of the innocence movement is that, ultimately, there is no real *problem* of wrongful conviction. Such an argument has been long-standing. In the early 20th century, Judge Learned Hand referred to the conviction of an innocent person as an "unreal dream,"[50] and a Massachusetts district attorney reportedly said, "Innocent men are never convicted. Don't worry about it, it never happens in the world. It is a physical impossibility."[51] Such confidence in the justice system, and disbelief about errors, has persisted. The U.S. attorney general in 1985 said that the notion of an innocent suspect was "contradictory," because an innocent person would not be a suspect.[52]

While these points seem to suggest that a wrongful conviction could not happen, this line of critique has evolved to some degree. Most modern advocates of this position do not suggest that protecting the innocent is not worthwhile or that mistakes cannot happen; on the contrary, most acknowledge that some errors are inevitable and highly unfortunate. However, they believe that innocence movement advocates have blown the issue far out of proportion, perpetuating a false notion that wrongful convictions are epidemic. In their minds, wrongful convictions may occur, but there is not an "innocence problem" in the United States.

Most estimates put the rate of wrongful convictions at 1%–5%. Arguably the most empirically grounded estimate, reported in a study published by the National Academy of Sciences, conservatively suggests that 4.1% of capital convictions may be erroneous.[53] However, the true number and rate of wrongful convictions is unknowable; by definition, wrongful convictions are hidden from view. Critics, however, tend to suggest not only that it may be possible to establish an error rate but that the rate is astonishingly low.

A leading proponent of this criticism is Paul Cassell, a former lawyer and judge who is now a law professor at the University of Utah. Cassell has been outspoken in his criticism of innocence advocacy since the late 1980s, when he coauthored a critique of the Bedau-Radelet study. While he has referred to the conviction of a factually innocent person as "the ultimate miscarriage of justice,"[54] he believes there are ways to estimate the prevalence of false confessions in particular and wrongful convictions in general and that those rates are low. This perspective has been adopted by a number of others, including former Supreme Court justice Antonin Scalia, whose dissent in *Kansas v. Marsh* cited the work of the Clatsop County, Oregon, district attorney Joshua Marquis, suggesting that a high estimate of the error rate in felony cases is only 0.027%.[55] Similarly, Morris Hoffman, a Denver district-court judge and adjunct professor at the University of Colorado, made a similar calculation. In his view, the myth is not that wrongful convictions occur but is "a myth about the frequency with which innocent people are caught in the net of criminal law."[56] According to his calculations, the actual wrongful conviction rate may be as low as 0.00065% and, though unlikely, as high as 1.95%.[57] Yet another calculation, by Northwestern law professor Ronald Allen and investigator Larry Laudan, came to an error rate of 0.84%.[58]

These estimates are shaky, at best—there are serious empirical problems with the calculations that call into question the legitimacy of the specific numbers—but the nature of the critique in general is worth noting. Marquis summed up this perspective when we spoke, acknowledging that wrongful convictions do happen on occasion, as would be expected from any human system, but pointing out that the concern is a matter of scale: "The overriding question has to be, how significant is it [the prevalence of wrongful convictions]?" Nobody wants to see an error happen—"Who could possibly be against protecting innocent people?" he asked—but the question must be whether the problem is "epidemic or episodic." Marquis and others believe that it is episodic but that innocence advocates and the media have created the perception that innocents are routinely convicted through the work of rogue cops and prosecutors.[59]

For critics, the episodic nature of wrongful convictions does not warrant major reforms to the justice system, particularly in regard to the death penalty; indeed, much of the skepticism about wrongful convictions has come from proponents of capital punishment. Marquis told me that there is some reason for apprehension; the execution of an innocent person is a "logical and reasonable concern" that many people have. "I think everybody would agree that, if in fact there had been a wrongful conviction in a death penalty case, that would be a grave concern," he said. This concern extends to prosecutors as well, whose "worst nightmare" is not the acquittal of a guilty offender or losing a case but sentencing an innocent person to death.[60] However, in his and others' view, the fear is based on something other than reality. Cassell, for example, has written that while "the most important error rate" is that of mistaken executions, rather than of wrongful convictions in general, there are no documented cases of an innocent person being put to death, and thus that most important rate is zero.[61] Even if there were such cases, critics still believe it would not warrant major changes to capital punishment. A common point is that many human activities involve mistakes that harm innocent citizens, but those pursuits are continued because they have other benefits for society.[62] Ronald Allen and Amy Shavell note that "a common feature of social planning is that it affects the incidence of death. Virtually all social policies and decisions quite literally determine who will live and who will die." More specifically, they point out that as many as 40,000 people die every year in car accidents, but we do not necessarily lower speed limits or require further safety devices on vehicles. "Merely permitting people on the roads guarantees a slaughter," they wrote, but "the mere fact of innocent deaths is not sufficient to put an end to the slaughter."[63] Similarly, Marquis told me that pharmacists and surgeons unintentionally kill tens of thousands of people every year, yet "you don't ban those things. You try to go back and figure out what went wrong."[64] For all of these things, we continue them as a benefit to society at large, and innocence critics suggest the death penalty should be treated no differently.

The "myth of innocence," according to critics, is due largely to the work of innocence advocates, who have been disingenuous, or at least unclear, when defining what does and does not count as a wrongful conviction and exoneration. Cassell has suggested that many alleged cases of wrongful conviction and false confession actually involve guilty offenders and that innocence advocates have been inaccurate in their definition of "actual innocence."[65] Marquis suggested the same, arguing that many of the supposed wrongful convictions are not cases in which defendants are actually innocent. Part of the problem, in his view, is that the meaning of "wrongful conviction" and "exoneration" has been warped by innocence advocates: "I believe that what is happening the last couple of years in America is that innocence and exoneration are being redefined. I think we all agree that if somebody really didn't do it, that's exonerated." On the other hand, he said, advocates and organizations such as the Innocence Project draw on cases that are extraordinary and grab headlines but, "when you dig deep, turn out not to be wrongful convictions at all." He pointed to examples such as Roger Coleman, who was proven to be guilty more than a decade after his execution despite the fact that many people believed him to be innocent, and Ricky McGinn, who was proven guilty after a media campaign encouraged the testing of biological evidence because many people believed in his innocence.[66]

While neither of these men were exonerated, and no innocence organizations claim that they were, this is a disturbing trend for folks like Marquis, who said that one of the problems is that innocence advocates "make broad, sweeping statements" but that people who take the issue seriously on what he called "my side" are hesitant to talk about cases "unless we break them down and read them, and that is incredibly time-consuming." Thus, innocence advocates use the media, where sensationalist headlines are the focus and wrongful conviction is "the flavor de jour," to perpetuate the perception that errors are a widespread problem. He mentioned a *New York Times* article that suggested that approximately 4% of death row inmates would end up exonerated, a figure with which Marquis would be deeply troubled but which he believes to be far off base; such a rate would be a "catastrophic failure," and if the rate was even close to that, Marquis told the reporter, "I would quit my job and become a Buddhist monk." Innocence advocates are thus spreading a false reality by warping the meaning of terms. He said the meaning of exoneration has been twisted to refer to many who are, in fact, guilty. "By [innocence advocates'] definition," Marquis said, "O. J. Simpson has been exonerated in the murder of Nicole Brown because he wasn't convicted."[67] While this last statement is untrue—most collections of exonerations state their standards for a case to be included, and exonerations are generally counted only if someone is convicted and later found to be innocent in some way, while acquittals at first trial (like Simpson's) are not considered exonerations—the larger point of Marquis and others is

worth considering: are wrongful convictions actually a common occurrence, at least enough to justify major alterations to the justice system?

Proponents of the "innocence myth" perspective suggest that errors
are not common and believe that the false notion that they are has important repercussions for the justice system and society at large. The
"costs of the myth," as Hoffman has called them, include the public's loss
of confidence in the justice system and American culture's overvaluing
of lawyers in general while undervaluing the abilities of jurors to evaluate facts and make accurate decisions. Perhaps more interestingly, Hoffman argues that the myth that wrongful convictions are common will
actually increase the number of innocents who plead guilty for serious
crimes out of fear that they would be mistakenly convicted at trial.[68]

Ultimately, at the heart of all of these concerns is the error rate, and
this line of critique does not derive from an empirically sound estimate
of error but from a social constructionist perspective, which suggests
that problems are not objective realities but rather are interpretive con-
structs that are developed and shaped by a variety of cultural factors.
Just as many people have suggested that the crime-control sentiment
over the past several decades was driven or reinforced by social constructions of what a criminal is and what justice is, Marquis and other
critics suggest that there is no innocence problem in the justice system
but rather a perception of one created by savvy and opportunistic advocates and groups.[69]

The legitimacy of this critique notwithstanding—again, uncovering
the rate of wrongful convictions is virtually impossible—it is one with
which innocence advocates can, should, and do sometimes engage. If
a handful of outspoken scholars, lawyers, and judges have expressed
such concerns about the innocence movement, it is entirely possible
that many more in the legal world share them. And perhaps more importantly, this critique is based largely on a confidence in the justice
system to avoid wrongful convictions, a sentiment that may be shared
among the general public. This confidence was perhaps best summarized in *Herrera v. Collins*, in which the Supreme Court, while expressing some constitutional concern about the execution of an innocent
person, emphasized the "constitutional provisions" that that help protect
"against the risk of convicting an innocent person."[70] Justice Sandra Day
O'Connor wrote in her concurring opinion that a wrongful execution

"would be a constitutionally intolerable event" but implied that such an event is unlikely to occur. "Our society has a high degree of confidence in its criminal trials," she wrote, "in no small part because the Constitution offers unparalleled protections against convicting the innocent."[71] Such confidence may certainly permeate the public sphere and serve as a barrier to broader reform for innocence advocates, and thus they must engage with such discourse and dissent going forward.

Retribution and Due Process Concerns

Beyond the simple belief that wrongful convictions do not occur frequently enough to justify the reform efforts, some people have expressed concern that an innocence focus may take attention away from other issues that are equally or more important. Importantly, these concerns come from varying perspectives. Allen and Laudan point out that there are many "horrifying mistakes" that occur in the "highly complicated matrix of relationships" in which wrongful convictions occur and that these errors must be balanced.[72]

More specifically, several people have expressed concern that too much emphasis on factual innocence complicates the retributive element of punishment. Hoffman, for instance, has suggested that focusing on whether someone actually committed a crime takes the emphasis away from the importance of moral guilt, which leaves juries unprepared to evaluate the intentions and mental state of offenders, which they are required to do.[73] Virginia law professor Josh Bowers, who has argued that erroneously pleading guilty actually helps most innocent defendants,[74] placed more emphasis on "normative innocence," or the deservingness of offenders to be condemned by the justice system and the community.[75] From a different perspective, law professors Carol and Jordan Steiker have pointed out that an innocence focus may undermine retributive arguments against the death penalty. In particular, an emphasis on the fact that innocent defendants are underserving of the retribution provided by the death penalty takes away from the many cases in which offenders may be guilty but in which a death sentence is still excessive.[76]

Some people have also expressed concern about the negative effects of the innocence focus on defense work. Hoffman has suggested that it undervalues the work of public defenders, while Steiker and Steiker have argued that institutional innocence projects undermine the due process values traditionally associated with public defense work.[77] These are perhaps the most interesting critiques, because they do not stem from the perspective of criticizing the innocence movement per se but support the mission while still expressing some concern about the potential implications of the movement for due process. A leading proponent of this position is Abbe Smith. A Georgetown law professor and indigent criminal defense attorney, Smith really became aware of wrongful convictions "when friends stopped becoming defense lawyers and started innocence projects." She realized it might become a phenomenon in the mid- to late 1990s and has become somewhat concerned about the potential impact of the innocence movement on up-and-coming lawyers. In particular, she said that just as *Law and Order* helped create a generation of young prosecutors, the innocence movement is creating a generation of students who enter law school specifically to do innocence work. "That's their orientation," Smith said, and although "there's nothing wrong with that," she expressed concerns about the long-term impact of the movement on young lawyers: "My chief concern is I don't want to teach young lawyers or law students that the work is worthwhile only if it's on behalf of the innocent, because the innocence movement is happening at a time when we continue to lead the world in incarceration. So the innocence movement is not going to stop what, I would argue, in some ways is a much more devastating problem: the fact that we lock up so many people and for so long and that they're disproportionately people who come from communities that are already hard-pressed."[78]

Smith's critique is rather different from the "myth of innocence" perspective outlined earlier. She was very complimentary of innocence advocates and supports their ideals: "They've done real good," she said of innocence projects and have "made a lot of improvements to the criminal justice system. . . . [Their work] is changing law enforcement for the better in many ways" and has shed light on previously under-examined areas like eyewitness accuracy and false confessions. Smith also thinks that innocence work is a great introduction for students into the practice of criminal defense work; her most formative experience as a student was working on the case of Patsy Kelly Jarrett, whom Smith and many others believe was innocent of the murder for which she was convicted. However, the reality is that "we don't operate a system where innocents are often prosecuted. The vast majority of people are guilty." Her concern is that a focus solely on innocence can detract from the importance of ensuring high-quality representation for all offenders and that motivating students to be passionate about the myriad issues in the system can be difficult when innocence is their goal: "If that's your source of outrage, it's going to be harder to get it up for somebody who is overcharged. . . . It's hard to have that student get indignant about prosecutorial overcharging or over-punishment" if the offender is truly guilty, even though that defendant deserves the same level of zealous representation as the innocent client.[79]

Steve Drizin, an innocence movement insider, expressed a similar sentiment: "What I am a little bit worried about is that the obsessive focus, if you will, on innocence may create a generation of lawyers who think that the only kind of criminal defense work is representing innocent people. And that would be a perversion, because most of the people who founded this movement came to it after representing people who were charged with crimes who very well may have been guilty."[80] The concern, ultimately, is that innocence can "kind of suck the air out of the room" for traditional criminal defense work and distract from other important issues, according to Smith: "The attention is all on the stories. The narrative force of a story about innocence is just so compelling. Inevitably, it's more compelling than the story of a guilty person who has served much, much, much too much time and is now completely changed and ought not to be in jail. That's a harder story to tell."[81] Again, this critique is not necessarily one that seeks to diminish the value of innocence organizations or of concern with wrongful convictions. It does suggest, however, that the narrow focus on innocence may detract from other, possibly more important matters. To this end, some people have suggested that the innocence movement's agenda should be expanded "to broader questions about the structure and administration of the justice system."[82] In fact, several prominent thinkers who generally support the movement's ideals have proposed more fundamental reforms of the U.S. adversary system that go beyond the commonly advocated innocence reforms like recording interrogations and altering eyewitness procedures. For example, a special New York Law School symposium explored pretrial reforms that could help deal with wrongful convictions,[83] and law professors Daniel Medwed, D. Michael Risinger, and Lesley Risinger have suggested reforms to criminal procedure to make the U.S. justice system more fundamentally "innocentric."[84]

Beyond concerns about an innocence focus drawing attention away from fundamental problems with the U.S. justice system, there is also the matter of resources. As Abbe Smith told me, finding money to support any criminal defense work is difficult, but it is even more so when that defense is for clients who may well be guilty. "There are lots of foundations that love the innocence projects," she said. "It's a much harder sell to support efforts to do ordinary criminal defense, which tends to be representing the guilty."[85]

The innocence movement is too young to know if and when these concerns will bear out. Some people in the innocence community, such as Steve Drizin, seem to share them, while others do not.[86] Still, they exist and are particularly interesting as they come not from the law enforcement community or the political right but from the criminal defense community, traditionally a friend of the movement.

Coalitions and Organizational Issues

The innocence movement has a relatively strong organizational infrastructure, but as with any movement, that structure may need to change and adapt as the movement evolves. As it stands, the Innocence Network remains a loose affiliation of organizations whose primary function, in some ways, is to serve as a vessel for communication between advocates and organizations. Some are happy with such a structure, according to the director of the Innocence Network Support Unit, Meredith Kennedy: "It's really the essence of what the Network is, people talking to each other," she said, "and some people feel quite strongly that that's really all they want the Network to be." Not everyone agrees, though, as some people want the Network to become something concrete: "Some say, 'We can be more than just a group that's learning from each other. We can really get things done. We can really push things, use our collective voice to elevate issues.'"[87]

Another important part of the organizational coalition is the role of the Innocence Project, an issue over which there seems to be some tension within the movement. Although the Innocence Project is much larger than any other member organization, in terms of both budget and staff, it is in some ways just another Network member. During my informal conversations with a variety of people, some suggested that there are problems with having such a structure; that is, having an organization like the Innocence Project serve as the face of the movement yet be treated as just another one of the group creates problems.

There are several reasons for this. The first, as Theresa Newman worded it, is "brand confusion."[88] If smaller organizations use the term "Innocence Project" in their name, there may be confusion when they achieve something and receive media attention. A newspaper reporter may just say something was achieved by "the Innocence Project," not realizing that the organization that accomplished it is a separate, independent entity from *the* Innocence Project based in New York. Such confusion may not only impact a small group's opportunity to receive publicity but can directly impact fund-raising. For example, when Gregory Taylor was exonerated in North Carolina in a case that received national attention, a number of donations were made to the Innocence Project in New York rather than to local North Carolina groups.[89] I heard a number of such stories throughout my interviews and informal conversations, of people donating to the New York–based Innocence Project, rather than a local organization that actually handled a case, because they heard in the news that "the Innocence Project" had freed someone and an Internet search invariably leads to the largest one.

For these and other reasons, the Innocence Network has engaged in strategic planning processes for people to offer suggestions and voice their opinions about the structure of the Network. However, as Kennedy said, "people are all over the spectrum on that," and the variety of organizational types within the Network makes it difficult to secure agreement:

> You have a whole lot of people who are at one end of the spectrum and say, "I want a loose affiliation. In fact, because I'm a member of a law school clinic, I actually couldn't be a part of something that was any more than a loose affiliation. And what the Network is right now is absolutely meeting my needs and expectations, and it should stay as it is now"— all the way down to people who say, "I think the Innocence Network needs to become a legal entity, and go into, sort of, competition against

the Innocence Project for funds and be bigger than the Innocence Project and work globally." So you have a million people in between those viewpoints.[90]

Thus, changing the structure of the Innocence Network would be difficult and may cause "a lot of collateral damage," because "the different organizations that are part of the Network all need and want different things." Kennedy suggested that by changing into something more formal, the Network may actually lose member organizations, in part because law school clinics may not be able to become part of a more formal organizational network.[91]

There are more in-between approaches, and Kennedy said Network members have discussed a variety of them. Other issues discussed have included doing joint fund-raising campaigns, giving members more input into the policy strategies of the Innocence Project, and having the Innocence Project become the official national headquarters for the Network.

Another organizational challenge for the innocence movement is how to handle international growth. More than ten Innocence Network members are based outside the United States, and much of the talk about the future revolves around how to handle the innocence movement globally. Kennedy said that much of the Network's growth is international, and it is "struggling from an organizational standpoint . . . with determining how best to really encourage and foster that growth." Given how different the legal systems and issues are in different countries and regions of the world, there is some question about whether having "a one-size-fits-all Network that covers the whole world" is the best way to handle the international growth of the movement. For example, she pointed out that in India, the issues are often less about postconviction than about preconviction, wherein people are held for years before ever going to trial and being acquitted. The question is thus how to handle the international organization of the movement:

One of the things that we're thinking about is, do we establish sister networks in other parts of the world; convert the Innocence Network to just being a U.S.-based network but encourage the establishment of a network in South America, Europe; spin the Canadian projects off and have them create their own innocence network; and then do some kind of international secretariat or an advisory group or something that gets together once a year, once every two years, and talks about the global innocence issues and figures out if it makes sense to do some kind of global campaign that different networks could join in on?

Kennedy said she thinks the Network's future is actually one with "many innocence networks in different parts of the world, all working together to help push the whole movement forward globally." With how "nitty-gritty" the work is, she said having the entire global movement headquartered in the United States could be a "round-peg-square-hole" type of scenario. It is different from something like Amnesty International, for which the issues are more universal, such as abolishing the death penalty. Instead, reform in the United States might be "totally irrelevant" to organizations working overseas, and so having one universal network may not be the best approach.[92]

The Longevity of the DNA Era

DNA has been an established part of the legal landscape for about two decades; as time has worn on, testing on the front end of cases, during the investigatory and prosecution phases, has become more common, leading to important questions for the innocence movement: Is the DNA-exoneration era coming to an end? And if so, what might that mean for the movement, given how important DNA exonerations have been?

The numbers paint an interesting picture. On the basis of the list maintained by the Innocence Project, which tracks only DNA exonerations, there were fewer secured in 2013 and 2014 than in any year since 1999. To some people, this suggests a trend toward decreasing DNA exonerations overall, though others, like Peter Neufeld, are quick to point out that this is only two years' worth of information. "There's not enough data to know whether the rate of DNA exonerations is going to continue to drop," he said. "We've had drops in the past, and it turned out to be a blip and it went back up."[93]

It is also important to note that the other major source of information about exonerations, the National Registry of Exonerations, does not necessarily support the idea that DNA exonerations are on the decline. While the *proportion* of exonerations secured through DNA has declined over the past decade, the decline is due in large part to an increase in non-DNA exonerations, rather than an actual decrease in DNA cases, as shown in table C.1.

TABLE C.1. Exonerations since 2000, National Registry of Exonerations

Year	DNA exonerations	Total exonerations	% DNA exonerations
2000	15	75	20
2001	21	89	23.6
2002	23	58	39.7
2003	23	77	29.9
2004	13	57	22.4
2005	23	61	37.7
2006	23	64	35.9
2007	21	72	29.2
2008	19	66	28.8
2009	29	89	32.6
2010	23	74	31.1
2011	21	72	29.2
2012	20	99	20.2
2013	18	96	18.7
2014	22	142	15.5
2015	26	153	17

Note: Numbers current as of June 27, 2016

Still, there is reason to suspect that there may be a decrease in DNA exonerations going forward. As Neufeld pointed out, many exonerations have come in cases that were prosecuted in the 1980s and 1990s, and as DNA has become more common in the early stages of cases, it makes sense that postconviction DNA exonerations would decrease.[94] Similarly, Rob Warden, who told me that he erroneously predicted that the era of DNA exonerations was winding down more than a dozen years ago, said that there will ultimately be a trend away from such cases and toward more non-DNA cases. As he pointed out, many of the DNA exonerations are still coming from cases that were prosecuted before DNA testing was common, and it is only natural that those cases will eventually run out.[95] So the decline of DNA is "a legitimate concern, but of course it hasn't happened yet."[96]

On the other hand, there are reasons to suspect that DNA exonerations will not necessarily decrease, at least not in the near future. Instead, the types of DNA exonerations may change. The vast majority of DNA exonerations were in sexual assault cases, in which there was most likely to be biological material to test; in more recent cases, Warden said, DNA exonerations are occurring in other, non–sexual assault cases.[97] This is partially due to the improvements in DNA technology, which Neufeld pointed out has gotten "stronger and more sensitive." In addition to testing bodily fluids, DNA testing can now be conducted on hair and skin cells, allowing for new types of cases, both old and recent, to be reexamined with DNA technology. In other words, Neufeld told me, groups like the Innocence Project may be able to look at cases they had to pass on previously:

> There were cases that we turned down 15 years ago where there was no rape, so there's no semen. [Or] there was no trail of blood that the assailant left, but he had clubbed his victim with a baseball bat. Well, we would have turned down that case 15 years ago. Now, we'll take that case. So, while, in one sense there would be reason to think that [the number of DNA exonerations] would drop, in another sense, there are many more opportunities to test other types of evidence that we couldn't have tested ten years ago. So in that sense, it will expand, and it's too soon to tell how that's all going to fall out. We're going to have to wait several more years. But I know that we're doing more and more complicated cases, more and more cases where we're looking at skin cells and we're looking at hairs and mitochondrial DNA, and we're getting results and exonerating people. So one of the things we haven't even done is go back and look at all the cases we closed out because it didn't involve semen or blood and take a fresh look at those cases.[98]

Thus, the nature of wrongful conviction work will continually change, and Neufeld said it is important to make sure advocates remain current on the latest scientific advancements to keep up with the times and continue working on DNA cases. Scheck similarly noted that new aspects of

DNA science come with questions that will continually need to be evaluated. As he put it, "DNA is foolproof, except any fool can do it."[99] That is, there will always be the possibility for error, and advocates must remain vigilant in exploring potential problems as the technology advances.

Even if DNA exonerations do decrease, it is clear that exonerations overall have not been trending downward, as there were more in 2015 than ever before. And several people, including Neufeld, pointed out that the majority of innocence organizations work on non-DNA cases, despite the fact that such cases "are more challenging for the projects": "The people who do exclusively non-DNA cases and roll up their sleeves and figure out all the ways to investigate a case, they are doing the really challenging criminal justice work, because those are much harder cases to win. They always have been. When you have a 95-year-old woman who has been raped, and they recover semen, and we can prove that the semen didn't come from our client, you don't have to do much lifting to get an exoneration. But if you're talking about witness recantations, it's a much tougher hole. It just is."[100] Although the number of non-DNA exonerations has increased in recent years, given how difficult the work is, it is possible that the number of exonerations may ultimately decrease. Judy Royal pointed out that there are more and more people "excited about the idea of doing this kind of work," but she did wonder "if that enthusiasm will remain if there are fewer exonerations." Still, she believes that there are enough people "who are very dedicated and will be working on these more difficult cases" for some time.[101]

One of the biggest questions when it comes to this issue is whether the Innocence Project will itself become more involved in non-DNA cases. While everyone recognizes that the organization has a backlog that will keep it busy with DNA for the short term, they also see some movement into other types of cases.[102] Both Scheck and Neufeld, for their part, are unsure of what the future holds, but both are open to expanding their work. "Will we do non-DNA cases?" Neufeld pondered. "We may, you know? We'll see. We'll see where things lead us."[103]

Scheck pointed out that, although the Innocence Project's specialty is DNA work, it has already been involved in other types of cases and may continue to expand that way in the future: "There may well come a time when our project does both DNA and non-DNA cases. We've managed to get a number of people out of prison without DNA evidence, already six or seven of them, all interesting and important cases. We've been working on cases now that involve non-DNA evidence, whether it's the Cameron Todd Willingham arson case or cases involving other forms of invalidated science. These matters are not just DNA."[104] The important thing is to heed the lessons learned from DNA exonerations, with their high level of certainty, and apply them to other types of cases. According to Raley, "the beauty of the DNA exoneration is that it opened a window" into the causes of wrongful convictions and made people understand how errors can happen throughout the criminal justice system.[105] Therefore, as Nick O'Connell said, "it needs to be more about DNA highlighting this in an unequivocal way." The number of DNA exonerations, which are pulled from only a small subset of all cases in which DNA is even present, can be extrapolated to suggest that there are far more wrongful convictions than most people want to believe, and thus O'Connell does not see the movement dying down. "I really don't. I think people are going to be able to see that this is a systemic issue," he said. He sees DNA as "just what was needed to put this into discussion, into people's frame."[106] Karen Newirth agreed and thinks DNA exonerations will continue to help in the non-DNA cases: "Maybe this is idealistic," she said, "but I think the DNA exonerations will set the stage for people to believe in the innocence of exonerees who were freed without DNA. . . . I think we are creating a dialogue around what goes wrong, and that will help people to understand and believe in wrongful convictions where there isn't DNA."[107]

If DNA exonerations do decrease, there are some potential ramifications. One is that, with how much focus has been placed on DNA cases, there may be an expectation of DNA testing that makes securing non-DNA exonerations more difficult.[108] Theresa Newman also said she thinks a decline in DNA exonerations could potentially hurt the movement in part because prosecutors may become less willing to acknowledge errors without strong scientific evidence and governors may be less willing to offer pardons, which is necessary in some states to secure compensation for exonerees. It is thus important, she said, that the innocence movement makes as much progress as possible while DNA exonerations are still occurring at a fairly high rate.[109]

There is also some concern from people outside the innocence movement that if DNA exonerations dwindle, it may hurt perceptions about the problems in the criminal justice system more generally. "If the DNA cases dry up," Abbe Smith said, "people will think, 'See? We're good now. We found all the really bad cases, and now nobody innocent is in prison. So we don't give a shit about anybody else in prison,' no matter the circumstances." She worries that concerns about policies like life without parole and solitary confinement will slip from the collective consciousness, because "the people in prison are guilty, so we stop thinking and caring too much about them."[110]

From all angles, then, the future of DNA exonerations will have an impact on the innocence movement. Steve Drizin said he does not think DNA exonerations are going to decrease significantly in the immediate future but that when they eventually do, "the Network will be put to the test":

> There are a number of projects that only do DNA cases and don't have the expertise in postconviction law and practice to handle a non-DNA case. And so either those projects will accept non-DNA cases, or they will cease to exist. Non-DNA cases are in some respects harder than DNA cases. You have to spend more time on investigations, getting out in the field, reinterviewing witnesses, trying to locate the true perpetrator or identify the true perpetrator without the benefit of DNA evidence. These cases can take longer to resolve and require great creativity and stamina on the part of lawyers and projects. The payoff when you win is huge, but we'll see how many projects are in it for the long haul.[111]

The Future of Innocence

Clearly, the innocence movement has its share of challenges ahead. It has its critics and skeptics, and it is important that innocence advocates engage with them and try to find common ground. They also must continue to work hard at garnering publicity. In a changing media culture and during a time when the story of a wrongful conviction may be perceived as less spectacular, unique, and newsworthy than it once was, it is up to advocates to use new media and social media to ensure that the public and policy makers remain informed and engaged with their issues. The movement must also continue to nurture its organizational structure and expand its coalitions, both within and outside the criminal justice system, to ensure it is poised to combat the resistance that reform-ers will certainly face. And advocates and organizations must be willing to change course and adapt to the shifting nature of criminal justice in general and wrongful convictions and exonerations in particular.

Despite these very real challenges, the sense within the movement seems to be fairly optimistic. Regardless of the changes in evidence and case types, innocence advocates have, as Maurice Possley said, amassed a "great body of work" that "shows that people are getting the courage to admit that they got something wrong, . . . and that's saying some-thing."[112] As challenging as the work is and despite the many roadblocks, many people within the movement see improvement, such as Aimee Maxwell: "I think one of the things about being a criminal defense law-yer for so long [is] I knew how bad it was. And so I see all these glim-mers of hope where I'm sure new ones are like, 'Holy crap, this is awful!' I'm like, 'No, it's getting better!'"[113]

The innocence movement is also not lacking in passion. Those who have dedicated themselves to this work show a level of commitment that makes it easy to see that the movement will continue, in some form, at least for the immediate future. They are reformers, inspired by those who came before them and by the men and women whose lives are changed through their work. As long as people like them exist, progres-sive reform movements will likely remain an important thread in the fabric of social and political life in the United States.

If nothing else, there is a very practical reason to think that the in-nocence movement will not disappear anytime too soon: supply and demand. There is a market for the movement. "I don't think wrongful convictions are decreasing or have stopped by any stretch of the imagi-nation," Paul Casteleiro told me. He said it is really "remarkable" to think about. When Jim McCloskey started doing this work and founded Centurion Ministries in the early 1980s, "nobody else was doing it as a project or a business. But these types of entities have multiplied," which "proves the point that wrongful convictions are not going down." It is a very economic approach to thinking about the movement. "The sys-tem has the capacity for these groups," Casteleiro said. "The market is there."[114]

For the advocates who are dedicated to the innocence movement, there will always be innocent men and women who can be freed from the shackles of erroneous confinement, and that may be enough to keep the movement going. McCloskey, the "godfather of the industry" who founded the nonprofit innocence business, does not see the movement going anywhere. The sources of error are so common, so ingrained in the people and organizations and processes of the criminal justice system, that wrongful convictions will never cease to exist. "It's human nature," he said. "There have always been wrongful convictions. There always will be wrongful convictions. It's the old Field of Dreams thing: build it, and they will come."[115]

Perhaps this perspective is overly optimistic, but it should not be surprising. Without the belief that the cause is a worthy one and that change is possible, the innocence movement would be dead where it stands. Innocence advocates are well aware of the challenges they face and will continue to face, but they must believe that they can and will overcome those hurdles. Only time will tell if their beliefs come to pass. Given the divisive state of discourse about the justice system and in American political and cultural life more generally, having opposing sides come together to achieve progressive reform seems challenging at best and near-impossible at worst. On the other hand, perhaps McCloskey is right; perhaps it is the "old Field of Dreams thing," and the innocence movement will continue to build until it can no longer be ignored or avoided. With persistence, maybe advocates can accomplish the spectacular.

Regardless of the long-term prospects of the innocence movement, it has taught us and will continue to teach us important lessons about the U.S. criminal justice system, which affects millions of lives every single day. By heeding those lessons, we can grow, improve, and ultimately promote a system that truly emphasizes justice for all.

APPENDIX

Data, Methods, and Limitations

This study may best be thought of as a "history of the present." This phrase, popularized by philosopher Michel Foucault and, more recently, sociologist David Garland,[1] reflects a combination of historical narrative and social scientific inquiry and provides a useful tool for thinking about this study of the innocence movement. It differentiates the work from pure narrative history but also from much traditional social scientific research. I do not claim to have presented a fully comprehensive history of the modern criminal justice system or even of the innocence movement itself. Furthermore, this is a case study of a single movement and has little to say about the generalizability of its findings.

My goal was a history that is both narrative and analytic. This study traces many of the key actors, organizations, and events that were involved in the rise of the innocence movement in the United States. Constructing this narrative and filtering it through the lenses of social science allow us to better understand how this phenomenon came to be, why it has the characteristics it has, and its current state.

To that end, the approach taken in this study is a combination of historical and qualitative methods. This is fairly standard for social movement research, particularly case studies of individual movements, which are seldom defined by any one particular methodological approach or data source but rather a combination of methods that often includes "one or more qualitative approaches."[2] The data sources used here can be separated into three general categories: archival materials, qualitative interviews, and observational data.

ARCHIVAL MATERIALS

Archival materials consisted of primary and secondary accounts of key events, people, and organizations. Again, the goal was not necessarily to be fully comprehensive—no historical account can make such a claim—but to collect enough information to develop a thorough understanding of each key element of the innocence movement I cover. The specific documents consulted are cited throughout the study, but I provide here a brief general discussion about the data sources.

One source of data was the National Death Penalty Archive, located on the campus of the University at Albany. The archive contains a variety of collections, but I focused on just a few that contained materials from prominent anti–death penalty activists and organizations. In particular, I viewed the collections from the Southern Coalition on Jails and Prisons, the Illinois Coalition to Abolish the Death Penalty, Catholics Against the Death Penalty, and the Steven Hawkins collection. Materials included pamphlets and other informational materials, internal memorandums, news reports, notes, and other documents.

For a key piece of legislation, the 2004 Innocence Protection Act, I constructed a legislative history by collecting documents from the Library of Congress's online archive. These covered the years from the bill's introduction in 2000 to its passage in 2004 and included bill drafts, congressional statements, and committee notes.

Additionally, I drew on legal documents, newspaper articles, and other published materials such as older academic publications. Court decisions were used for key cases discussed throughout. Newspaper reports were particularly useful for filling in details, gauging reactions to key cases and events, and gaining a sense of the broader discourse surrounding these developments. And finally, given that this study is in some ways designed to trace the history of an idea, older academic publications—particularly research published in the 1980s in both the hard and social sciences and articles written by key actors such as Scheck and Neufeld, for example—were treated as historical data rather than as simple literature-review materials.

INTERVIEWS

The second major source of information came from semi-structured interviews with 37 people involved in innocence work; 17 interviews were conducted in person, 16 were conducted over the phone, and four involved both a phone call and an in-person meeting. While in-person interviews are generally best, due to resource constraints, they were not always possible. And while "it's better to be there, . . . telephone interviews are the next best thing."[3] My telephone interviews still provided a wealth of information, and given that I was not asking about sensitive material, I do not believe that anything particularly significant was lost. Similar to oral history interviews, these conversations were aimed at generating "a robust or 'thick' description of a historical period or situation from the perspective of those who lived through that time."[4] Such interviews are particularly useful for understanding earlier periods of current movements such as the innocence movement.

Interviewees are listed in table A.1, along with their affiliations at the time of the interview. These individuals were chosen for a number of reasons. First, I wanted to ensure that I spoke with key individuals who were responsible for starting the movement. Without speaking to people from Centurion Ministries, the Innocence Project, and the Northwestern Center on Wrongful Convictions, constructing a story of the movement would have been near-impossible, as they are largely responsible for its existence. However, I did not want to speak only with the movement founders and leaders but also with some who came into this area of work later or who are involved with smaller, less well-known organizations. Thus, I spoke with a number of other individuals who work for the three seminal organizations just named and also several who work with smaller innocence projects.

I did not want to speak solely with those who work within the innocence movement. I spoke to a few key scholars who conducted the early research into wrongful convictions and a couple of journalists who have been involved in wrongful conviction work. I also wanted to get the perspectives of people who have expressed hesitations, concerns, or criticisms of the innocence movement. While not many have been publicly outspoken against the movement, I was able to arrange interviews with two such people, law professor Abbe Smith and the Clatsop County, Oregon, district attorney Joshua Marquis. Finally, there was a slight snowballing element to the interviewee list. In a few instances, an interviewee would recommend that I speak with someone else, and in many cases, I did so.

TABLE A.1. Interviewees

Name	Position at time of interview	Formal interview date
Erika Applebaum	Executive Director, Innocence Project of Minnesota	1/14/14
Janet Baxendale	Case Development Manager, Centurion Ministries	1/16/14
Adele Bernhard	Director, Post-Conviction Innocence Clinic, New York Law School	7/28/14
Rebecca Brown	Director of State Policy, Innocence Project	4/16/14
Paul Casteleiro	Attorney at Law	1/14/14
Ryan Costello	Student, Life After Innocence, Loyola University	1/22/14
Madeline deLone	Executive Director, Innocence Project	10/31/13
Richard Dieter	Executive Director, Death Penalty Information Center	5/29/14
Steve Drizin	Staff Attorney, Former Legal Director, Center on Wrongful Convictions	6/4/14
Jim Dwyer	Columnist, *New York Times*	5/29/14
Kate Germond	Director, Investigator, Centurion Ministries	1/16/14
Samuel Gross	Editor, Cofounder, National Registry of Exonerations	6/11/14
C. Ronald Huff	Professor Emeritus of Criminology, Law and Society, University of California–Irvine	11/21/13
Meredith Kennedy	Director, Innocence Network Support Unit, Innocence Project	2/25/14
Shannon Leitner	Research Fellow, National Registry of Exonerations	1/21/14
Alan Maimon	Case Investigator, Centurion Ministries	1/16/14
Joshua Marquis	District Attorney, Clatsop County, Oregon	7/22/14
Aimee Maxwell	Executive Director, Georgia Innocence Project	11/22/13
James McCloskey	Founder, Executive Director, Centurion Ministries	12/14/13
Christine Mumma	Executive Director, North Carolina Center on Actual Innocence	3/17/14
Peter Neufeld	Codirector, Cofounder, Innocence Project	4/16/14
Karen Newirth	Senior Fellow, Strategic Litigation Unit, Innocence Project	7/3/14
Theresa Newman	Codirector, Wrongful Convictions Clinic, Duke University Law	7/3/14
Laura Nirider	Codirector, Center on Wrongful Convictions of Youth	6/18/14
Nick O'Connell	Development Director, Centurion Ministries	1/16/14
Maurice Possley	Senior Researcher, National Registry of Exonerations	1/9/14
Vanessa Potkin	Senior Staff Attorney, Innocence Project	7/3/14
Michael Radelet	Professor of Sociology, University of Colorado Boulder	5/28/14
Jane Raley	Codirector, Center on Wrongful Convictions	6/12/14
Judy Royal	Staff Attorney, Center on Wrongful Convictions	6/13/14

TABLE A.1. Interviewees (*cont.*)

Name	Position at time of interview	Formal interview date
Stephen Saloom	Policy Director, Innocence Project	10/30/13
Barry Scheck	Codirector, Cofounder, Innocence Project	2/25/14
Abbe Smith	Professor, Director of Criminal Defense and Prisoner Advocacy Clinic, Georgetown Law	7/23/14
Joshua Tepfer	Codirector, Center on Wrongful Convictions of Youth	6/4/14
Jeremy Travis	President, John Jay College of Criminal Justice; Former Director, National Institute of Justice	7/22/14
Rob Warden	Executive Director, Cofounder, Center on Wrongful Convictions; Cofounder, National Registry of Exonerations	2/1/14
Emily West	Research Director, Innocence Project	2/25/14

With two exceptions, interviews and meetings lasted anywhere from 30 to 90 minutes.[5] In most cases, I was able to digitally record my interviews with permission. All participants consented to the use of their real names.

I developed a separate list of questions for each of the interviewees depending on their role and when they became involved in innocence work. In general, however, questions fell into four topical domains. First, all were asked questions about their individual backgrounds (e.g., how they became involved in innocence work, what it was like when they did, why they do it). Second, those who work for specific organizations were asked about the organization and their role(s) within it. Third, depending on when they became involved, they were asked about different key events and what those events meant in the greater scheme of things. Finally, all were asked about their thoughts on the broader movement (e.g., innocence as a social movement, movement frames, prospects for the future).

While this structure provided a general flow to the interviews, the nature and ordering of questions varied. And the interviews were only semi-structured, allowing interviewees to expand on some topics and not others, highlight things they thought were important, and take the conversations in new directions.

In addition to personal interviews, I found several recorded and/or published interviews with movement actors, including Barry Scheck, Peter Neufeld, and Rob Warden. These interviews supplemented my own and together allowed me to get something of an "inside perspective" on the innocence movement, including the thoughts and motivations of those who are driving it forward.

OBSERVATION AND PARTICIPATION

In addition to my two main sources of data just described, I had several opportunities to visit with innocence organizations and attend events. First, I attended the national Innocence Network conferences in 2013, 2014, and 2016. This served a couple of purposes. First, it allowed me to meet a number of advocates and initiate contacts for interviews. But more importantly, it allowed me to see the innocence movement "in action." Part of doing so is seeing very concrete things—what types of issues are discussed and how the conference is structured, for example—but there is also an element that is harder to define. Spending time around innocence advocates and exonerees allowed me to gain a sense of the movement's vibe, for lack of a better word. Seeing how people interacted and having informal conversations with those involved provided an invaluable source of information that, while difficult to describe, contributed immensely to my thinking about the innocence movement.

I also made several visits to two key innocence organizations. I visited the Innocence Project's office in New York twice. Seeing its headquarters and interacting with the employees and volunteers was immensely helpful. I also had a stroke of good fortune during my first visit in October 2013. During one of my interviews, an exoneree from Texas who happened to be in New York stopped by the office. A group of employees and students gathered in the conference room to speak with him, and they were kind enough to invite me into the room.

In addition to the Innocence Project, I spent an afternoon at the Centurion Ministries office in Princeton, New Jersey. I met staff members (and the office dog), was shown around the office, and had several informal conversations.

Kate Germond, Centurion's director, also invited me to a very special event just a couple of weeks after my visit. One of the organization's most generous donors was William Scheide. A collector of rare books, Bach scholar, and lover of classical music, Scheide and his wife held an event each year on his birthday and raised money for a local organization. Each year, he invited the staff and exonerees from Centurion to attend. Germond invited me to the events for Scheide's 100th birthday celebration. Thus, I was able not only to attend a very special event but to spend a weekend with the staff and more than a dozen exonerees from Centurion Ministries.

Like my attendance at the Innocence Network conference, the benefits of my visits with Centurion and the Innocence Project are difficult to articulate. Undoubtedly, however, they contributed to my understanding of and thinking about the innocence movement.

LIMITATIONS AND FUTURE DIRECTIONS

Like any study, this one has its limitations. I will mention two major ones here.

First, while I described the early history (i.e., pre-1980s) of wrongful convictions in brief, the historical scope of my focus is limited to the past few decades. This is by design. I wanted to focus on the modern innocence movement and how it developed and thus focused on the time period during which the key players joined, organizations developed, and ideas emerged. This should not, however, be interpreted to mean that the earlier history is less important or less worthy of further study. In fact, a longer-term examination of wrongful convictions and of the idea of innocence in criminal justice and in U.S. culture more generally would be exceedingly valuable and might highlight the historical preconditions that allowed the narrative of my study to unfold.

Second, there are key limitations to my data. The archival sources are far from complete; the National Death Penalty Archive alone contains a significant amount of information that was not consulted, innocence organizations may have records that I was unable to view for this project, and countless other news reports speak of the people and events covered in this study.

Perhaps more importantly, my interview sample was relatively small and did not cover the full spectrum of individuals involved in innocence work, and those I did interview could certainly have been asked additional questions about a number of other topics. In attempting to examine the emergence and development of the movement, I focused largely on the people and organizations who were involved at the earliest stages (e.g., early journalists and scholars, Centurion Ministries, the Innocence Project, and the Northwestern Center on Wrongful Convictions). As much of the early attention and action revolved around innocence and capital punishment, I also explored elements of the anti–death penalty movement (e.g., the Death Penalty Information Center). Regarding the current period, I focused mostly on Innocence Network organizations, as the Network is the structural backbone of the entire movement. However, I did not interview exonerees, their families, or others who have become involved in innocence advocacy to some degree (e.g., victims, practitioners). While this element is a vital part of the modern movement, and researchers should absolutely study this element of innocence advocacy, there were practical constraints to interviewing such individuals, and their participation is mostly recent and beyond the scope of this particular study. The movement largely grew out of the advocacy efforts of lawyers and investigators who were doing wrongful conviction work, and to that end, I aimed to provide a thorough narrative and analysis of those efforts and their results.

Still, these data limitations are noteworthy and valid critiques. I do not think, however, that they disrupt the basic validity of my narrative or my analytical interpretations. While I did not consult every possible source of information or interview every possible person, I made sure to speak with many of the key actors who were responsible for the growth of the innocence movement, including the founders of the movement, and with a decent variety of others involved in wrongful conviction advocacy through formal organizations, and the data I collected provide important and interesting information about the movement.

The foregoing critiques, of both the limited historical lens and of the data limitations, are important to consider when interpreting the narrative and analysis presented in this study. However, I think that both speak to issues about the scope and focus of this project. Garland points out that many studies aimed at understanding social life face "tension between broad generalization and the specification of empirical particulars."[6] Those that attempt to paint general pictures using broad strokes often miss specifics and details, some of which may not fit or clearly contradict the ideas presented; on the other hand, case studies emphasizing empirical specifics and historical details can lose sight of larger trends and patterns and fail to make connections that are historically and analytically important. I hope that this study walks this line and achieves some of both, but it certainly faces shortcomings from both sides. In some ways, it is very specific, focusing on individual stories that together make up a single, larger narrative; in other ways, it speaks to much larger issues, like the implications of civil rights discourse, how change happens, and what it means to be a social movement.

There are a number of specific ideas that do not receive the depth they warrant. Many issues brought up throughout the book are worthy of their own in-depth study. A few come immediately to mind. As noted earlier, I did not focus on exoneree advocacy, but such efforts seem to be more common now than ever before. A number of exonerees have founded their own organizations, including Witness to Innocence, Exonerated Nation, the Jeffrey Deskovic Foundation for Justice, and more. These are interesting and potentially powerful initiatives, but relatively few have been operating for more than a few years. Given the difficulties of sustaining a nonprofit organization in an expensive but underfunded area, it is too soon to fully examine the long-term success and impact of such organizations. However, scholars can and should explore these initiatives, and I am aware of several efforts to do so that are under way by talented researchers. Related to organizational efforts, the innocence movement provides a unique opportunity for research in that the entire population is relatively small and can be examined in terms of the organizational structures, tactics, resources, and more. Using innocence projects as the unit of analysis, scholars could devise and carry out interesting studies of the innocence movement. More emphasis could also be put on the cause-lawyering element of the innocence movement, as it is driven in large part by lawyers who are dedicated to changing the system.

Scholars might also focus on media. I have noted throughout that innocence has seemingly come to the forefront of debate and conversation, and one way to gauge such a development is in tracking coverage of wrongful convictions in media and popular culture. More extensive, systematic research on the media's coverage of innocence would provide valuable information about the innocence movement. In addition, with the mainstream popularity of recent cultural phenomena like the podcast *Serial* and the Netflix series *Making a Murderer*, the public seems to be getting a glimpse into flaws in the justice system more than ever before. Again, the long-term impact of these ventures is unknown, but research can begin and continue to explore the effects of such media on public perceptions and opinions. Finally, a more public-policy-oriented approach to the study of the movement can be taken. Scholars can focus on examining specific reform efforts. Case studies could, for example, unpack the 2004 Justice for All Act in far greater detail to uncover the politics of reform. On the other hand, studies can examine patterns and identify factors that influence reform, or the lack thereof, at the state, county, or agency level.

This list is far from exhaustive. These (and many other) ideas and topics raised throughout this study are worthy of detailed research. Rather than focus on any one individual area, however, I aimed to cover a broad array of issues. This was done, in part, because the innocence movement has yet to be examined in great depth. Thus, I wanted to use the information gathered about a relatively small number of key people, organizations, and events to speak to larger themes about legal reform, movements, and social change. To that end, while the limitations of this particular study are quite real and ought to be acknowledged, I hope that by touching on a number of issues that are interesting and important, this work serves as a starting point, raising new questions for scholars (and advocates and critics, for that matter) and ultimately broadening the scope of research in the field. This might mean more studies of the innocence movement, of course, but also of other issues relating to miscarriages of justice.

I also hope that this study highlights some of the utility of using social movement research to think about change in criminal justice; in a system that seems to undergo major shifts every other decade or so, that seems so prone to flights of fancy, drawing on research about how change happens and how people mobilize is a useful way to think about how and why that evolution happens. And movement scholars can and should look to criminal justice and legal movements for examples that may be useful for building, refining, and ultimately testing their theoretical ideas.

NOTES

1. As of October 7, 2016, the National Registry of Exonerations lists 1,896 exonerations.
2. In the mid-18th century, for instance, William Blackstone famously said, "It is better that ten guilty persons escape than that one innocent suffer" (*Commentaries*, 358).
3. *United States v. Garsson*, 291 F. 646, 649 (S.D.N.Y. 1923).
4. Meese said this in an interview with *U.S. News and World Report*, published on October 14, 1985. According to one *Chicago Tribune* report, legal experts were shocked by his statement. Knight-Ridder Newspapers, "Meese's Miranda Reply."
5. Zalman, "Edwin Borchard," 332.
6. Findley, "Innocence Found."
7. Based on data from the National Registry of Exonerations as of June 27, 2016, in the six years from 2010 to 2015, there was an average of 2.04 exonerations per week. In 2015 alone, there were 153 exonerations, an average of 2.94 per week.
8. National Registry of Exonerations, "First 1,600 Exonerations."
9. See, for example, Gross et al., "Rate of False Conviction"; Risinger, "Innocents Convicted"; Poveda, "Estimating Wrongful Convictions."
10. This is based on the fact that the United States has approximately 2.2 million people in prisons and jails and approximately 4.7 million people under community supervision through probation or parole. See Glaze and Kaeble, *Correctional Populations in the United States*.
11. National Registry of Exonerations, "First 1,600 Exonerations"; For DNA exonerations, the common contributing factors are similar: eyewitness misidentifications, contaminated confessions, forensic errors, informants and snitches, poor lawyering, and government misconduct. See, generally, Garrett, *Convicting the Innocent*.
12. Norris and colleagues examined state-level reforms in five areas: eyewitness identification procedures, forensic oversight commissions, recording of interrogations, use of jailhouse informants, and state-created innocence commissions. See Norris et al., "Than That One Innocent Suffer"; Norris et al., "Preventing Wrongful Convictions."
13. According to the Innocence Project, all states currently have a DNA access law on the books, though many contain significant shortcomings. In addition, over half of the states and the District of Columbia have an evidence preservation law.

Innocence Project, "Access to Post-conviction DNA Testing"; Innocence Project, "Preservation of Evidence."

14. As of October 2016, 30 states, the District of Columbia, and the federal government have compensation statutes in place. The number of states with such a policy has doubled since 2000. See Norris, "Exoneree Compensation," 294; Innocence Project, "Compensating the Wrongly Convicted."

15. It is difficult to parse out exactly which of these agencies are and are not in states that require recording, because little systematic research has been conducted on this topic. The Innocence Project reports, "More than a thousand additional law enforcement agencies voluntarily record interrogations," but it is unclear whether these include those in states where recording is required. See Innocence Project, "False Confessions or Admissions."

16. See, for example, Emily, "Dallas County"; "Manhattan District Attorney." There are now at least 24 Conviction Integrity Units in the United States, and they were involved in at least 58 exonerations in 2014 alone. See National Registry of Exonerations, "Recent Findings."

17. Grisham, *Innocent Man*; Grisham, *Confession*.

18. Nyman, "Just How Popular Is 'Making a Murderer'?"; Hesse, "'Serial' Takes the Stand"; "This American Life—'Serial.'"

19. Nededog, "Here's How Popular." It is worth noting that there are no official statistics or formal ratings for Netflix programs.

20. Bedau, "Innocence and the Death Penalty."

21. Dieter, "Crisis of Confidence."

22. Baumgartner, De Boef, and Boydstun, *Decline of the Death Penalty*.

23. Warden, "Illinois Death Penalty Reform"; Wills, "Illinois Gov. Pat Quinn Abolishes Death Penalty."

24. This argument was made by Justice Stephen Breyer in his dissent in *Glossip v. Gross*, 135 U.S. 2726 (2015), an opinion that was joined by Justice Ruth Bader Ginsburg. The case dealt with the constitutionality of Oklahoma's execution method, specifically its use of midazolam as the initial drug in the lethal injection mixture.

25. Findley, "Pedagogy of Innocence"; see also Hartung, "Legal Education in the Age of Innocence." It is worth noting that there has been some skepticism and concern about the growth of innocence projects, which I discuss in the conclusion.

26. Medwed, "Innocentrism," 1550.

27. Marshall, "Innocence Revolution and the Death Penalty."

28. See, for example, Findley, "Pedagogy of Innocence"; Stiglitz, Brooks, and Shulman, "Hurricane Meets the Paper Chase"; Suni, "Ethical Issues for Innocence Projects."

29. Zalman, "Integrated Justice Model," 1467.

30. McAdam, "Conceptual Origins," 25.

31. McCarthy and Zald, "Resource Mobilization and Social Movements."

32. Snow et al., "Frame Alignment Processes."

33. McAdam, *Political Process*, 48.

34. It is worth noting that I am not the first scholar to invoke social movement research in relation to the innocence movement. Jon Gould, in his analysis of the Innocence Commission for Virginia, discusses theories of social change in light of that specific organization. However, his work does not draw heavily on such concepts. Rather, his work may be thought of as a seed idea that influenced the approach taken in this study. See Gould, *Innocence Commission*, 47–52.

35. Garland, "Culture of High Crime Societies," 350.

CHAPTER 1. "VOICES IN THE WILDERNESS"

1. It should be noted that there is an imposter theory, which suggests that the man who returned to Vermont was not, in fact, the same Russell Colvin who had been supposedly murdered. See McFarland, *Counterfeit Man*. This theory is, however, unlikely to be true—the man was examined in open court and was seen and spoken to by town members who had known him for his entire life. Warden, "First Wrongful Conviction."

2. The Boorn case is considered the first wrongful conviction by the Center on Wrongful Convictions at Northwestern University. The Center's cofounder, Rob Warden, published a reprint of *The Dead Alive* with a side-by-side discussion of the actual Boorn case in 2005. Warden, *Wilkie Collins's The Dead Alive*.

3. There is some debate about the number of victims who can be linked to Jack the Ripper with certainty. The "Canonical Five" are generally accepted as the victims of the same killer: Mary Ann Nichols, Annie Chapman, Elizabeth Stride, Catherine Eddowes, and Mary Jane Kelly. See "Whitechapel Murder Victims." An academic analysis of the modus operandi of 11 potential Jack the Ripper murders suggests that six could actually be attributed to the same killer. See, generally, Keppel et al., "Jack the Ripper Murders."

4. There were, of course, other likely wrongful conviction cases during the 1800s, including the cases of Stain and Cromwell, Andrew Toth, Will Purvis, and Percy Sullivan. See Borchard, *Convicting the Innocent*. It is also worth noting that some of the more well-known innocence action in the 19th century occurred overseas. For instance, Francois Picaud was framed for being a British spy in France in 1807, and his story later served as the inspiration for Alexandre Dumas's *The Count of Monte Cristo*, serialized in the 1840s. Similarly, in 1895, the French captain Alfred Dreyfus was framed, wrongly accused, and imprisoned for being a spy. In addition, Sir Arthur Conan Doyle, the creator of fictional detective Sherlock Holmes, was involved in several cases of alleged miscarriages of justice in the late 19th and early 20th centuries. For a discussion, see Yant, "Media's Muddled Message."

5. Between the collections of Borchard and Radelet and colleagues, more than 25 wrongful convictions are collected that occurred in the first decade of the 20th century. Borchard, *Convicting the Innocent*; Radelet, Bedau, and Putnam, *In Spite of Innocence*.

6. Borchard, "European Systems," 684.

7. Bedau and Radelet suggest that Borchard's proposals would not have prevented a large number of the 400 wrongful convictions they discuss in their book. The reason, they say, is because Borchard's proposals do not touch on the specific issues that led to the convictions, such as mistaken eyewitnesses, unreliable polygraphs, perjury, and the like, which cannot be eradicated with changes to criminal procedure. Bedau and Radelet, "Miscarriages of Justice," 86–89.

8. C. Clark, "Edwin Borchard," 1072.

9. Leo, "Rethinking the Study of Miscarriages of Justice," 203.

10. Zalman, "Integrated Justice Model," 1478.

11. See Zalman, "Edwin Borchard."

12. By this time, three states—Wisconsin, North Dakota, and California—had passed some type of compensation statute. And Borchard continued to write about and advocate for exoneree compensation. See Borchard, "State Indemnity for Errors of Criminal Justice." One particular aspect of Borchard's proposed compensation bill is worth discussing. He proposed that an individual who "contributed to bring about his arrest or conviction" (211) should be excluded from compensation eligibility. This included individuals who concealed evidence or made a voluntary false confession. As he noted, this provision "follows the well-known maxims that a claimant must come into court with clean hands, and that no one shall profit by his own wrong" (209). Given what we now know about false confessions and the individuals who are prone to making them, and the frequency with which we see them in known wrongful convictions, this is a particularly interesting element of Borchard's proposed reform. With all that psychological science and legal scholarship has taught us about criminal interrogations and confessions, it now seems common that those who falsely confess should not be excluded from compensation.

13. These works were well intentioned, no doubt, but they tended to be redundant. Leo refers to these books in his review as the "big-picture" books and points out that they often follow a very similar structure. Leo, "Rethinking the Study," 203.

14. Frank and Frank, *Not Guilty*, 31.

15. Ibid., 241.

16. Radin, *Innocents*, 232.

17. See, generally, Watson, *Sacco & Vanzetti*.

18. "Governor Dukakis Discusses."

19. Gardner, *Court of Last Resort*; Yant, "Media's Muddled Message."

20. See, generally, Carter and Klonsky, *Eye of the Hurricane*; Hirsch, *Hurricane*.

21. Death Penalty Information Center.

22. Weinberg, "Miracle Worker."

23. McCloskey, quoted in Frankel, "Burden of Proof."

24. McCloskey, quoted in Cox, "McCloskey Labors."

25. McCloskey, quoted in Frankel, "Burden of Proof."

26. McCloskey, quoted in Weinberg, "Exonerator."

27. Jim McCloskey, interview with author, December 2013; Frankel, "Burden of Proof"; Cox, "McCloskey Labors"; Jones, "He Helps Innocent Prisoners"; Alperin, "Finding Truth"; Weinberg, "Exonerator."

28. McCloskey, quoted in Alperin, "Finding Truth."

29. McCloskey, interview with author.

30. McCloskey, quoted in Alperin, "Finding Truth."

31. McCloskey, interview with author.

32. McCloskey, quoted in Alperin, "Finding Truth."

33. McCloskey, quoted in Weinberg, "Exonerator."

34. Weinberg, "Miracle Worker"; Weinberg, "Exonerator"; Casteleiro told me that he has since worked with Centurion on at least 12 exonerations, plus "a couple more cases than that." Paul Casteleiro, interview with author, January 2014. Since our interview, he has become an official staff member at Centurion, now serving as its legal director.

35. Casteleiro, interview with author.

36. McCloskey, interview with author.

37. Centurion Ministries, "Jorge De Los Santos"; Alperin, "Finding Truth"; Weinberg, "Exonerator."

38. McCloskey, quoted in Frankel, "Burden of Truth"; McCloskey, interview with author.

39. Centurion Ministries, "1980–1989"; Princeton Theological Seminary; Jones, "He Helps Innocent Prisoners"; Frankel, "Burden of Truth."

40. McCloskey, interview with author.

41. Kate Germond explained to me that wealthy Princeton widows sought out male seminary students as tenants, often offering rent-free housing in exchange for taking the landlord to meetings and appointments. McCloskey had an arrangement with "a delightful and interesting woman," and that room served as the first Centurion office. Kate Germond, interview with author, January 2014.

42. McCloskey, interview with author.

43. Frankel, "Burden of Truth."

44. McCloskey, interview with author.

45. Ibid.; Alperin, "Finding Truth."

46. McCloskey, interview with author.

47. Germond says she was "sort of" a volunteer: "I was paid $100 dollars a month." Germond, interview with author.

48. Ibid.

49. McCloskey, interview with author.

50. Germond, interview with author; Alperin, "Finding Truth."

51. Centurion Ministries, "1980–1989"; Jones, "He Helps Innocent Prisoners."

52. McCloskey, interview with author.

53. Ibid.

54. Centurion Ministries, "Clarence Brandley"; Pressley, "Speedy Justice Can Be Dead Wrong."

55. Centurion Ministries, "Joyce Ann Brown."

56. C. Ronald Huff, interview with author, November 2013; Yant, "Media's Muddled Message."

57. Maurice Possley, interview with author, January 2014.

58. McCloskey, interview with author.

59. Warden, interview by Campbell.

60. Rob Warden, interview with author, February 2014.

61. Ibid.

62. Warden, interview by Campbell.

63. Northwestern University Center on Wrongful Convictions, "Lavelle Burt," accessed November 20, 2013, www.law.northwestern.edu/legalclinic/wrongfulconvictions/; Warden, interview by Campbell.

64. Ron Huff, for instance, appeared on the morning show to discuss wrongful convictions. Huff, interview with author.

65. Warden, interview with author.

66. Williams, "Mirrors without Memories," 11.

67. Ebert, "Thin Blue Line."

68. Rafferty, "True Detective."

69. Ibid.; Gershman, "Thin Blue Line," 317.

70. Rafferty, "True Detective."

71. E. Morris, "Thin Blue Line."

72. National Film Preservation Board, "National Film Registry."

73. J. Anderson, "Op-ed Films for the Ages."

74. Morris once remarked in an interview that he was prouder of the investigation into the murder than he was of the film itself and that the investigation is what led to Adams's release, not the film. In investigating the case, Morris found a variety of evidence that pointed strongly to Adams's innocence. E. Morris, interview by *The Believer*.

75. Ibid.

76. Gershman, "Thin Blue Line," 276. Gershman later adds, "By providing a devastating account of an almost certain miscarriage of justice, *The Thin Blue Line* offers an enormously compelling critique of the utility and fairness of the adversary trial process" (302).

77. Huff, interview with author.

78. Ibid.

79. Huff et al., "Guilty until Proved Innocent," 518.

80. Huff, Rattner, and Edward Sagarin, *Convicted but Innocent*. Sagarin passed away before the book was completed, but his name remained attached to the volume. Huff, interview with author.

81. Samuel Gross, interview with author, June 2014.

82. Ibid. See also Gross, "Loss of Innocence," 396.

83. Gross, interview with author.

84. Gross, "Loss of Innocence," 449.

85. Ehrmann, "For Whom the Chair Waits."
86. Radelet told me that they responded to every single letter they received, explaining that they were not lawyers and could not offer proper legal advice. Michael Radelet, interview with author, May 2014.
87. Van den Haag, "Ultimate Punishment," 1665.
88. Bedau and Radelet, "Miscarriages of Justice," 21.
89. Markman and Cassell, "Protecting the Innocent," 121.
90. Bedau and Radelet, "Myth of Infallibility," 169; Radelet remarked to me that this exchange was rather unbalanced. As representatives of the Justice Department, Markman and Cassell had resources unavailable to Bedau and Radelet. Radelet, interview with author.
91. Zalman, "Integrated Justice Model."
92. Radelet, interview with author; Radelet, Bedau, and Putnam, *In Spite of Innocence*.
93. Radelet, interview with author.
94. Huff, interview with author.
95. Huff et al., "Guilty Until Proved Innocent," 522.
96. Radelet, interview with author.
97. Huff, interview with author.
98. Janet Baxendale, interview with author, January 2014. During a visit with McCloskey, I mentioned to him that he had been referred to as "the godfather" of innocence work. He laughed and said, "Ah, that makes me sound old." I then informed him that Kate Germond had referred to him as the "granddaddy" and to the two of them as the "grandparents." To this, McCloskey just smiled and nodded.

CHAPTER 2. "A EUREKA MOMENT"

1. Department of Genetics, "History of Genetic Fingerprinting."
2. Jeffreys, "Century of Human Genetics."
3. Aronson, *Genetic Witness*.
4. Department of Genetics, "History of Genetic Fingerprinting"; Aronson, *Genetic Witness*.
5. Aronson, *Genetic Witness*, 13; The papers included Jeffreys, Wilson, and Thein, "Hypervariable 'Minisatellite' Regions"; Jeffreys, Wilson, and Thein, "Individual-Specific 'Fingerprints.'"
6. Department of Genetics, "History of Genetic Fingerprinting"; Newton, "Discovering DNA Fingerprinting."
7. For a more in-depth description of the case, see Aronson, *Genetic Witness*, 7–15.
8. Ibid., 13; For examples of press coverage in England, see Silcock, "Genes Tell Tales"; Veitch, "Son Rejoins Mother."
9. Department of Genetics, "History of Genetic Fingerprinting."
10. Ibid.
11. McKie, "Eureka Moment"; BBC News, "DNA Pioneer's 'Eureka' Moment."
12. Newton, "Discovering DNA Fingerprinting"; Wambaugh, *Blooding*.
13. Wambaugh, *Blooding*, 220.

14. Aronson, *Genetic Witness*, 17.
15. Department of Genetics, "History of Genetic Fingerprinting."
16. Jeffreys, "Century of Human Genetics."
17. McKie, "Eureka Moment."
18. Aronson, *Genetic Witness*, 15, 18.
19. Ibid., 19.
20. Ibid., 19–20, 30.
21. Giusti et al., "Application of Deoxyribonucleic Acid"; Kanter et al., "Analysis of Restriction Fragment Length Polymorphisms." For a more in-depth discussion of these publications, see Aronson, *Genetic Witness*, 30–31.
22. Michael Baird, quoted in Aronson, *Genetic Witness*, 31.
23. Aronson, *Genetic Witness*; Lewis, "DNA Fingerprints."
24. Lewis, "DNA Fingerprints," 50.
25. Ibid., 51–52.
26. The term "*Wesley-Bailey* hearing" was used by Jay Aronson. Aronson, *Genetic Witness*, 42.
27. C. Woodruff, "Wesley Jailed 38 1/3 Years-Life."
28. "DNA Test Case."
29. *Frye v. United States*, 293 F. 1013 (D.C. Cir. 1923).
30. *People of the State of New York v. George Wesley, People of the State of New York v. Cameron Bailey*, 140 Misc. 2d 306 (1988); Aronson, *Genetic Witness*, 45–48.
31. *People v. Wesley, People v. Bailey*.
32. Ibid.
33. Aronson, *Genetic Witness*, 56; Lewin, "DNA Typing."
34. Neufeld, quoted in Lewin, "DNA Typing," 1033.
35. Aronson, *Genetic Witness*, 56.
36. Scheck, Neufeld, and Dwyer, *Actual Innocence*, 8–10.
37. As an interesting and entertaining aside, Neufeld and Scheck recall the first time they ever spoke, after which Scheck wanted Neufeld fired. They were running a mock trial to allow the lawyers to hone their lines of questioning. Scheck was the attorney, and Neufeld served as a mock potential juror. When explaining to Neufeld that the trial would not be like it is portrayed on television and that not all police officers would be "Kojaks," Neufeld reported that he did not know what that meant, saying, "I don't watch much TV." Scheck then told their supervisor that Neufeld was not suitable as a mock juror or as a lawyer, because he was "so elitist, so out of touch with mass culture and entertainment," that he could not relate to juries. After their supervisor declined to fire Neufeld, the two formed a close friendship. Scheck, Neufeld, and Dwyer, *Actual Innocence*, 7–8.
38. Scheck, interview by Kreisler; Parloff, "How Barry Scheck and Peter Neufeld."
39. Barry Scheck, interview with author, February 2014.
40. Scheck, interview by Kreisler; Neufeld, interview by Kreisler.
41. Neufeld, interview by Kreisler.
42. Scheck, interview with author.

43. Scheck, interview by Kreisler.
44. Neufeld, interview by Kreisler; Scheck echoes this point: "I didn't take any biology, I didn't really take math courses, and I wasn't science-oriented. . . . I wound up being an American studies major, taking courses with Robert Penn Warren, reading all these great books. I was much more interested in literature and the arts and cinema, the theater. Those became my principal interests—sociology, psychology. I was not at all oriented towards any of the hard sciences." Scheck, interview by Kreisler.
45. Parloff, "How Barry Scheck and Peter Neufeld," 52.
46. *People of the State of New York v. Joseph Castro*, 545 N.Y.S. 2d 985 (Sup. Ct. 1989); Parloff, "How Barry Scheck and Peter Neufeld"; Patton, "DNA Fingerprinting"; Lewin, "DNA Typing."
47. Parloff, "How Barry Scheck and Peter Neufeld," 50.
48. Lifecodes report, quoted in Lewin, "DNA Typing."
49. As was written in the *Castro* decision, "all the available legal precedents agree that DNA forensic evidence is admissible, and none have held that this evidence fails to pass the Frye standard." *Castro*, 545 N.Y.S. 2d at 987.
50. Parloff, "How Barry Scheck and Peter Neufeld"; Lewin, "DNA Typing."
51. Neufeld, quoted in Lewin, "DNA Typing."
52. Neufeld, quoted in Parloff, "How Barry Scheck and Peter Neufeld," 53.
53. Ibid.
54. Neufeld, quoted ibid.
55. Neufeld, quoted in Lewin, "DNA Typing."
56. Parloff, "How Barry Scheck and Peter Neufeld."
57. Lander, quoted in Lewin, "DNA Typing."
58. Parloff, "How Barry Scheck and Peter Neufeld," 53.
59. Lander, quoted in Lewin, "DNA Typing."
60. Lander, quoted in Parloff, "How Barry Scheck and Peter Neufeld," 53.
61. Lewin, "DNA Typing."
62. Scheck, quoted in Parloff, "How Barry Scheck and Peter Neufeld," 53.
63. Roberts, quoted in Lewin, "DNA Typing."
64. Roberts, quoted ibid.
65. The four experts in attendance included Lander, Roberts, Carl Dobkin, and Lorraine Flaherty. Lewin, "DNA Typing."
66. Neufeld, quoted in Lewin, "DNA Typing."
67. Report, quoted in Parloff, "How Barry Scheck and Peter Neufeld," 55.
68. Ibid., 55.
69. Report, quoted in Lewin, "DNA Typing."
70. Ibid.
71. Neufeld, quoted ibid.
72. The court essentially ruled that forensic DNA evidence passes the *Frye* test but that the test was insufficient on its own to determine admissibility of the evidence. As the opinion states, "It is the view of this court that given the complexity of the

DNA multi-system identification tests and the powerful impact that they may have on a jury, passing muster under *Frye* alone is insufficient to place this type of evidence before a jury without a preliminary, critical examination of the actual testing procedures performed in a particular case." *Castro*, 545 N.Y.S. 2d at 987.

73. Sugarman, quoted in Parloff, "How Barry Scheck and Peter Neufeld," 56.
74. Unnamed New York State jurist, quoted ibid., 52.
75. Neufeld and Colman, "When Science Takes the Witness Stand," 52.
76. Neufeld, quoted in Parloff, "How Barry Scheck and Peter Neufeld," 56.
77. Scheck, quoted ibid.
78. Ibid., 56.
79. Aronson, *Genetic Witness*, 87.
80. Lander, quoted in Lewin, "DNA Typing."
81. Jay Aronson details the process through which the FBI developed its forensic crime analysis program. Aronson, *Genetic Witness*, 90–117.
82. The term "DNA Wars" in the section title is borrowed from Aronson, *Genetic Witness*, 120.
83. *United States v. Bonds, Verdi, and Yee*, 12 F.3d 540 (6th Cir. 1994).
84. Labaton, "DNA Fingerprinting Showdown"; *Bonds*, 12 F.3d 540.
85. Ronald Kuby, quoted in Labaton, "DNA Fingerprinting Showdown," 1990.
86. *United States v. Yee et al.*, 134 F.R.D. 161 (N.D. Ohio 1991); *Bonds*, 12 F.3d 540.
87. Lander, "Invited Editorial."
88. Harmon, "Please Leave Law to the Lawyers," 891.
89. Lander, "Lander Reply," 903.
90. Chakraborty and Kidd, "Utility of DNA Typing"; Lewontin and Hartle, "Population Genetics in Forensic DNA Typing."
91. Roberts, "Fight Erupts over DNA Fingerprinting"; Roberts, "Was *Science* Fair to Its Authors?"
92. Roberts, "Science in Court," 732.
93. Aronson, *Genetic Witness*, 151.
94. National Research Council, *DNA Technology in Forensic Science*; National Research Council, *Evaluation of Forensic DNA Evidence*.
95. For more, see Aronson, *Genetic Witness*, 146–172.
96. Ibid., 175.
97. The sketch that Cromwell produced with police does resemble Dotson in some ways. Interestingly, though, the sketched perpetrator did not have facial hair, and Dotson wore a mustache. Ibid.
98. Ibid.
99. Associated Press, "Gary Dotson Set Free."
100. Sam Adam, quoted in Shipp, "Debate Surrounds Rape Decision."
101. "Recantation, Incantation and Rape."
102. Shipp, "Debate Surrounds Rape Decision."
103. UPI, "Rape Case Judge."
104. Shipp, "Sentence Is Commuted."

105. "Governor Thompson's Justice": "Buffeted by public puzzlement and advice, [Governor James Thompson] calmly resolved this anomalous case with fairness to the complainant, the prisoner, the legal system and the society it is supposed to serve."

106. McDowell, "Key Figures in Illinois Rape Case."

107. Associated Press, "Parole Revoked"; Dotson was actually released again on Christmas Eve 1987 but again wound up in trouble after an incident in a restaurant where, after drinking, he allegedly struck a waitress because his sandwich was not as he ordered it. The charges were dropped, however, after several witnesses cast doubt on the version of events recounted by the waitress. The Prisoner Review Board still revoked his parole since he failed to call his parole officer on the day he was initially released and ordered him back to prison for six months. Northwestern University Center on Wrongful Convictions, "First DNA Exoneration."

108. As Warden made clear to me in our conversation, he was "right there at the very beginning of the DNA era," and was "totally immersed in it at the time." This is not surprising, particularly given his later heavy involvement in the innocence movement, which is discussed in later chapters. Rob Warden, interview with author, February 2014.

109. Northwestern University Center on Wrongful Convictions, "First DNA Exoneration."

110. Associated Press, "Illinois Governor Withholds Decision."

111. Warden, "Illinois Death Penalty Reform," 397. It is also worth noting that even Jeffreys wrote a critical letter urging quick action in the case due to the "conclusive nature" of the DNA evidence. "It is clear that rejection of this evidence by the judiciary would constitute a gross miscarriage of justice," Jeffreys wrote. Northwestern University Center on Wrongful Convictions, "First DNA Exoneration."

112. Associated Press, "Prosecutors Drop Charges."

113. See Warden, "Illinois Death Penalty Reform"; Zalman, "Integrated Justice Model."

114. Priest, "Wrongly Jailed Man."

115. National Registry of Exonerations, "David Vasquez," accessed June 3, 2015, www.law.umich.edu.

116. Priest, "Va. Man Pardoned."

117. Priest, "Arlington Detective's Hunch."

118. Priest, "Arlington Reopens 1984 Rape-Murder Case." The *Alford* plea comes from a 1970 case in North Carolina. See *North Carolina v. Alford*, 400 U.S. 25 (1970).

119. Priest, "Arlington Reopens 1984 Rape-Murder Case"; Innocence Project, "David Vasquez."

120. National Registry of Exonerations, "David Vasquez."

121. Priest, "Pardon Urged for Man Convicted of Va. Murder."

122. Priest, "Va. Man Pardoned after Five Years in Prison."

123. This is based on newspaper searches through ProQuest and Lexis Nexis for the names "Gary Dotson" and "David Vasquez," along with various combinations and variations of "wrongful conviction," "exoneration," and "innocence." This is also a point raised in Zalman, "Integrated Justice Model."

124. Zalman, "Integrated Justice Model."
125. Warden, interview with author.
126. The Innocence Project maintains information only about DNA exonerations, and David Vasquez is listed as one of the cases on its website. Furthermore, it does not include him on a short list of clients who were exonerated through non-DNA evidence. It is logical, then, to assume that it counts Vasquez as a "DNA exoneration." Thus, on the basis of the dates of exoneration, Vasquez can logically be considered the first DNA exoneree in the United States.
127. It is also worth noting that the Dotson profile on the Northwestern Center's website refers to his case as the "first DNA exoneration." And although it has since been removed, their profile of the Vasquez case described David as "the first prisoner in the United States—probably the world—to be exonerated by DNA."
128. Scheck, interview by Kreisler.
129. Neufeld, interview by Kreisler.
130. Peter Neufeld, interview with author, April 2014. Freedom schools were alternative schools for African American children, mostly in the South. After the Supreme Court's 1954 ruling in *Brown v. Board of Education*, a number of jurisdictions still maintained separate but unequal schooling for white and black children. Activists set up freedom schools as a response to these practices. There is a significant body of scholarship on freedom schools and the civil rights movement, much of it focusing specifically on Mississippi. See, for example, Howe, "Mississippi's Freedom Schools"; Rothschild, "Volunteers and the Freedom Schools."
131. Neufeld, interview by Kreisler.
132. Neufeld, interview with author.
133. Scheck, interview with author. For more on the McLaughlin case, see Kennedy, "Wrongly Convicted Man Wins $1.9-Million Judgment"; Christianson, *Innocent*, 34–36.
134. Scheck, interview with author.
135. Neufeld, interview with author.
136. Scheck, interview with author.
137. Scheck, interview by Kreisler.
138. Neufeld, interview with author.
139. Ibid.
140. Ibid.
141. Kate Germond, interview with author, January 2014; Scheck, interview with author.
142. Germond, interview with author.
143. Scheck, interview with author.
144. Neufeld, interview with author.
145. Rabinovitz, "Rape Conviction Overturned."
146. All details of the events leading up to the crime and its aftermath are drawn from Junkin, *Bloodsworth*, 31, 34–38, 44–46.

147. Ibid., 75–77; see also Goldstein, "DNA Test May Free Man"; Valentine, "Jailed for Murder, Freed by DNA"; Valentine, "Man Cleared by DNA Gets Pardon."

148. Goldstein, "DNA Test May Free Man."

149. Police had previously put a rock on the table when questioning Bloodsworth. Assuming it was the murder weapon, he had talked about it. They later used the fact that he knew what the murder weapon was against him. Junkin, *Bloodsworth*, 97.

150. Apparently, the "terrible" things Bloodsworth had been talking about in relation to his marriage included his neglect of his wife and smoking marijuana. Goldstein, "DNA Test May Free Man."

151. Valentine, "Man Cleared by DNA Gets Pardon."

152. Innocence Project, "Kirk Bloodsworth."

153. Associated Press, "Fantastic!"

154. Castaneda, "DNA Evidence Spells Freedom."

155. Goldstein, "DNA Test May Free Man."

156. Associated Press, "Fantastic!"

157. Valentine, "Man Cleared by DNA Gets Pardon." The investigation for Dawn Hamilton's real killer continued, though at the time, there were no clear suspects. Nine years later, however, a forensic biologist found stains that had not yet been analyzed. The sample was run through the state DNA database, and a hit was found for a man named Kimberly Ruffner, who, incidentally, had occupied the cell directly below Kirk's and with whom he had lifted weights. After this, Ann Brobst, from the state attorney's office, apologized to Kirk for what had been done to him. Junkin, *Bloodsworth*, 273–277.

158. There were 31 executions in 1992 and 38 in 1993. There had not been more than 30 executions in one year since 1976. Death Penalty Information Center, "Executions by Year since 1976."

159. Richard Dieter, interview with author, May 2014.

160. Ibid.

161. Staff Report by the Subcommittee on Civil and Constitutional Rights, Committee on the Judiciary, 103rd Cong., 1st sess., October 21, 1993.

162. Radelet, Bedau, and Putnam, *In Spite of Innocence*.

163. Dieter, interview with author.

164. Ibid.

165. Ibid.

166. *Herrera v. Collins*, 506 U.S. 390 (1993).

167. Dieter, interview with author.

168. Ibid.

169. Samuel Gross, interview with author, June 2014.

170. Dieter, interview with author; DPIC produced its second innocence report in 1997. Dieter, *Innocence and the Death Penalty*.

171. The folks at DPIC were aware of this fact. One agenda for a DPIC board meeting from 2001 stated, "Many articles and speakers make reference to the number of innocent people released from death row. DPIC has become the key source

for this list." Death Penalty Information Center, "Proposed Agenda for the DPIC Board Meeting," July 30, 2001, Steven Hawkins Collection, National Death Penalty Archive, Albany, NY.

172. Jim McCloskey, interview with author, December 2013.

173. Stevens, quoted in "Justice Stevens Criticizes."

174. Transcripts from the O. J. Simpson trial and other information about the case are available at http://walraven.org/simpson.

175. Scheck, interview by Kreisler. Scheck also recounts this in another interview: "It was clear in 1994 that Peter Neufeld and I knew a lot about forensic DNA testing and serology and forensic evidence. And so I was in Madison Square Garden watching a play-off game when we got a phone call from Gerry Uelmen, who was the dean of Santa Clara Law School, and Bob Shapiro saying, 'We are representing Mr. Simpson and we're coming up on a preliminary hearing, and there is blood on the crime scene and other forensic evidence. Could you just advise us what questions to ask about technical detail?'" Gitschier, "Innocence Project at Twenty."

176. Margolick, "Day of Familiar Dueling."

177. The reaction to the verdict followed the circus-like atmosphere that had been present throughout the duration of the trial. In many ways, the reaction was divided along racial lines, though not exclusively so. See, for example, "Reaction to O. J. Verdict."

178. Aronson, *Genetic Witness*, 173.

179. Neufeld, interview in "What Jennifer Saw."

180. Scheck, interview in "What Jennifer Saw."

181. Scheck, interview by Kreisler.

182. Scheck, quoted in Gitschier, "Innocence Project at Twenty."

183. Aronson, *Genetic Witness*, 180.

184. On the basis of a ProQuest search of the *New York Times* archive, the actual number appears to be over 180.

185. For example, Scheck's cross-examination of Dennis Fung, who had handled the police evidence, "brought him instant, worldwide notoriety and applause." Margolick, "Simpson Lawyer Makes New York Style Play."

186. Span, "Gene Team."

187. Margolick, "Simpson Lawyer Makes New York Style Play." There were other criticisms levied at them (as well as at the rest of Simpson's defense team) after the trial concluded. At one point, it was reported that Scheck and Neufeld were "headed for new careers in Hollywood," working with CBS to develop a television drama based on their lives. Egan, "After Simpson Trial, Inquiries and Deals."

188. Span, "Gene Team."

189. Germond, interview with author.

190. San Martin and Gibson, "Reno May Be Nominated."

191. Marcus, "Clinton Nominates Reno."

192. San Martin and Gibson, "Reno May Be Nominated."

193. Marcus, "Clinton Nominates Reno."

194. San Martin and Gibson, "Reno May Be Nominated"; Reno actually once remarked that she would have never thought she would be a prosecutor because she thought prosecutors "were more interested in securing convictions than in seeking justice." Marcus, "Clinton Nominates Reno."

195. New York Times News Service, "3rd Try"; San Martin and Gibson, "Reno May Be Nominated."

196. *Furman v. Georgia*, 408 U.S. 238 (1972).

197. Chin and Grant, "Convicted of Murdering One of His Children."

198. Reno's memorandum, quoted in Sherrer, "Arcadia and the Twenty Year Effort."

199. For more on the James Richardson case, see Lane, *Arcadia*; Sherrer, "Arcadia and the Twenty Year Effort"; National Registry of Exonerations, "James Joseph Richardson." The Richardson case has recently come up in the news again, as a bill to compensate Richardson passed the Florida House and Senate at the tail end of the 2014 legislative session. Cummings, "Richardson Compensation Bill Passes."

200. Connors et al., *Convicted by Juries*, 2; Jeremy Travis mentioned to me that of all of his contributions to the project, coming up with the title may have been the one of which he was proudest. Jeremy Travis, interview with author, July 2014.

201. The three types of evidence they found common among these cases are now commonly associated with wrongful convictions: eyewitness identification, forensic evidence, and government misconduct.

202. Connors et al., *Convicted by Juries*, 24.

203. Zalman, "Integrated Justice Model," 1488.

204. Travis, interview with author.

205. Ibid.

206. Neufeld and Scheck cite data from the FBI stating that of the roughly 10,000 sexual assault cases since 1989 in which DNA testing was performed, approximately 2,000 have been inconclusive, 2,000 excluded the primary suspect, and 6,000 were inclusive. Thus, of those in which a result was obtained, one-fourth of them were exclusions. Neufeld and Scheck, "Commentary," xxviii.

207. Ibid., xxxi.

208. Ibid., xxx–xxxi.

209. Travis, interview with author.

210. Zalman, "Integrated Justice Model," 1488.

211. Madeline deLone, interview with author, October 2013.

212. Scheck, interview by Kreisler.

CHAPTER 3. "WE'RE ALL TOGETHER ON THIS"

1. Peter Neufeld, interview with author, April 2014.

2. A popular myth traces the "Windy City" nickname to the long-winded nature of early Chicago politicians. According to this story, the term was made popular when New York and Chicago were competing to hold the 1893 Columbian Exposition, or world's fair, and the *New York Sun* editor Charles Dana used the phrase

as a derogatory remark toward Chicago. This story, however, is known to be false. See Wilton, *Word Myths*.

3. Death Penalty Information Center, "Innocence Cases."

4. See Protess and Warden, *Promise of Justice*.

5. Terry, "After 18 Years in Prison." Don Terry covers the Ford Heights Four exonerations and discusses the debate over limiting the federal death penalty appeals process.

6. Rob Warden, interview with author, February 2014.

7. Cantwell, "Brandley Free after 10 Years."

8. Warden, interview with author.

9. Ibid.

10. Ibid.

11. Ibid.

12. Davis, "Hope Sought for Innocents."

13. Hentoff, "Not Dead Yet."

14. Associated Press, "Death Row Survivors Meet."

15. Warden, interview with author; At the time, there were more than 70 death row exonerees in all. However, some could not make it, some were in prison, some died, and others could not be found. Associated Press, "Death Row Survivors Meet."

16. Getting an exact number of attendees is difficult. Newspaper reports suggested that anywhere from 300 to 1,200 were in attendance. Davis, "Hope Sought for Innocents"; Associated Press, "Death Row Survivors Meet"; Tuft, "Ex-Death Row Inmates"; Gumbel, "Death Row Survivors Call"; Levinson, "Conference Honors"; In my interview with Rob Warden, he mentioned an auditorium that holds more than 750 people reaching standing-room-only, and multiple news reports suggest more than 1,000 attendees, so I am inclined to lean towards the higher end of this spectrum.

17. Howlett, "Time Lost to Death Row."

18. Gumbel, "Death Row Survivors Call."

19. Terry, "Survivors Make the Case"; Tuft, "Ex-Death Row Inmates."

20. Levinson, "Conference Honors."

21. Gumbel, "Death Row Survivors Call."

22. Levinson, "Conference Honors."

23. Terry, "Survivors Make the Case."

24. Gumbel, "Death Row Survivors Call"; Tuft, "Ex-Death Row Inmates."

25. Terry, "Survivors Make the Case."

26. Dwyer, "System's Dead Wrong."

27. Kate Germond, interview with author, January 2014.

28. Tuft, "Ex-Death Row Inmates."

29. Howlett, "Time Lost to Death Row."

30. Michael Radelet, interview with author, May 2014.

31. Warden, interview by Campbell.

32. Steve Drizin, interview with author, June 2014.

33. Gumbel, "Death Row Survivors Call."

34. Richard Dieter, interview with author, May 2014.

35. Death Penalty Information Center, "Executions by Year since 1976."

36. Terry, "Survivors Make the Case." See also Davis, "Hope Sought for Innocents"; McLaughlin, "Tales of Journey."

37. Terry, "Survivors Make the Case."

38. Marshall, quoted in Levinson, "Death Row's Survivors."

39. Marshall, quoted in Terry, "Survivors Make the Case."

40. Levinson, "Death Row's Survivors."

41. "Death Penalty States Kill the Innocent Sometimes."

42. Drizin, interview with author.

43. Warden, interview with author.

44. McLaughlin, "Tales of Journey."

45. Dwyer, "System's Dead Wrong."

46. Terry, "Survivors Make the Case."

47. Tuft, "Ex-Death Row Inmates."

48. Howlett, "Time Lost to Death Row."

49. Warden, interview by Campbell.

50. National Registry of Exonerations, "Anthony Porter." It is worth noting that this case recently reemerged after it was discovered that the investigator who secured Simon's confession may have used some questionable and potentially coercive techniques to do so. Cook County state's attorney Anita Alvarez recently threw out Simon's convictions and freed him from prison. The saga has called into question the guilt or innocence of both Porter and Simon, the integrity of investigators, and the decisions of former prosecutors and the former governor George Ryan. It has also added a wrinkle to the story of Illinois's recent abolition of the death penalty, in which Porter's exoneration played a major role. See Mills, Schmadeke, and Hinkel, "Prosecutors Free Inmate"; Madhani, "Man's Release Twists."

51. Warden, interview with author.

52. For instance, in a memo to DPIC board members, Richard Dieter discussed an article that appeared in *American Spectator* from "the conservative perspective about the death penalty" in which the author wrote "an 'expose' on how the death penalty movement has used the innocence issue to undermine capital punishment." They did not seem too concerned, however, as Dieter wrote, "My own reaction is that the author probably gives us too much credit, and that, if this is the worst our enemies can say of us, we're doing pretty well." Dieter, "Memo to DPIC Board Members and Consultants from Richard Dieter, RE: Agenda; articles," April 6, 2000, Steven Hawkins Collection, National Death Penalty Archive, Albany, NY.

53. Ryan was actually the head of the Illinois campaign for Bush. Johnson, "Illinois, Citing Faulty Verdicts."

54. Warden, interview by Campbell.
55. "Timeout on the Death Penalty."
56. Ryan, quoted in Johnson, "Illinois, Citing Faulty Verdicts." He was also quoted similarly in Taylor, "Death Penalty," 450–451.
57. Associated Press, "Illinois Governor Plans."
58. Johnson, "Illinois Governor Hopes."
59. Getz, "Local Lawyers Have Varied Reactions."
60. Meinert, "Clinton Praises Ryan."
61. Johnson, "Illinois, Citing Faulty Verdicts."
62. "Timeout on the Death Penalty."
63. A number of documents from the organization, found in the National Death Penalty Archive, show support for Ryan's decision.
64. Kernek, "Cross Walk."
65. See Bright, "Smooth Road to the Death House."
66. Frum, "Justice Americans Demand." It is worth noting that this editorial generated a number of letters to the editor, mostly disagreeing with the original piece. See "Death Penalty in a Democracy."
67. Johnson, "Illinois, Citing Faulty Verdicts."
68. Ryan, quoted in ibid.
69. Johnson, "No Executions in Illinois."
70. Warden, interview with author.
71. Ryan's moratorium was the top news story "according to Associated Press member newspaper editors and broadcasters," even topping the gasoline price surge that year. D'Alessio, "Execution Freeze Tops News."
72. Dieter, interview with author.
73. Ibid.
74. "Letter from Gara LaMarche, Director of U.S. Programs for OSI, to 'Colleagues' Inviting Them to a Luncheon Entitled, 'Capital Punishment in America: How the Death Penalty Is Changing the National Debate on Crime and Justice,'" October 30, 2000, Steven Hawkins Collection, National Death Penalty Archive, Albany, NY.
75. Liebman, "New Death Penalty Debate," 539.
76. Jim Dwyer, interview with author, May 2014; see also Warden, "Role of the Media."
77. Dwyer, interview with author.
78. Leo and Gould, "Studying Wrongful Convictions," 13.
79. Will, "Innocent on Death Row."
80. Simonich, "Actual Innocence."
81. Long, "Actual Innocence."
82. Simonich, "Actual Innocence."
83. Lain, "Deciding Death," 45.
84. "Actual Innocence."
85. Will, "Innocent on Death Row."

86. Dieter, "Memo to DPIC Board Members," April 6, 2000.

87. "Governor Ryan's Brave Example."

88. See Holmes, "Look Who's Questioning the Death Penalty": "'The political climate is shifting,' said Tim Lynch, director of the Project on Criminal Justice for the Cato Institute, a conservative-libertarian research and advocacy organization. 'I think a lot of conservatives may not go as far as liberals and say it should be abolished. But what happened in Illinois is getting people to rethink whether sufficient safeguards are in place.'"

89. When asked about this time, Maurice Possley said, "Politicians were afraid to touch [the death penalty] because it was a moral issue. Now the debate changed to 'Are there flaws in the system?' and politicians are open to wrestling with that." Possley, interview with author, January 2014.

90. Johnson, "Illinois, Citing Faulty Verdicts."

91. United States Senate, "Statements on Introduced Bills and Joint Resolutions," April 26, 2000; United States Senate, "The Need for a Moratorium on Executions," June 6, 2000; "Reforming the Death Penalty System."

92. See "New Death Penalty Politics"; Seelve, "Firmly for Death Penalty."

93. Seelve, "Firmly for Death Penalty."

94. Johnson, "No Executions in Illinois."

95. Death Penalty Information Center, *DPIC Year End Report*, December 2000, Steven Hawkins Collection, National Death Penalty Archive, Albany, NY.

96. Baumgartner et al., *Decline of the Death Penalty*, 119–121. Baumgartner and colleagues report that "innocence/fairness has shown a dramatic increase from virtually no coverage before the 1980s to constituting more than half of the entire amount of coverage annually in many recent years," 120.

97. Death Penalty Information Center, *DPIC Year End Report*.

98. Byrne, "To Kill a 'Legacy.'"

99. Schaper, "Former Illinois Gov."; Associated Press, "Former Ill. Governor George Ryan."

100. "No Blanket Clemency."

101. Barnum, "Birkett Sues over Clemencies."

102. Associated Press, "Illinois Governor's Blanket Pardon."

103. Parsons and Mellen, "House Bill Seeks Limit."

104. Byrne, "To Kill a 'Legacy.'"

105. Keilman, "Relatives of Victims."

106. Associated Press, "Illinois Governor's Blanket Pardon."

107. Keilman, "Relatives of Victims."

108. Associated Press, "Illinois Governor's Blanket Pardon."

109. See Keilman, "Murder Victims' Families."

110. Olsen, "Law Profs Back Ryan."

111. Chase, "Final Appeal for Clemency Made."

112. Bush, "Jackson Asks Total Clemency."

113. Associated Press, "Illinois Governor's Blanket Pardon."

114. Ryan, "Deadline Clip."
115. "In Ryan's Words."
116. Robert Torricelli, "Agriculture, Rural Development, Food and Drug Administration, and Related Agency Programs Appropriations Act, 2001—Conference Report," United States Senate, October 18, 2000.
117. Proposed bills included, for example, the Criminal Justice Integrity and Law Enforcement Assistance Act, the Paul Coverdell National Forensic Sciences Improvement Act, and the DNA Analysis Backlog Elimination Act, all of which were proposed in 2000.
118. Patrick Leahy, "Statements on Introduced Bills and Joint Resolutions," United States Senate, June 7, 2000.
119. Dieter, "Memo to DPIC Board Members and Consultants from Richard Dieter, RE: Minutes; Up-date," March 17, 2000, Steven Hawkins Collection, National Death Penalty Archive, Albany, NY.
120. "New Looks at the Death Penalty."
121. "The Innocence Protection Act," United States Senate, October 19, 2000.
122. "Bills to Stop Executing the Innocent."
123. The bill was fairly popular in Congress. By October 2000, it had 14 co-sponsors in the Senate and nearly 80 in the House of Representatives. "Innocence Protection Act."
124. Death Penalty Information Center, "Understanding the Death Penalty: A Guide for Those Concerned about the Issue," October 2000, Steven Hawkins Collection, National Death Penalty Archive, Albany, NY.
125. Patrick Leahy, "Statements on Introduced Bills and Joint Resolutions," United States Senate, March 7, 2001.
126. Dianne Feinstein, "Statements on Introduced Bills and Joint Resolutions," United States Senate, April 30, 2001.
127. "Protecting against Wrongful Convictions," United States Senate, August 3, 2001.
128. Neufeld, interview with author.
129. The full text of the Justice for All Act is easily accessible through the Innocence Project's website at www.innocenceproject.org.
130. Richard Dieter, "Memo to DPIC Board Members," July 2, 1999, Steven Hawkins Collection, National Death Penalty Archive, Albany, NY.
131. "Letter from Gara LaMarche."
132. Herbert, "Criminal Justice Breakdown."
133. Lushing, "Death-Sentence Errors."
134. Herbert, "Criminal Justice Breakdown."
135. Korecki, "How Death Penalty Has Changed."
136. Warden, interview with author.
137. Barry Scheck, interview with author, February 2014.
138. See Hentoff, "Not Dead Yet"; Howlett, "Time Lost to Death Row."
139. Terry, "Survivors Make the Case."
140. Warden, "Four Decades."

141. Ibid.
142. Drizin, interview with author.
143. Scheck, interview with author.
144. Theresa Newman, interview with author, July 2014.
145. Scheck, interview with author.
146. Ibid.; Newman, interview with author.
147. Newman, interview with author.
148. Scheck, interview with author.
149. Ibid.
150. Ibid.
151. Flyer for National Association of Criminal Defense Lawyers (NACDL) Midwinter Meeting and Seminar, February 23–26, 2000, National Death Penalty Archive, Albany, NY. It is also worth noting that just a few years later, Scheck served as the president of the NACDL. See National Association of Criminal Defense Lawyers, "Past Presidents."
152. Innocence Network, "About the Innocence Network."
153. Newman, interview with author.
154. Ibid.; Innocence Network, "Innocence Network History."
155. Innocence Network, "Innocence Network Membership Guidelines."
156. Newman, interview with author.
157. Neufeld, interview with author.
158. Newman, interview with author.
159. Christine Mumma, interview with author, March 2014.
160. Newman, interview with author.
161. Ibid.
162. Scheck, interview with author.
163. Newman, interview with author.
164. Scheck, interview with author.
165. Madeline deLone, interview with author, October 2013; Stephen Saloom, interview with author, October 2013.
166. DeLone, interview with author.
167. From 2002 to 2004, Nina Morrison, now a senior staff attorney, served as the Innocence Project's director.
168. Scheck, interview with author.
169. Saloom, interview with author.
170. Ibid.
171. Ibid.
172. Ibid.
173. Aimee Maxwell, interview with author, November 2013.
174. For more, see Findley and Golden, "Innocence Movement," 98.
175. These are not exclusive. The Innocence Project is always looking at compensation and may become involved in some other issues, but it tends to stick with a small set of priority reforms.

176. Karen Newirth, interview with author, July 2014.

177. Maxwell, interview with author; see also Findley and Golden, "Innocence Movement," 96. Meredith Kennedy told me that the Network Support staff are all employees of the Innocence Project. This is because that group is the only one with the resources and infrastructure to support it. Meredith Kennedy, interview with author, February 2014.

178. Kennedy, interview with author.

179. Ibid.

180. Drizin, interview with author.

181. The Arizona Innocence Project is headed by Robert Schehr in the Department of Criminology and Criminal Justice at Northern Arizona University. The Illinois Innocence Project also seems to be interdisciplinary, headed by professors and former instructors from departments of political studies, legal studies, and criminal justice. The Idaho Innocence Project is housed in the Biology Department at Boise State University.

182. Innocence Network, *2014 Innocence Network Annual Report Summary*.

183. Mumma, interview with author.

184. Innocence Network, *2014 Innocence Network Annual Report Summary*.

185. Ibid.

186. Ibid.

187. Gross et al., "Rate of False Conviction."

188. See Risinger, "Innocents Convicted"; Poveda, "Estimating Wrongful Convictions."

189. These critiques and concerns are discussed in-depth in the conclusion of the book.

190. Garrett, *Convicting the Innocent*.

191. Samuel Gross, interview with author, June 2014.

192. Ibid.; Possley, interview with author.

193. Possley, interview with author.

194. Gross, interview with author.

195. Possley, interview with author.

196. Scheck, interview with author.

197. For more on the struggles faced by exonerees post-release, see Westervelt and Cook, *Life after Death Row*.

198. Witness to Innocence is a Philadelphia-based organization dedicated specifically to death row exonerees. Resurrection After Exoneration, founded by exoneree John Thompson, is based in New Orleans. A third Network member dedicated to post-release work, Life After Innocence, is based out of Loyola University's School of Law in Chicago and helps exonerees secure legal and social services after release.

199. For more on exoneree compensation, see Norris, "Assessing Compensation Statutes"; Norris, "Exoneree Compensation."

200. Newman, interview with author. Sessions such as these, as well as others on topics such as fund-raising basics, were on the agenda at all of the Innocence Network conferences I attended.

201. Jane Raley, interview with author, June 2014.

202. Judy Royal, interview with author, June 2014.

203. Erika Applebaum, interview with author, January 2014.

204. Kennedy, interview with author.

205. Newman, interview with author.

206. Maxwell, interview with author. The Innocence Network maintains a list of all amicus briefs filed, which totals more than 100. See Innocence Network, "Brief Bank."

207. Newman, interview with author.

208. Maxwell, interview with author.

209. The session at the 2014 Innocence Network conference was titled "The International Association of Chiefs of Police: Plans for Preventing Wrongful Convictions and the Potential Collaborations with Network Members" and featured three International Association of Chiefs of Police representatives discussing their summit, policy recommendations, and what needs to be done moving forward.

210. See, generally, National Research Council, *Strengthening Forensic Science*.

211. Hsu, "Justice Dept., FBI to Review."

212. FBI, "FBI Testimony on Microscopic Hair Analysis."

213. Hsu, "After FBI Admits." Perrot's conviction was overturned in early 2016, and he was released. See Augenstein, "1992 Rape Conviction."

214. Allocca, "FBI Admits Flaws"; Augenstein, "1992 Rape Conviction."

215. Hsu, "After FBI Admits"; Hsu, "Justice Dept., FBI to Review"; Hsu, "FBI Admits Flaws"; Lithwick, "Pseudoscience in the Witness Box"; Pilkington, "Thirty Years in Jail."

216. See Hsu, "Justice Dept. to Expand Review."

217. Mumma, interview with author.

218. See New York State Justice Task Force home page, accessed June 29, 2016, www.nyjusticetaskforce.com.

219. *Glossip v. Gross*, 135 U.S. 2726 (2015).

220. Mumma, interview with author; see also the North Carolina Innocence Inquiry Commission, "Cases."

221. Schultz, "Review: *Serial*."

222. J. Woodruff, "What 'Serial'-mania Says."

223. Barone, "Podcasts Seek Visibility"; Hesse, "'Serial' Takes the Stand"; Larson, "'Serial': The Podcast We've Been Waiting For"; Maine, "TV Show Based on the Serial Podcast"; Nyman, "Just How Popular."

224. M. Murphy, "Story behind a True Crime Documentary."

225. Hale, "Review: 'Making a Murderer.'"

226. Tassi, "Why 'Making a Murderer.'"

227. Nededog, "Here's How Popular."

228. Tassi, "Why 'Making a Murderer.'"

229. It is worth noting that President Barack Obama responded to the petition, encouraging citizen participation but pointing out that he has no authority to issue a pardon in a state case.

230. This appears to have been a clear trend, on the basis of the documents I found in the National Death Penalty Archive. For example, Rev. Augustine Judd, "Respect Life: The Gospel of Life and the Sentence of Death: Catholic Teaching on Capital Punishment"; "National Press Club Luncheon with Cardinal Roger Mahony, Archbishop of Los Angeles Archdiocese, The Death Penalty, Moderator Jack Cushman," May 25, 2000; Taylor, "Death Penalty," 451.

231. Richard Dieter, "Memo to DPIC Board Members," June 18, 1999, Steven Hawkins Collection, National Death Penalty Archive, Albany, NY.

232. Ibid.

CHAPTER 4. "IT DID GO AGAINST THE GRAIN"

1. Zalman, "Integrated Justice Model," 1485.

2. Walker, *Popular Justice*, 180–181.

3. *Mapp v. Ohio*, 367 U.S. 643 (1961); *Miranda v. Arizona*, 384 U.S. 436 (1966).

4. *Gideon v. Wainwright*, 372 U.S. 335 (1963).

5. This is far from an extensive account of all prison reform during this era. Samuel Walker provides more detail in his history of criminal justice in the United States. Walker, *Popular Justice*.

6. Ibid., 188.

7. See Haines, *Against Capital Punishment*, 189–191.

8. *Furman v. Georgia*, 408 U.S. 238 (1972).

9. See Scheingold, *Politics of Rights*; Walker, *Popular Justice*, 191–193.

10. Walker, *Popular Justice*, 195–197.

11. Retrieved from the FBI's Uniform Crime Report online database, available at www.fbi.gov.

12. Walker, *Popular Justice*, 205, 209.

13. Figures retrieved from the Sourcebook of Criminal Justice Statistics, available at www.albany.edu/sourcebook/.

14. See Packer, *Limits of the Criminal Sanction*.

15. *United States v. Salerno*, 481 U.S. 739 (1979).

16. For a review of the Court's involvement in issues of prisoners' rights, see Call, "Supreme Court and Prisoners' Rights." For specific case examples of the Supreme Court backing off of its regulation of prison conditions, see *Bell v. Wolfish*, 441 U.S. 520 (1979); *Rhodes v. Chapman*, 452 U.S. 337 (1981).

17. In *United States v. Leon*, 468 U.S. 897 (1984), the Supreme Court created a "good faith" exception to the exclusionary rule. The ruling held that if a warrant was mistakenly issued, evidence seized would still be admissible, in part because in such cases, the exclusionary rule could lead to the guilty going unpunished, causing the public to lose respect for the law.

18. In *New York v. Quarles*, 467 U.S. 649 (1984), the Supreme Court created a public safety exception to the *Miranda* requirements.

19. See, for example, Wilson, *Thinking about Crime*; van den Haag, *Punishing Criminals*.

20. Sentencing Project, "Trends in U.S. Corrections."
21. For more on crack-cocaine sentencing policy, see Sentencing Project, "Crack Cocaine Sentencing Policy."
22. Three-strikes laws were popular, at least in theory; offenders who twice before were convicted and released, yet still continued to commit serious crimes, would be given long-term sentences. In practice, however, they often resulted in long sentences for relatively minor offenses. Perhaps the most notable example of this is the case of the "pizza thief," in which a repeat offender was given 25 years to life for what is usually a petty theft. See Slater, "Pizza Thief Receives Sentence."
23. Walker, *Popular Justice*, 227–230; Laqueur, Rushin, and Simon, "Wrongful Conviction."
24. Justice Policy Institute, "Punishing Decade"; Sentencing Project, "Trends in U.S. Corrections."
25. Garland, *Culture of Control*, 12.
26. Garland, "Culture of High Crime Societies," 350.
27. These figures are based on information retrieved from the Death Penalty Information Center, available at www.deathpenaltyinfo.org.
28. Walker, *Popular Justice*, 239–241; see, generally, Garland, *Culture of Control*.
29. Walker, *Popular Justice*, 240.
30. Scheingold, *Politics of Law and Order*; see also McGarrell and Castellano, "Integrative Conflict Model."
31. Garland, *Culture of Control*, viii.
32. Beckett, *Making Crime Pay*; Beckett and Sasson, *Politics of Injustice*.
33. Tonry, *Thinking about Crime*.
34. Simon, *Governing through Crime*.
35. Alexander, *New Jim Crow*; Cohn, Barkan, and Halteman, "Punitive Attitudes toward Criminals."
36. Barak, "Between the Waves"; Ericson, "Mass Media, Crime, Law, and Justice."
37. Barry Scheck has referred to DNA as a "magic bullet." Scheck, interview by Kreisler.
38. Peter Neufeld, interview with author, April 2014.
39. Neufeld, interview by Kreisler.
40. Paul Casteleiro, interview with author, January 2014.
41. Madeline deLone, interview with author, October 2013.
42. Maurice, Possley, interview with author, January 2014.
43. Casteleiro, interview with author.
44. Possley, interview with author.
45. Warden, "Four Decades."
46. Casteleiro, interview with author.
47. Possley, interview with author.
48. DeLone interview with author.
49. Possley, interview with author.
50. Barry Scheck, interview with author, February 2014.

51. Aronson, *Genetic Witness*, 19.
52. Zalman, "Integrated Justice Model."
53. McCarthy and Zald, "Resource Mobilization and Social Movements."
54. Jim McCloskey, interview with author, December 2013.
55. Scheck, interview by Kreisler.
56. Neufeld, interview by Kreisler.
57. Menkel-Meadow, "Causes of Cause Lawyering," 37.
58. See Higginbotham, *In the Matter of Color*; Forbath, *Law and the Shaping of the American Labor Movement*; see also Menkel-Meadow, "Causes of Cause Lawyering," 42–43.
59. McCann and Dudas, "Retrenchment . . . and Resurgence?," 49.
60. Krishnan, "Lawyering for a Cause," 575–576; McCann and Dudas, "Retrenchment . . . and Resurgence?," 49; Menkel-Meadow, "Causes of Cause Lawyering," 43; Greenberg, *Crusaders in the Courts*.
61. Neufeld, interview by Kreisler.
62. Scheck, interview by Kreisler.
63. Ibid.
64. Ibid.
65. Kate Germond, interview with author, January 2014.
66. Warden, "Four Decades."
67. C. Ronald Huff, interview with author, November 2013.
68. DeLone, interview with author.
69. Germond, interview with author.
70. Casteleiro, interview with author.
71. Neufeld, interview for "What Jennifer Saw."
72. Warden, "Four Decades."
73. See Munsterberg, *On the Witness Stand*.
74. See, for example, Loftus, *Eyewitness Testimony*; Wells and Loftus, *Eyewitness Testimony*.
75. Huff, interview with author.
76. Huff et al., "Guilty until Proved Innocent," 523.
77. Bedau and Radelet, "Miscarriages of Justice."
78. Radelet, Bedau, and Putnam, *In Spite of Innocence*.
79. Warden, "Four Decades."
80. Reno, "Message from the Attorney General," iii.
81. Aronson, *Genetic Witness*, 17.
82. Department of Genetics, "History of Genetic Fingerprinting."
83. Jeffreys, quoted in Wellcome Trust: The Human Genome, "DNA Fingerprinting Enters Society."
84. Aronson, *Genetic Witness*, 19.
85. Ibid., 31–32.
86. Reno, "Message from the Attorney General," iii.
87. Zalman, "Integrated Justice Model," 1485.

88. See Garland, *Culture of Control.*
89. Baumgartner, De Boef, and Boydstun, *Decline of the Death Penalty*, 8.
90. Neufeld, interview with author.
91. Scheck, interview with author.
92. Possley, interview with author.
93. Kate Germond and Ron Huff both mentioned this issue to me specifically during our interviews, and similar points were made by others, including Madeline deLone, Stephen Saloom, and more. It is also worth mentioning that Huff and colleagues pointed this out in their 1986 article, when they said that even if the system were accurate 99.5% of the time, it "could still generate nearly 6,000 erroneous convictions (for index crimes alone) each year." Huff et al., "Guilty until Proved Innocent," 523.
94. DeLone, interview with author.
95. Wilson, *Thinking about Crime*, 128.
96. Stephen Saloom, interview with author, October 2013.
97. Possley, interview with author.
98. Richard Dieter, interview with author, May 2014.
99. Saloom, interview with author.
100. Scheck, interview in "What Jennifer Saw."
101. Neufeld, interview in "What Jennifer Saw." Maurice Possley said something remarkably similar during our conversation, saying that DNA "gave us a window into the criminal justice room in a way that hadn't been seen before." Possley, interview with author.
102. Saloom, interview with author.
103. Warden, "Role of the Media," 40.
104. McAdam, McCarthy, and Zald, *Comparative Perspectives on Social Movements*, 8.

CHAPTER 5. "IT'S JUST JUSTICE . . . REAL JUSTICE"
1. See, generally, Garrett, *Convicting the Innocent.*
2. Peter Neufeld, interview with author, April 2014.
3. Trabasso, "Power of the Narrative," 187–188.
4. See, for example, Pennington and Hastie, "Explaining the Evidence."
5. See Posner, "Law and Literature"; Seaton, "Law and Literature."
6. For instance, Jane Murphy discusses cause lawyering and narrative power in efforts to secure changes to domestic-violence laws. See Murphy, "Lawyering for Social Change."
7. Barry Scheck, interview with author, February 2014.
8. Aimee Maxwell, interview with author, November 2013.
9. Stephen Saloom, interview with author, October 2013.
10. It is worth noting that there is much debate about whether Stalin actually ever said this. A simple search-engine query will bring up a number of blogs, forums, and other websites disputing the origin of the quotation. Regardless of whether it was correctly quoted or misattributed, it is useful for making the larger point.

11. See Slovic, "If I Look at the Mass," 80.
12. Maurice Possley, interview with author, January 2014.
13. Madeline deLone, interview with author, October 2013.
14. Terry, "Survivors Make the Case"; see also Davis, "Hope Sought for Innocents"; McLaughlin, "Tales of Journey."
15. Michael Radelet, interview with author, May 2014.
16. Ibid.
17. Scheck, interview with author.
18. Maxwell, interview with author.
19. Jane Raley, interview with author, June 2014.
20. Innocence Network, *2014 Innocence Network Annual Report Summary.*
21. Scheck, interview with author.
22. DeLone, interview with author.
23. Ryan Costello, interview with author, January 2014; Laura Nirider, interview with author, June 2014.
24. Shannon Leitner, interview with author, January 2014.
25. Costello, interview with author.
26. DeLone, interview with author.
27. Ibid.
28. See Munson, *Making of Pro-Life Activists.*
29. Costello, interview with author.
30. Nirider, interview with author.
31. Rob Warden, interview with author, February 2014.
32. Steve Drizin, interview with author, June 2014.
33. Christine Mumma, interview with author, March 2014.
34. McAdam, *Political Process,* 45–46.
35. See, for example, Flam and King, *Emotions and Social Movements*; Goodwin, Jasper, and Polletta, *Passionate Politics.*
36. Centurion Ministries, "Press Release from James C. McCloskey."
37. Frankel, "Burden of Proof."
38. Maxwell, interview with author.
39. Casteleiro, interview with author.
40. Maxwell, interview with author.
41. Warden, "Four Decades."
42. Possley, interview with author.
43. Casteleiro, interview with author.
44. Ibid.
45. Leitner, interview with author.
46. Scheck, interview in "Case for Innocence."
47. McCloskey, quoted in Alperin, "Finding Truth."
48. Leitner, interview with author.
49. Neufeld, interview by Kreisler.
50. Alan Maimon, interview with author, January 2014.

51. McCloskey described two examples of volunteers who have stayed with the organization. One was a math teacher who saw one of Centurion's cases in the newspaper and cut it out. When he retired eight years later, he joined Centurion as a volunteer and worked on case investigation. He has been with the organization since the late 1990s. Another volunteer, a former fraternity brother of McCloskey's and corporate executive, expressed interest in volunteering for McCloskey at a college reunion. Jim McCloskey, interview with author, December 2013.

52. McCloskey, quoted in Alperin, "Finding Truth."

53. Germond, quoted ibid.

54. Warden, interview with author.

55. Neufeld, interview by Kreisler.

56. Ibid.

57. Karen Newirth, interview with author, July 2014.

58. Kate Germond, interview with author, January 2014. Regarding the mementos in the office, at Centurion Ministries in particular, a number of staff members made references to the pictures and news articles on the walls when describing what they do, why they do it, and why they enjoy it so much.

59. McCloskey, interview with author.

60. Maxwell, interview with author.

61. Scheck, interview by Kreisler.

62. Newirth, interview with author.

63. McAdam, *Political Process*, 48.

64. Saloom, interview with author.

65. Ibid.

66. Saloom, interview with author.

67. Neufeld, interview with author.

68. Ibid.

69. Erika Applebaum, interview with author, January 2014.

70. Maxwell, interview with author.

71. Saloom, interview with author.

72. Ibid.

73. See Acker, "Flipside Injustice."

74. McCann and Dudas, "Retrenchment . . . and Resurgence?" 44.

75. C. Ronald Huff, interview with author, November 2013.

76. Mumma, interview with author.

77. Neufeld, interview by Kreisler.

78. Neufeld, interview with author.

79. Scheck, interview by Kreisler.

80. Neufeld, interview by Kreisler. See also Findley, "Toward a New Paradigm."

81. Neufeld, interview with author. Others, including Kate Germond, also agreed with the importance of packaging wrongful convictions as a public safety issue in order to generate widespread support.

82. Scheck, interview with author.

83. See Travis and Waul, "Reflections on the Crime Decline"; see also Zimring, *Great American Crime Decline.*

84. Commonly suggested factors include the increase in imprisonment, new policing strategies, demographic shifts, and a successful economy. For a summary, see Barker, "Explaining the Great American Crime Decline."

85. Neufeld, interview with author.

86. Maxwell, interview with author.

87. See Vitiello, "Alternatives to Incarceration."

88. Maxwell, interview with author.

CHAPTER 6. THE "NEW CIVIL RIGHTS"?

1. Diani, "Concept of Social Movement."

2. McCarthy and Zald, "Resource Mobilization and Social Movements," 1218.

3. Gamson and Meyer, "Framing Political Opportunity," 283.

4. Rosen, "Reflections on Innocence," 237; see also Redlich and Petrila, "Age of Innocence."

5. Findley, "Innocence Found."

6. See Marshall, "Innocence Revolution," 573; Godsey and Pulley, "Innocence Revolution," 266; Medwed, "Emotionally Charged," 2187.

7. See Innocence Project, "As 100th Innocent Prisoner Is Freed"; see also Associated Press, "Spread of Innocence Projects."

8. Medwed, "Innocentrism," 1550.

9. Zalman, "Integrated Justice Model," 1468.

10. Rosen describes some of the popular beliefs about the system that existed as recently as the 1990s, including guilty defendants getting off on technicalities, judges and legislators dismissing innocence, and the desire for swifter executions. He does note that the possibility of convicting the innocent was not completely ignored and that it might be "more accurate to say that wrongful convictions just were not considered enough of a problem to warrant a lot of attention." Rosen, "Reflections on Innocence," 238. Similarly, Mark Godsey and Thomas Pulley describe widespread beliefs that the "system was highly accurate" and suggest that innocence, particularly DNA testing, "have demonstrated the fallacy and naiveté of these beliefs." Godsey and Pulley, "Innocence Revolution," 265–266.

11. Stephen Saloom, interview with author, October 2013.

12. Ibid.

13. Madeline deLone, interview with author, October 2013.

14. Scheck, interview by Kreisler.

15. DeLone, interview with author.

16. Marshall, "Innocence Revolution," 573–574.

17. Scheck, interview by Big Think.

18. Theresa Newman, interview with author, July 2014.

19. Karen Newirth, interview with author, July 2014.

20. C. Ronald Huff, interview with author, November 2013.

21. Jim McCloskey, interview with author, December 2013.
22. Kate Germond, interview with author, January 2014.
23. Erika Applebaum, interview with author, January 2014.
24. Richard Dieter, interview with author, May 2014.
25. Michael Radelet, interview with author, May 2014.
26. Abbe Smith, interview with author, July 2014; Laura Nirider, interview with author, June 2014.
27. Jim Dwyer, interview with author, May 2014.
28. Samuel Gross, interview with author, June 2014.
29. Neufeld, interview by Kreisler.
30. Ibid.
31. Scheck, interview by Kreisler.
32. Peter Neufeld, interview with author, April 2014.
33. This point was raised by an anonymous reviewer of the first draft of this manuscript. Neufeld, Scheck, and Brustin, LLP is a New York–based civil rights law firm, but it is worth noting that its work is not limited only to innocence cases. It handles a variety of civil issues inside and outside New York.
34. Jeremy Travis, interview with author, July 2014.
35. Paul Casteleiro, interview with author, January 2014.
36. Christine Mumma, interview with author, March 2014.
37. Germond, interview with author.
38. Maurice Possley, interview with author, January 2014.
39. Neufeld, interview with author.
40. Steve Drizin, interview with author, June 2014.
41. Nick O'Connell, interview with author, January 2014.
42. Barry Scheck, interview with author, February 2014.
43. Ibid.
44. Griffin, "True Lessons of True Crime."
45. Aimee Maxwell, interview with author, November 2013.
46. Ibid.
47. DeLone, interview with author.
48. See, for example, Sappenfield, "Can Ferguson Spark New Civil Rights Movement?"
49. Rebecca Brown, interview with author, April 2014.
50. Judy Royal, interview with author, June 2014.
51. Brown, interview with author.
52. Newirth, interview with author.
53. Neufeld, interview with author.
54. Ibid.
55. Rob Warden, interview with author, February 2014.
56. Ryan Costello, interview with author, January 2014.
57. Meredith Kennedy, interview with author, February 2014.
58. Alan Maimon, interview with author, January 2014.

59. Shannon Leitner, interview with author, January 2014; Emily West, interview with author, February 2014.
60. See, generally, McAdam, *Political Process*; Morris, *Origins of the Civil Rights Movement*.
61. For more on the gay rights movement, see, generally, Clendinen and Nagourney, *Out for Good*.
62. See, for example, Andersen, *Out of the Closets and into the Courts*.
63. Adele Bernhard, interview with author, July 2014.
64. Nirider, interview with author.
65. Bryan Stevenson said this during his TED Talk. See Stevenson, "We Need to Talk about Injustice."

CONCLUSION

1. Zalman, "Criminal Justice System Reform," 470.
2. For more on preventive policy reforms generally, see Norris et al., "Than That One Innocent Suffer."
3. For more on the post-release struggles of exonerees generally, see Westervelt and Cook, *Life after Death Row*. For more on compensation policies, see Norris, "Assessing Compensation Statutes"; Norris, "Exoneree Compensation."
4. For more on postconviction relief standards, including actual innocence claims, see Brooks, Simpson, and Kaneb, "If Hindsight Is 20/20."
5. An illustrative case and counterpoint is that of Michael Morton, who was convicted of murdering his wife in Texas and spent nearly 25 years in prison. The prosecutor in the case, Ken Anderson, eventually became a judge. However, in 2013, Anderson was sentenced to ten days in jail for intentionally failing to disclose exculpatory evidence in Morton's case. However, Anderson was released after only five days. Godsey, "For the First Time Ever"; Osborn, "How Ken Anderson Was Released."
6. Scheck, interview by Kreisler.
7. Rebecca Brown, interview with author, April 2014.
8. Neufeld, interview by Kreisler.
9. Scheck, interview by Kreisler.
10. A recent exchange in psychology has debated the potential for eyewitness reforms proposed by innocence advocates not only to reduce erroneous identifications but also to reduce correct identifications. See S. Clark, "Costs and Benefits"; S. Clark, "Eyewitness Identification Reform"; Wells, Steblay, and Dysart, "Eyewitness Identification Reforms."
11. Scheck, interview by Kreisler.
12. Nick O'Connell, interview with author, January 2014.
13. Scheck, interview by Kreisler.
14. Ibid.
15. O'Connell, interview with author.
16. Neufeld, interview by Kreisler.

17. In my viewing of an information file developed for legislative-reform priority areas, I saw a section titled "Opponents," though advocates are quick to say that such language is not quite accurate. As Rebecca Brown said, "It's really a bipartisan issue. . . . I think using the term 'opponent' is probably even too extreme. I think there are people that need to be brought along." Brown, interview with author.

18. Ibid.

19. O'Connell, interview with author.

20. Paul Casteleiro said that it "has probably not changed prosecutorial misconduct, presumptions of guilt, [and] bias in the system." Casteleiro, interview with author, January 2014.

21. In this context, noble-cause corruption would suggest that doing things to solve cases—cutting corners, violating certain policies, and so forth—is acceptable because the outcome is to catch criminals and protect society.

22. O'Connell, interview with author.

23. Christine Mumma, interview with author, March 2014.

24. Ibid.

25. Jim Dwyer, quoted in the film *The Central Park Five*. The Central Park Five were a group of black and Latino teens who were convicted of the brutal rape and assault of a woman in New York City's Central Park in April 1989. The boys were finally exonerated in 2002 after DNA showed they were not the rapists and the real offender confessed to the crime. See also Burns, *Central Park Five*.

26. Adele Bernhard, interview with author, July 2014.

27. Theresa Newman, interview with author, July 2014.

28. Barry Scheck, interview with author, February 2014; Scheck, interview by Kreisler.

29. Peter Neufeld, interview with author, April 2014.

30. Scheck, interview by Kreisler.

31. Casteleiro, interview with author.

32. Sloan, "ABA Tackles Law School Debt."

33. Casteleiro, interview with author.

34. Newman, interview with author.

35. Steve Drizin, interview with author, June 2014.

36. Bernhard, interview with author.

37. Scheck, interview by Kreisler.

38. Bernhard, interview with author; Newman, interview with author; Scheck, interview by Kreisler.

39. Jane Raley, interview with author, June 2014.

40. Casteleiro, interview with author.

41. Jim McCloskey, interview with author, December 2013.

42. Stephen Saloom, interview with author, October 2013.

43. Aimee Maxwell, interview with author, November 2013.

44. Erika Applebaum, interview with author, January 2014.

45. Maurice Possley, interview with author, January 2014.

46. McCloskey, interview with author.
47. Judy Royal, interview with author, June 2014.
48. Applebaum, interview with author.
49. Griffin, "True Lessons."
50. *United States v. Garsson*, 291 F. 646, 649 (S.D.N.Y. 1923).
51. Borchard, *Convicting the Innocent*, v.
52. Knight-Ridder Newspapers, "Meese's Miranda Reply."
53. Gross et al., "Rate of False Conviction."
54. Cassell, "Guilty and the 'Innocent,'" 536.
55. *Kansas v. Marsh*, 548 U.S. 163, 197–198 (2006); Scalia cited Marquis, "Innocent and the Shammed."
56. Hoffman, "Myth of Factual Innocence," 668.
57. Ibid., 673; Hoffman, "'Innocence' Myth."
58. Allen and Laudan, "Deadly Dilemmas," 71.
59. Joshua Marquis, interview with author, July 2014.
60. Ibid.
61. Cassell, "We're Not Executing the Innocent."
62. This was a major point for the death penalty supporter Ernest van den Haag, who said that activities such as trucking and construction regularly involve deaths but are continued. Van den Haag, "Ultimate Punishment," 1665.
63. Allen and Shavell, "Further Reflections on the Guillotine," 628.
64. Marquis, interview with author.
65. Markman and Cassell, "Protecting the Innocent"; Cassell, "Guilty and the 'Innocent.'"
66. Marquis, interview with author.
67. Ibid.
68. Hoffman, "Myth of Factual Innocence," 684–689.
69. For more on the social constructionist perspective and innocence issues, see Norris and Bonventre, "Advancing Wrongful Conviction Scholarship."
70. *Herrera v. Collins*, 506 U.S. 390, 398 (1993).
71. Ibid., 420.
72. Allen and Laudan, "Deadly Dilemmas," 68.
73. Hoffman, "Myth of Factual Innocence," 688–689.
74. Bowers argues that most innocent defendants are repeat offenders and that most crimes with which they are wrongly charged are minor ones, so pleading guilty actually helps them reduce their punishment, since there are such high pretrial process costs. See Bowers, "Punishing the Innocent."
75. See Bowers, "Legal Guilt."
76. Steiker and Steiker, "Seduction of Innocence," 597–600.
77. Hoffman, "Myth of Factual Innocence," 685–687; Steiker and Steiker, "Seduction of Innocence," 618–621.
78. Abbe Smith, interview with author, July 2014; see also Abbe Smith, "In Praise of the Guilty Project."

79. Smith, interview with author.
80. Drizin, interview with author.
81. Smith, interview with author.
82. Siegel, "Moving Down the Wedge of Injustice," 1222.
83. See Bakken and Steel, "Exonerating the Innocent."
84. Medwed, "Innocentrism"; Risinger and Risinger, "Innocence is Different."
85. Smith, interview with author.
86. For example, Adele Bernhard said that she does not see this as a legitimate critique, as she has not seen any decrease in interest among students in representing clients in general. "In terms of being on the ground at the law school level, I have not seen any diminishing interest on the students' part. They're still just as interested in joining the criminal defense clinic or the prosecution clinic, even if they've been in my [innocence] clinic." Bernhard, interview with author.
87. Meredith Kennedy, interview with author, February 2014.
88. Newman, interview with author.
89. Mumma, interview with author.
90. Kennedy, interview with author.
91. Ibid.
92. Ibid.
93. Neufeld, interview with author.
94. Ibid.
95. Rob Warden, interview with author, February 2014.
96. Bernhard, interview with author.
97. Warden, interview with author.
98. Neufeld, interview with author.
99. Scheck, interview with author.
100. Neufeld, interview with author.
101. Royal, interview with author.
102. Both Maurice Possley and Rob Warden pointed this out specifically. For instance, Warden mentioned how involved the Innocence Project was in the Cameron Todd Willingham arson case in Texas, a highly questionable arson case that did not involve DNA, in which a man was executed despite serious doubts about his guilt. Possley, interview with author; Warden, interview with author.
103. Neufeld, interview with author.
104. Scheck, interview with author.
105. Raley, interview with author.
106. O'Connell, interview with author.
107. Karen Newirth, interview with author, July 2014.
108. Casteleiro, interview with author.
109. Newman, interview with author.
110. Smith, interview with author.
111. Drizin, interview with author.
112. Possley, interview with author.

113. Maxwell, interview with author.
114. Casteleiro, interview with author.
115. McCloskey, interview with author.

APPENDIX

1. See Foucault, *Discipline and Punish*, 31; Garland, "What Is a 'History of the Present'?"; see also Garland, *Culture of Control*, 2.
2. Snow and Trom, "Case Study," 150.
3. Weiss, *Learning from Strangers*, 59.
4. Blee and Taylor, "Semi-Structured Interviewing," 102.
5. My conversation with Jim Dwyer lasted only 16 minutes and occurred on the phone while he was driving. On the other side of the spectrum, my conversation with Joshua Marquis lasted more than two hours.
6. Garland, *Culture of Control*, vii.

REFERENCES

Acker, James R. "The Flipside Injustice of Wrongful Convictions: When the Guilty Go Free." *Albany Law Review* 76 (2013): 1629–1712.

"Actual Innocence: Five Days to Execution, and Other Dispatches from the Wrongly Convicted." *Publishers Weekly*, January 31, 2000. http://publishersweekly.com.

Alexander, Michelle. *The New Jim Crow: Mass Incarceration in the Age of Colorblindness*. New York: New Press, 2012.

Allen, Ronald J., and Larry Laudan. "Deadly Dilemmas." *Texas Tech Law Review* 41 (2008): 65–92.

Allen, Ronald J., and Amy Shavell. "Further Reflections on the Guillotine." *Journal of Criminal Law and Criminology* 95 (2005): 625–636.

Allocca, Sean. "FBI Admits Flaws in Hair Analysis Spanning Two Decades." *Forensic Magazine*, April 20, 2015.

Alperin, Michele. "Finding Truth That May Set Someone Free." *U.S. 1* (Princeton, NJ), January 14, 2009.

Andersen, Ellen Ann. *Out of the Closets and into the Courts: Legal Opportunity Structure and Gay Rights Litigation*. Ann Arbor: University of Michigan Press, 2006.

Anderson, John. "Op-ed Films for the Ages." *Variety*, February 19, 2006.

Aronson, Jay D. *Genetic Witness: Science, Law and Controversy in the Making of DNA Profiling*. New Brunswick, NJ: Rutgers University Press, 2007.

Associated Press. "Death Row Survivors Meet at Law School Conference: 'Where I've Been and Not to Be Able to Hate Is a Miracle,' Ex-Prisoner Says." *St. Louis Post-Dispatch*, November 15, 1998.

———. "'Fantastic!': Innocent Man Out of Prison after 9 Years." *Palm Beach (FL) Post*, June 29, 1993.

———. "Former Ill. Governor George Ryan Released from Custody." *USA Today*, July 3, 2013.

———. "Gary Dotson Set Free on Bond in Rape Case." *New York Times*, May 2, 1985.

———. "Illinois Governor Plans to Halt Death Penalty, a Report Says." *New York Times*, January 31, 2000.

———. "Illinois Governor's Blanket Pardon Spares Lives of 167 Condemned Inmates." *Fox News*, January 11, 2003.

———. "Illinois Governor Withholds Decision in 1977 Rape Case." *New York Times*, October 25, 1988.

———. "Parole Revoked in Case of Commuted Rape Term." *New York Times*, September 5, 1987.

———. "Prosecutors Drop Charges of Rape 4 Years after Accuser Recanted." *New York Times*, August 15, 1989.

———. "Spread of Innocence Projects Seen as 'New Civil Rights Movement.'" *Dallas Morning News*, June 6, 2002.

Augenstein, Seth. "1992 Rape Conviction Overturned Due to Flawed FBI Hair Analysis." *Forensic Magazine*, February 3, 2016.

Bakken, Tim, and Lewis M. Steel. "Exonerating the Innocent: Pretrial Innocence Procedures." *New York Law School Law Review* 56 (2011–2012): 825–834.

Barak, Gregg. "Between the Waves: Mass-Mediated Themes of Crime and Justice." *Social Justice* 21 (1994): 133–147.

Barker, Vanessa. "Explaining the Great American Crime Decline: A Review of Blumstein and Wallman, Goldberger and Rosenfeld, and Zimring." *Law and Social Inquiry* 35 (2010): 489–516.

Barnum, Art. "Birkett Sues over Clemencies." *Chicago Tribune*, February 6, 2003.

Barone, Joshua. "Podcasts Seek Visibility via Festivals." *New York Times*, July 25, 2015.

Baumgartner, Frank R., Suzanna L. De Boef, and Amber E. Boydstun. *The Decline of the Death Penalty and the Discovery of Innocence*. New York: Cambridge University Press, 2008.

BBC News. "DNA Pioneer's 'Eureka' Moment." September 9, 2009. http://news.bbc.co.uk.

Beckett, Katherine. *Making Crime Pay: Law and Order in Contemporary American Politics*. New York: Oxford University Press, 1997.

Beckett, Katherine, and Theodore Sasson. *The Politics of Injustice: Crime and Punishment in America*. Thousand Oaks, CA: Sage, 2004.

Bedau, Hugo Adam, ed. *The Death Penalty in America: Current Controversies*. New York: Oxford University Press, 1997.

———. "Innocence and the Death Penalty: Assessing the Danger of Mistaken Executions." In *The Death Penalty in America: Current Controversies*, edited by Hugo Adam Bedau, 344–360. New York: Oxford University Press, 1997.

Bedau, Hugo Adam, and Michael L. Radelet. "Miscarriages of Justice in Potentially Capital Cases." *Stanford Law Review* 40 (1987): 21–179.

———. "The Myth of Infallibility: A Reply to Markman and Cassell." *Stanford Law Review* 41 (1988): 161–170.

Bell v. Wolfish, 441 U.S. 520 (1979).

"Bills to Stop Executing the Innocent." *New York Times*, April 4, 2000.

Blackstone, William. *Commentaries on the Laws of England*. Oxford, UK, 1769.

Blee, Kathleen M., and Verta Taylor. "Semi-structured Interviewing in Social Movement Research." In *Methods of Social Movement Research*, edited by Bert Klandermans and Suzanne Staggenborg, 92–117. Minneapolis: University of Minnesota Press, 2002.

Borchard, Edwin M. *Convicting the Innocent: Errors of Criminal Justice*. New Haven, CT: Yale University Press, 1932.

———. "European Systems of State Indemnity for Errors of Criminal Justice." *Journal of the American Institute of Criminal Law and Criminology* 3 (1913): 684–718.

———. "State Indemnity for Errors of Criminal Justice." *Boston University Law Review* 21 (1941): 201–211.

Bowers, Josh. "Legal Guilt, Normative Innocence, and the Equitable Decision Not to Prosecute." *Columbia Law Review* 110 (2010): 1655–1726.

———. "Punishing the Innocent." *University of Pennsylvania Law Review* 156 (2008): 1117–1179.

Bright, Stephen B. "A Smooth Road to the Death House." *New York Times*, February 7, 2000.

Brooks, Justin, Alexander Simpson, and Paige Kaneb. "If Hindsight Is 20/20, Our Justice System Shouldn't Be Blind to New Evidence of Innocence: A Survey of Post-conviction New Evidence Statutes and a Proposed Model." *Albany Law Review* 79 (2016).

Burns, Sarah. *The Central Park Five: A Chronicle of a City Wilding*. New York: Knopf, 2011.

Bush, Rudolph. "Jackson Asks Total Clemency." *Chicago Tribune*, January 1, 2003.

Byrne, Dennis. "To Kill a 'Legacy.'" *Chicago Tribune*, October 21, 2002.

Call, Jack E. "The Supreme Court and Prisoners' Rights." *Federal Probation* 50 (1995): 36–46.

Cantwell, Guy. "Brandley Free after 10 Years." *Houston Post*, January 24, 1990.

Carter, Rubin, and Ken Klonsky. *Eye of the Hurricane: My Path from Darkness to Freedom*. Chicago: Lawrence Hill Books, 2011.

Cassell, Paul G. "The Guilty and the 'Innocent': An Examination of Alleged Cases of Wrongful Conviction from False Confessions." *Harvard Journal of Law and Public Policy* 22 (1999): 523–603.

———. "We're Not Executing the Innocent." *Wall Street Journal*, June 16, 2000.

Castaneda, Carol J. "DNA Evidence Spells Freedom." *USA Today*, June 29, 1993.

Central Park Five, The. Directed by Ken Burns, David McMahon, and Sarah Burns. New York: IFC Video, 2013. DVD.

Centurion Ministries. "Clarence Brandley." Accessed November 15, 2013, www.centurionministries.org.

———. "Jorge De Los Santos." Accessed November 15, 2013, www.centurionministries.org.

———. "Joyce Ann Brown." Accessed November 15, 2013, www.centurionministries.org.

———. "1980–1989." Accessed June 27, 2016, www.centurionministries.org.

———. "Press Release from James C. McCloskey, Executive Director of Centurion Ministries, Inc. on the Roger Coleman DNA Testing Results." January 12, 2006. www.centurionministries.org.

Chakraborty, Ranajit, and Kenneth Kidd. "The Utility of DNA Typing in Forensic Work." *Science* 254 (1991): 1735–1739.

Chase, John. "Final Appeal for Clemency Made." *Chicago Tribune*, January 10, 2003.

Chin, Paula, and Meg Grant. "Convicted of Murdering One of His Children, James Richardson Hopes the Truth Will Set Him Free." *People*, March 6, 1989.

Christianson, Scott. *Innocent: Inside Wrongful Conviction Cases.* New York: NYU Press, 2004.

Clark, Charles E. "Edwin Borchard." *Yale Law Journal* 60 (1951): 1071–1072.

Clark, Steven E. "Costs and Benefits of Eyewitness Identification Reform: Psychological Science and Public Policy." *Perspectives on Psychological Science* 7 (2012): 238–259.

———. "Eyewitness Identification Reform: Data, Theory, and Due Process." *Perspectives on Psychological Science* 7 (2012): 279–283.

Clendinen, Dudley, and Adam Nagourney. *Out for Good: The Struggle to Build a Gay Rights Movement in America.* New York: Touchstone, 1999.

Cohn, Steven F., Steven E. Barkan, and William A. Halteman. "Punitive Attitudes toward Criminals: Racial Consensus or Racial Conflict?" *Social Problems* 38 (1991): 287–296.

Connors, Edward, Thomas Lundregan, Neal Miller, and Tom McEwen. *Convicted by Juries, Exonerated by Science: Case Studies in the Use of DNA Evidence to Establish Innocence after Trial.* Washington, DC: National Institute of Justice, June 1996.

Cox, Paul. "McCloskey Labors to Exonerate Innocent Prisoners." *Newark (NJ) Star-Ledger,* October 2, 2008.

Cummings, Ian. "Richardson Compensation Bill Passes." *Sarasota (FL) Herald-Tribune,* May 2, 2014.

D'Alessio, F. N. "Execution Freeze Tops News." *Chicago Sun-Times,* December 23, 2000.

Daubert v. Merrell Dow Pharmaceuticals, Inc., 509 U.S. 579 (1993).

Davis, Kevin. "Hope Sought for Innocents Sentenced to Die: Conference Will Feature Their Stories." *USA Today,* November 13, 1998.

"Death Penalty in a Democracy, The." *New York Times,* February 5, 2000.

Death Penalty Information Center. "Executions by Year since 1976." Accessed December 14, 2014, www.deathpenaltyinfo.org.

———. *Innocence and the Death Penalty: Assessing the Danger of Mistaken Executions.* 1993. Accessed December 14, 2014, www.deathpenaltyinfo.org.

———. "Innocence Cases." Accessed December 14, 2014, www.deathpenaltyinfo.org.

———. "The Innocence List." Accessed May 12, 2015, www.deathpenaltyinfo.org.

"Death Penalty States Kill the Innocent Sometimes: More than 30 Who Had Been Condemned to Die Are Witnesses." *Portland (ME) Press Herald,* November 14, 1998.

Department of Genetics, University of Leicester. "The History of Genetic Fingerprinting." Accessed December 10, 2014, https://le.ac.uk/.

Diani, Mario. "The Concept of Social Movement." *Sociological Review* 40 (1992): 1–25.

Dieter, Richard C. "A Crisis of Confidence: Americans' Doubts about the Death Penalty." In *Against the Death Penalty: International Initiatives and Implications,* edited by Jon Yorke, 187–203. Burlington, VT: Ashgate, 2008.

———. *Innocence and the Death Penalty: The Increasing Danger of Executing the Innocent.* Washington, DC: Death Penalty Information Center, July 1997.

"DNA Test Case." *Schenectady (NY) Gazette,* July 28, 1988.

Dwyer, Jim. "The System's Dead Wrong: Tales of Bad-Rap Capital Cases." *New York Daily News,* November 17, 1998.

Ebert, Roger. "The Thin Blue Line." Accessed December 10, 2014, www.errolmorris. com.

Egan, Timothy. "After Simpson Trial, Inquiries and Deals: Some Move to Market Celebrity, While Others Face New Scrutiny." *New York Times*, October 6, 1995.

Ehrmann, Sara. "For Whom the Chair Waits." *Federal Probation* 26 (1962): 14–25.

Emily, Jennifer. "Dallas County District Attorney's Conviction Integrity Unit to Focus on Non-DNA Cases." *Dallas Morning News*, May 23, 2010.

Ericson, Richard V. "Mass Media, Crime, Law, and Justice: An Institutional Approach." *British Journal of Criminology* 31 (1991): 219–249.

FBI. "FBI Testimony on Microscopic Hair Analysis Contained Errors in at Least 90 Percent of Cases in Ongoing Review." Press release. April 20, 2015. www.fbi.gov.

Findley, Keith. "Innocence Found: The Rise of the Innocence Movement in America." Presentation at the annual meeting of the American Society of Criminology, Chicago, IL, November 2012.

———. "The Pedagogy of Innocence: Reflections on the Role of Innocence Projects in Clinical Legal Education." *Clinical Law Review* 13 (2006): 1101–1148.

———. "Toward a New Paradigm of Criminal Justice: How the Innocence Movement Merges Crime Control and Due Process." *Texas Tech Law Review* 41 (2008): 133–175.

Findley, Keith A., and Larry Golden. "The Innocence Movement, the Innocence Network, and Policy Reform." In *Wrongful Conviction and Criminal Justice Reform: Making Justice*, edited by Marvin Zalman and Julia Carrano, 93–110. New York: Routledge, 2014.

Flam, Helena, and Debra King. *Emotions and Social Movements*. New York: Routledge, 2005.

Forbath, William E. *Law and the Shaping of the American Labor Movement*. Cambridge, MA: Harvard University Press, 1989.

Foucault, Michel. *Discipline and Punish: The Birth of the Prison*. New York: Vintage Books, 1979.

Frank, Jerome, and Barbara Frank. *Not Guilty*. New York: Da Capo, 1957.

Frankel, Glenn. "Burden of Proof." *Washington Post*, May 14, 2006.

Frum, David. "The Justice Americans Demand." *New York Times*, February 4, 2000.

Frye v. United States, 293 F. 1013 (D.C. Cir. 1923).

Furman v. Georgia, 408 U.S. 238 (1972).

Gamson, William A., and David S. Meyer. "Framing Political Opportunity." In *Comparative Perspectives on Social Movements*, edited by Doug McAdam, John D. McCarthy, and Mayer N. Zald, 275–290. New York: Cambridge University Press, 1996.

Gardner, Erle Stanley. *The Court of Last Resort*. New York: William Sloane Associates, 1952.

Garland, David. *The Culture of Control: Crime and Social Order in Contemporary Society*. Chicago: University of Chicago Press, 2001.

———. "The Culture of High Crime Societies: Some Preconditions of Recent 'Law and Order' Policies." *British Journal of Criminology* 40 (2000): 347–375.

———. "What Is a 'History of the Present'? On Foucault's Genealogies and Critical Preconditions." *Punishment and Society* 16 (2014): 365–384.

Garrett, Brandon L. *Convicting the Innocent: Where Criminal Prosecutions Go Wrong.* Cambridge, MA: Harvard University Press, 2011.

Gershman, Bennett L. "The Thin Blue Line: Art or Trial in the Fact-Finding Process?" *Pace Law Review* 9 (1989): 275–317.

Getz, Jim. "Local Lawyers Have Varied Reactions to Moratorium on Executions." *St. Louis Post-Dispatch*, February 1, 2000.

Gideon v. Wainwright, 372 U.S. 335 (1963).

Gitschier, Jane. "The Innocence Project at Twenty: An Interview with Barry Scheck." *PLOS Genetics*, August 8, 2013.

Giusti, Alan M., Michael Baird, S. Pasquale, Ivan Balazs, and J. Glassberg. "Application of Deoxyribonucleic Acid (DNA) Polymorphisms to the Analysis of DNA Recovered from Sperm." *Journal of Forensic Sciences* 31 (1986): 409–417.

Glaze, Lauren E., and Danielle Kaeble. *Correctional Populations in the United States, 2013.* Washington, DC: Bureau of Justice Statistics, U.S. Department of Justice, 2014.

Glossip v. Gross, 135 U.S. 2726 (2015).

Godsey, Mark A. "For the First Time Ever, a Prosecutor Will Go to Jail for Wrongfully Convicting an Innocent Man." *Huffington Post*, November 8, 2013. www.huffington-post.com.

Godsey, Mark A., and Thomas Pulley. "The Innocence Revolution and Our 'Evolving Standards of Decency' in Death Penalty Jurisprudence." *University of Dayton Law Review* 29 (2004): 265–292.

Goldstein, Amy. "DNA Test May Free Man Once Sentenced to Death." *Washington Post*, June 28, 1993.

Goodwin, Jeff, James M. Jasper, and Francesca Polletta. *Passionate Politics: Emotions and Social Movements.* Chicago: University of Chicago Press, 2001.

Gould, Jon B. *The Innocence Commission: Preventing Wrongful Convictions and Restoring the Criminal Justice System.* New York: NYU Press, 2008.

"Governor Dukakis Discusses Impending Exoneration of Sacco and Vanzeti." *Today Show*, July 19, 1977. Transcript accessed February 25, 2015.

"Governor Ryan's Brave Example." *New York Times*, July 3, 2000.

"Governor Thompson's Justice." *New York Times*, May 14, 1985.

Greenberg, Jack. *Crusaders in the Courts: How a Dedicated Band of Lawyers Fought for the Civil Rights Revolution.* New York: Basic Books, 1994.

Gregg v. Georgia, 428 U.S. 153 (1976).

Griffin, Lisa Kern. "The True Lessons of True Crime." *New York Times*, January 12, 2016.

Grisham, John. *The Confession.* New York: Doubleday, 2010.

———. *The Innocent Man.* New York: Doubleday, 2006.

Gross, Samuel R. "Loss of Innocence: Eyewitness Identification and Proof of Guilt." *Journal of Legal Studies* 16 (1987): 395–453.

Gross, Samuel R., Barbara O'Brien, Chen Hu, and Edward H. Kennedy. "Rate of False Conviction of Criminal Defendants Who Are Sentenced to Death." *Proceedings of the National Academy of Sciences of the United States of America* 111 (2014): 7230–7235.

Gumbel, Andrew. "Death Row Survivors Call for Abolition." *Independent* (UK), November 16, 1998.

Haines, Herbert H. *Against Capital Punishment: The Anti–Death Penalty Movement in America, 1972–1994*. New York: Oxford University Press, 1996.

Hale, Mike. "Review: 'Making a Murderer,' True Crime on Netflix." *New York Times*, December 16, 2015.

Harmon, Rockne P. "Please Leave Law to the Lawyers." *American Journal of Human Genetics* 49 (1991): 891.

Hartung, Stephanie Roberts. "Legal Education in the Age of Innocence: Integrating Wrongful Conviction Advocacy into the Legal Writing Curriculum." *Boston University Public Interest Law Journal* 22 (2013): 129–163.

Hentoff, Nat. "Not Dead Yet." *Washington Post*, October 31, 1998.

Herbert, Bob. "Criminal Justice Breakdown." *New York Times*, February 14, 2000.

Herrera v. Collins, 506 U.S. 390 (1993).

Hesse, Monica. "'Serial' Takes the Stand: How a Podcast Became a Character in Its Own Narrative." *Washington Post*, February 8, 2016.

Higginbotham, A. Leon. *In the Matter of Color: Race and the American Legal Process*. New York: Oxford University Press, 1978.

Hirsch, James S. *Hurricane: The Miraculous Journey of Rubin Carter*. New York: Houghton Mifflin, 2000.

Hoffman, Morris B. "The 'Innocence' Myth." *Wall Street Journal*, April 26, 2007.

———. "The Myth of Factual Innocence." *Chicago-Kent Law Review* 82 (2007): 663–690.

Holmes, Steven A. "Look Who's Questioning the Death Penalty." *New York Times*, April 16, 2000.

Howe, Florence. "Mississippi's Freedom Schools: The Politics of Education." *Harvard Educational Review* 35 (1965): 144–160.

Howlett, Debbie. "Time Lost to Death Row Scars Ex-Inmates: Forum Puts Faces on Wrongly Convicted." *USA Today*, November 16, 1998.

Hsu, Spencer S. "After FBI Admits Overstating Forensic Hair Matches, Focus Turns to Cases." *Washington Post*, April 20, 2015.

———. "FBI Admits Flaws in Hair Analysis over Decades." *Washington Post*, April 18, 2015.

———. "Justice Dept., FBI to Review Use of Forensic Evidence in Thousands of Cases." *Washington Post*, July 10, 2012.

———. "Justice Dept. to Expand Review of FBI Forensic Techniques beyond Hair Unit." *Washington Post*, February 25, 2016.

Huff, C. Ronald, Arye Rattner, and Edward Sagarin. *Convicted but Innocent: Wrongful Conviction and Public Policy*. Thousand Oaks, CA: Sage, 1996.

Huff, C. Ronald, Arye Rattner, Edward Sagarin, and Donald E. J. MacNamara. "Guilty until Proved Innocent: Wrongful Conviction and Public Policy." *Crime and Delinquency* 32 (1986): 518–544.

Innocence Network. "About the Innocence Network." Accessed October 3, 2016, www.innocencenetwork.org.

———. "Brief Bank." Accessed June 27, 2016, www.innocencenetwork.org.

———. "Innocence Network History." Accessed January 5, 2014, www.innocencenetwork.org.

———. "Innocence Network Membership Guidelines." Accessed January 5, 2014, www.innocencenetwork.org.

Innocence Project. "Access to Post-conviction DNA Testing." Accessed September 19, 2016, www.innocenceproject.org.

———. "As 100th Innocent Prisoner Is Freed by DNA Tests, Innocence Network Convenes to Map the Future of 'New Civil Rights Movement' in Criminal Justice." Press release. January 17, 2002. www.deathpenaltyinfo.org.

———. "Compensating the Wrongly Convicted." Accessed June 27, 2016, www.innocenceproject.org.

———. "David Vasquez." Accessed February 26, 2015, www.innocenceproject.org.

———. "False Confessions or Admissions." Accessed June 27, 2016, www.innocenceproject.org.

———. "Kirk Bloodsworth." Accessed December 14, 2014, www.innocenceproject.org.

———. "Preservation of Evidence." Accessed September 19, 2016, www.innocenceproject.org.

"In Ryan's Words: 'I Must Act.'" *New York Times*, January 11, 2003.

Jeffreys, Alec J. "A Century of Human Genetics." Paper presented at the Leicester Medical Society Bicentenary. Accessed December 10, 2014, www2.le.ac.uk.

Jeffreys, Alec J., Victoria Wilson, and Swee Lay Thein. "Hypervariable 'Minisatellite' Regions in Human DNA." *Nature* 314 (1985): 67–73.

———. "Individual-Specific 'Fingerprints' of Human DNA." *Nature* 316 (1985): 76–79.

Johnson, Dirk. "Illinois, Citing Faulty Verdicts, Bars Executions." *New York Times* February 1, 2000.

———. "Illinois Governor Hopes to Fix a 'Broken' Justice System." *New York Times*, February 19, 2000.

———. "No Executions in Illinois until System Is Repaired." *New York Times*, May 21, 2000.

Jones, Marilyn. "He Helps Innocent Prisoners Win Their Freedom." *Christian Science Monitor*, November 30, 2009.

Junkin, Tim. *Bloodsworth*. Chapel Hill, NC: Algonquin Books, 2004.

Justice Policy Institute. "The Punishing Decade: Prison and Jail Estimates at the Millennium." 2000. www.justicepolicy.org.

"Justice Stevens Criticizes Election of Judges: 'Profoundly Unwise' Process Like Letting Fans Pick Referees, He Says." *Washington Post*, August 4, 1996.

Kansas v. Marsh, 548 U.S. 163 (2006).

Kanter, Evan, Michael Baird, Robert Shaler, and Ivan Balazs. "Analysis of Restriction Fragment Length Polymorphisms in Deoxyribonucleic Acid (DNA) Recovered from Dried Bloodstains." *Journal of Forensic Sciences* 31 (1986): 403–408.

Keilman, John. "Murder Victims' Families Feel Twice Betrayed by Ryan." *Chicago Tribune*, January 12, 2003.

———. "Relatives of Victims Feel 'Cheated.'" *Chicago Tribune*, January 12, 2003.

Kennedy, Tony. "Wrongly Convicted Man Wins $1.9-Million Judgment, but Normal Life May Elude Him." *Los Angeles Times*, November 5, 1989.

Keppel, Robert D., Joseph G. Wels, Katherine M. Brown, and Kristen Welch. "The Jack the Ripper Murders: A *Modus Operandi* and Signature Analysis of the 1888–1891 Whitechapel Murders." *Journal of Investigative Psychology and Offender Profiling* 2 (2005): 1–21.

Kernek, Lisa. "Cross Walk: Local Walkers Spend Good Friday Reflecting on Contemporary Social Issues." *State Journal-Register* (Springfield, IL), April 22, 2000.

Knight-Ridder Newspapers. "Meese's Miranda Reply Shocking to Law Experts." *Chicago Tribune*, October 10, 1985.

Korecki, Natasha. "How Death Penalty Has Changed Since Ryan's Commutations." *Chicago Tribune*, January 11, 2004.

Krishnan, Jayanth K. "Lawyering for a Cause and Experiences from Abroad." *California Law Review* 94 (2006): 575–615.

Labaton, Stephen. "DNA Fingerprinting Showdown Expected in Ohio." *New York Times*, June 22, 1990.

Lain, Corinna Barrett. "Deciding Death." *Duke Law Journal* 57 (2007): 1–83.

Lander, Eric S. "Invited Editorial: Research on DNA Typing Catching Up with Courtroom Application." *American Journal of Human Genetics* 48 (1991): 819–823.

———. "Lander Reply." *American Journal of Human Genetics* 49 (1991): 899–903.

Lane, Mark. *Arcadia*. New York: Holt, Rinehart, and Winston, 1970.

Laqueur, Hannah, Stephen Rushin, and Jonathan Simon. "Wrongful Conviction, Policing, and the 'Wars on Crime and Drugs.'" In *Examining Wrongful Convictions: Stepping Back, Moving Forward*, edited by Allison D. Redlich, James R. Acker, Robert J. Norris, and Catherine L. Bonventre, 93–107. Durham, NC: Carolina Academic Press, 2014.

Larson, Sarah. "'Serial': The Podcast We've Been Waiting For." *New Yorker*, October 9, 2014.

Leo, Richard A. "Rethinking the Study of Miscarriages of Justice: Developing a Criminology of Wrongful Conviction." *Journal of Contemporary Criminal Justice* 21 (2005): 201–223.

Leo, Richard A., and Jon B. Gould. "Studying Wrongful Convictions: Learning from Social Science." *Ohio State Journal of Criminal Law* 7 (2009): 7–30.

Levinson, Arlene. "Conference Honors Those Wrongly Convicted and Condemned." *Washington Post*, November 15, 1998.

———. "Death Row's Survivors: They Represent a Challenge to Use of Capital Punishment." *State Journal-Register* (Springfield, IL), November 8, 1998.

Lewin, Roger. "DNA Typing on the Witness Stand." *Science* 244 (1989): 1033–1035.

Lewis, Ricki. "DNA Fingerprints: Witness for the Prosecution." *Discover*, June 1988, 44–52.

Lewontin, Richard C., and Daniel L. Hartle. "Population Genetics in Forensic DNA Typing." *Science* 254 (1991): 1745–1750.

Liebman, James S. "The New Death Penalty Debate: What's DNA Got to Do with It?" *Columbia Human Rights Law Review* 33 (2002): 527–554.

Lithwick, Dahlia. "Pseudoscience in the Witness Box." *Slate*, April 22, 2015. www.slate.com.

Loftus, Elizabeth F. *Eyewitness Testimony*. Cambridge, MA: Harvard University Press, 1979.

Long, Alden. "Actual Innocence—Case Studies of DNA Testing Freeing the Wrongfully Convicted in the US." World Socialist Web Site, September 14, 2000. www.wsws.org.

Lushing, Peter. "Death-Sentence Errors and Justice Denied." *New York Times*, February 6, 2000.

Madhani, Aamer. "Man's Release Twists Ill. Death Penalty Reform Narrative." *USA Today*, October 30, 2014.

Maine, Sammy. "A TV Show Based on the Serial Podcast Is Happening." NME.com, June 4, 2016.

"Manhattan District Attorney Hails Conviction Integrity Unit." Thomson Reuters News and Insight, June 21, 2012.

Mapp v. Ohio, 367 U.S. 643 (1961).

Marcus, Ruth. "Clinton Nominates Reno at Justice." *Washington Post*, February 12, 1993.

Margolick, David. "Day of Familiar Dueling at Simpson Trial." *New York Times*, May 4, 1995.

———. "A Simpson Lawyer Makes New York Style Play in Judge Ito's Courtroom." *New York Time*, April 17, 1995.

Markman, Stephen J., and Paul G. Cassell. "Protecting the Innocent: A Response to the Bedau-Radelet Study." *Stanford Law Review* 41 (1988): 121–160.

Marquis, Joshua. "The Innocent and the Shammed." *New York Times*, January 26, 2006.

Marshall, Lawrence C. "The Innocence Revolution and the Death Penalty." *Ohio State Journal of Criminal Law* 1 (2004): 1573–1584.

McAdam, Doug. "Conceptual Origins, Current Problems, Future Directions." In *Comparative Perspectives on Social Movements*, edited Doug McAdam, John D. McCarthy, and Mayer N. Zald, 23–40. New York: Cambridge University Press, 1996.

———. *Political Process and the Development of Black Insurgency, 1930–1970*. Chicago: University of Chicago Press, 1982.

McAdam, Doug, John D. McCarthy, and Mayer N. Zald. *Comparative Perspectives on Social Movements*. New York: Cambridge University Press, 1996.

McCann, Michael, and Jeffrey Dudas. "Retrenchment . . . and Resurgence? Mapping the Changing Context of Movement Lawyering in the United States." In *Cause Law-*

yers and Social Movements, edited by Austin Sarat and Stuart A. Scheingold, 37–59. Stanford, CA: Stanford University Press, 2006.

McCarthy, John D., and Mayer N. Zald. "Resource Mobilization and Social Movements: A Partial Theory." *American Journal of Sociology* 82 (1977): 1212–1241.

McDowell, Edwin. "Key Figures in Illinois Rape Case Appear on TV." *New York Times*, May 16, 1985.

McFarland, Gerald M. *The Counterfeit Man: The True Story of the Boorn-Colvin Murder Case*. Amherst: University of Massachusetts Press, 1990.

McGarrell, Edmund F., and Thomas C. Castellano. "An Integrative Conflict Model of the Criminal Law Formation Process." *Journal of Research in Crime and Delinquency* 28 (1991): 174–196.

McKie, Robin. "Eureka Moment That Led to the Discovery of DNA Fingerprinting." *Guardian* (UK), May 23, 2009.

McLaughlin, Abraham. "Tales of Journey from Death Row to Freedom." *Christian Science Monitor*, November 16, 1998.

Medwed, Daniel S. "Emotionally Charged: The Prosecutorial Charging Decision and the Innocence Revolution." *Cardozo Law Review* 31 (2010): 2187–2213.

———. "Innocentrism." *University of Illinois Law Review* 2008 (2008): 1549–1572.

Meinert, Dori. "Clinton Praises Ryan for Pause in Executions." *State Journal-Register* (Springfield, IL), February 17, 2000.

Menkel-Meadow, Carrie. "The Causes of Cause Lawyering: Toward an Understanding of the Motivation and Commitment of Social Justice Lawyers." In *Cause Lawyering: Political Commitments and Professional Responsibilities*, edited by Austin Sarat and Stuart Scheingold, 31–68. New York: Oxford University Press, 1998.

Mills, Steve, Steve Schmadeke, and Dan Hinkel. "Prosecutors Free Inmate in Pivotal Illinois Death Penalty Case." *Chicago Tribune*, October 30, 2014.

Miranda v. Arizona, 384 U.S. 436 (1966).

Morris, Alfred. *The Origins of the Civil Rights Movement*. New York: Free Press, 1984.

Morris, Errol. Interview by *The Believer*. April 2004. www.errolmorris.com.

———. "The Thin Blue Line: Synopsis." Errol Morris's website. Accessed December 10, 2014, www.errolmorris.com.

Munson, Ziad W. *The Making of Pro-Life Activists: How Social Movement Mobilization Works*. Chicago: University of Chicago Press, 2008.

Munsterberg, Hugo. *On the Witness Stand*. New York: McClure, 1908.

Murphy, Jane C. "Lawyering for Social Change: The Power of the Narrative in Domestic Violence Law Reform." *Hofstra Law Review* 21 (1993): 1243–1293.

Murphy, Mekado. "The Story behind a True Crime Documentary a Decade in the Making." *New York Times*, December 21, 2015.

National Association of Criminal Defense Lawyers. "Past Presidents." Accessed January 2, 2015, www.nacdl.org.

National Film Preservation Board. "National Film Registry." Accessed December 10, 2014, www.loc.gov.

National Registry of Exonerations. "Anthony Porter." Accessed December 15, 2014, www.law.umich.edu.

———. "David Vasquez." Accessed June 3, 2015, www.law.umich.edu.

———. "The First 1,600 Exonerations." Accessed June 20, 2016, www.law.umich.edu.

———. "James Joseph Richardson" Accessed October 14, 2014, www.law.umich.edu.

———. "Recent Findings." Accessed June 27, 2016, www.law.umich.edu.

National Research Council. *DNA Technology in Forensic Science*. Washington, DC: National Academy Press, 1992.

———. *The Evaluation of Forensic DNA Evidence*. Washington, DC: National Academy Press, 1996.

———. *Strengthening Forensic Science in the United States: A Path Forward*. Washington, DC: National Academies Press, 2009.

Nededog, Jethro. "Here's How Popular Netflix's 'Making a Murderer' Really Was According to a Research Company." *Business Insider*, February 12, 2016.

Neufeld, Peter J. Interview by Harry Kreisler for *Conversations with History*. April 27, 2001. www.youtube.com.

———. Interview in "What Jennifer Saw." *Frontline*, PBS, February 25, 1997. www.pbs.org.

Neufeld, Peter J., and Neville Colman. "When Science Takes the Witness Stand." *Scientific American* 262 (1990): 46–53.

Neufeld, Peter J., and Barry C. Scheck. "Commentary." In *Convicted by Juries, Exonerated by Science*, by Edward Connors, Thomas Lundregan, Neal Miller, and Tom McEwen, xxviii–xxxi. Washington, DC: National Institute of Justice, 1996.

"New Death Penalty Politics, The." *New York Times*, June 7, 2000.

"New Looks at the Death Penalty." *New York Times*, February 19, 2000.

Newton, Giles. "Discovering DNA Fingerprinting." Wellcome Trust: The Human Genome, April 2, 2004. http://genome.wellcome.ac.uk.

New York Times News Service. "3rd Try: Clinton Nominates Veteran Prosecutor." *Deseret News* (Salt Lake City, UT), February 12, 1993.

New York v. Quarles, 467 U.S. 649 (1984).

"No Blanket Clemency, Prosecutors Urge Ryan." *Chicago Tribune*, December 13, 2002.

Norris, Robert J. "Assessing Compensation Statutes for the Wrongly Convicted." *Criminal Justice Policy Review* 23 (2012): 352–374.

———. "Exoneree Compensation: Current Policies and Future Outlook." In *Wrongful Conviction and Criminal Justice Reform: Making Justice*, edited by Marvin Zalman and Julia Carrano, 289–303. New York: Routledge, 2014.

Norris, Robert J., and Catherine L. Bonventre. "Advancing Wrongful Conviction Scholarship: Toward New Conceptual Frameworks." *Justice Quarterly* 32 (2015): 929–949.

Norris, Robert J., Catherine L. Bonventre, Allison D. Redlich, and James R. Acker. "'Than That One Innocent Suffer': Evaluating State Safeguards against Wrongful Convictions." *Albany Law Review* 74 (2010–2011): 1301–1364.

Norris, Robert J., Catherine L. Bonventre, Allison D. Redlich, James R. Acker, and Carmen Lowe. "Preventing Wrongful Convictions: An Analysis of State Investigation Reforms." *Criminal Justice Policy Review* (2017, forthcoming).

North Carolina Innocence Inquiry Commission. "Cases." Accessed September 23, 2016, www.innocencecommission-nc.gov.

North Carolina v. Alford, 400 U.S. 25 (1970).

Northwestern University Center on Wrongful Convictions. "First DNA Exoneration: Gary Dotson." Accessed September 21, 2016, www.law.northwestern.edu.

———. "Lavelle Burt." Accessed November 20, 2013, www.law.northwestern.edu.

Nyman, Shane. "Just How Popular Is 'Making a Murderer'?" *Appleton (WI) Post-Crescent*, January 14, 2016.

Olsen, Patrick. "Law Profs Back Ryan on Blanket Clemency." *Chicago Tribune*, December 30, 2002.

Osborn, Claire. "How Ken Anderson Was Released after Only Five Days in Jail." *Austin (TX) American-Statesman*, November 15, 2013.

Packer, Herbert L. *The Limits of the Criminal Sanction*. Stanford, CA: Stanford University Press, 1968.

Parloff, Roger. "How Barry Scheck and Peter Neufeld Tripped Up the DNA Experts." *American Lawyer*, December 1989.

Parsons, Christi, and Karen Mellen. "House Bill Seeks Limit on Blanket Clemency." *Chicago Tribune*, January 17, 2003.

Patton, Stephen M. "DNA Fingerprinting: The Castro Case." *Harvard Journal of Law and Technology* 3 (1990): 223–240.

Pennington, Nancy, and Reid Hastie. "Explaining the Evidence: Tests of the Story Model for Juror Decision Making." *Journal of Personality and Social Psychology* 62 (1992): 189–206.

People of the State of New York v. George Wesley, People of the State of New York v. Cameron Bailey, 140 Misc. 2d 306 (1988).

People of the State of New York v. Joseph Castro, 545 N.Y.S. 2d 985 (Sup. Ct. 1989).

Pilkington, Ed. "Thirty Years in Jail for a Single Hair: The FBI's 'Mass Disaster' of False Conviction." *Guardian* (UK), April 21, 2015.

Posner, Richard A. "Law and Literature: A Relation Reargued." *Virginia Law Review* 72 (1986): 1351–1392.

Poveda, Tony G. "Estimating Wrongful Convictions." *Justice Quarterly* 18 (2001): 689–708.

President's Commission on Law Enforcement and Administration of Justice. *The Challenge of Crime in a Free Society*. Washington, DC: United States Government Printing Office, 1967.

Pressley, Sue Anne. "Speedy Justice Can Be Dead Wrong, Texas Case Shows: Death Row: Clarence Brandley Stands as Living Proof That an Innocent Man Could Be Executed." *Los Angeles Times*, February 19, 1995.

Priest, Dana. "Arlington Detective's Hunch Pays Off in Circumstantial Murder Case." *Washington Post*, October 13, 1988.

———. "Arlington Reopens 1984 Rape-Murder Case." *Washington Post*, May 4, 1988.

———. "Pardon Urged for Man Convicted of Va. Murder: New Evidence in 1984 Arlington Slaying Points to Richmond Felon." *Washington Post* , October 12, 1988.

———. "Va. Man Pardoned after Five Years in Prison: Baliles Acts after Evidence Links Murder to Arlington Killer." *Washington Post*, January 5, 1989.

———. "Wrongly Jailed Man Endures Ordeal by Fear." *Washington Post*, July 17, 1989.

Princeton Theological Seminary. "Bicentennial Moment: James McCloskey." Accessed October 22, 2013, www.ptsem.edu.

Protess, David, and Rob Warden. *A Promise of Justice: The Eighteen-Year Fight to Save Four Innocent Men.* New York: Hyperion, 1998.

Rabinovitz, Jonathan. "Rape Conviction Overturned on DNA Tests." *New York Times*, December 2, 1992.

Radelet, Michael L., Hugo Adam Bedau, and Constance E. Putnam. *In Spite of Innocence: The Ordeal of 400 Americans Wrongly Convicted of Crimes Punishable by Death.* Boston: Northeastern University Press, 1992.

Radin, Edward D. *The Innocents.* New York: William Morrow, 1964.

Rafferty, Terrence. "True Detective." *New Yorker*, September 5, 1988.

"Reaction to O. J. Verdict Exposes Chasm between Blacks, Whites." *Sun-Sentinel* (Broward County, FL), October 8, 1995.

"Recantation, Incantation and Rape." *New York Times*, April 6, 1985.

Redlich, Allison D., and John Petrila, ed. "The Age of Innocence: Miscarriages of Justice in the 21st Century." Special issue, *Behavioral Sciences and the Law* 27 (2009).

"Reforming the Death Penalty System." *New York Times*, May 8, 2000.

Reno, Janet. "Message from the Attorney General." In *Convicted by Juries, Exonerated by Science*, by Edward Connors, Thomas Lundregan, Neal Miller, and Tom McEwen, iii–iv. Washington, DC: National Institute of Justice, 1996.

Rhodes v. Chapman, 452 U.S. 337 (1981).

Risinger, D. Michael. "Innocents Convicted: An Empirical Justified Factual Wrongful Conviction Rate." *Journal of Criminal Law and Criminology* 97 (2007): 761–806.

Risinger, D. Michael, and Lesley C. Risinger. "Innocence Is Different: Taking Innocence into Account in Reforming Criminal Procedure." *New York Law School Law Review* 56 (2011–2012): 869–909.

Roberts, Leslie. "Fight Erupts over DNA Fingerprinting." *Science* 254 (1991): 1721–1723.

———. "Science in Court: A Culture Clash." *Science* 254 (1991): 732–736.

———. "Was *Science* Fair to Its Authors?" *Science* 254 (1991): 1722.

Rosen, Richard A. "Reflections on Innocence." *Wisconsin Law Review*, 2006, 237–289.

Rothschild, Mary Aickin. "The Volunteers and the Freedom Schools: Education for Social Change in Mississippi." *History of Education Quarterly* 22 (1982): 401–420.

Ryan, George. "Deadline Clip: Governor George Ryan's Clemency Speech." Death Penalty Information Center. Accessed December 29, 2014, www.youtube.com.

San Martin, Nancy, and William E. Gibson. "Reno May Be Nominated for Attorney General." *Sun-Sentinel* (Broward County, FL), February 10, 1993.

Sappenfield, Mark. "Can Ferguson Spark New Civil Rights Movement? How Times Have Changed." *Christian Science Monitor*, November 30, 2014. www.csmonitor.com.

Schaper, David. "Former Illinois Gov. George Ryan Heading to Prison." National Public Radio, November 6, 2007. www.npr.org.

Scheck, Barry. Interview by Big Think. Accessed December 13, 2013, http://bigthink.com.

———. Interview by Harry Kreisler for *Conversations with History*. July 25, 2003. www.youtube.com.

———. Interview in "The Case for Innocence." *Frontline*, PBS, January 11, 2000. www.pbs.org.

———. Interview in "What Jennifer Saw." *Frontline*, PBS, February 25, 1997. www.pbs.org.

Scheck, Barry, Peter Neufeld, and Jim Dwyer. *Actual Innocence: Five Days to Execution and Other Dispatches from the Wrongly Convicted*. New York: Doubleday, 2000.

Scheingold, Stuart A. *The Politics of Law and Order: Street Crime and Public Policy*. New York: Longman, 1984.

———. *The Politics of Rights: Lawyers, Public Policy, and Political Change*. 2nd ed. Ann Arbor: University of Michigan Press, 2004.

Schultz, Anya. "Review: *Serial*, a Captivating New Podcast." *Daily Californian* (Berkeley), October 10, 2014.

Seaton, James. "Law and Literature: Works, Criticism, and Theory." *Yale Journal of Law and the Humanities*, 1999, 479–507.

Seelve, Katharine Q. "Firmly for Death Penalty, Gore Is Open to a Review." *New York Times*, June 14, 2000.

Sentencing Project. "Crack Cocaine Sentencing Policy: Unjustified and Unreasonable." Accessed January 5, 2015, www.prisonpolicy.org.

———. "Trends in U.S. Corrections." September 2014. www.sentencingproject.org.

Sherrer, Hans. "Arcadia and the Twenty Year Effort to Exonerate James Joseph Richardson." *Justice Denied* (blog), December 2008. http://justicedenied.org/.

Shipp, E. R. "Debate Surrounds Rape Decision: Amid Outcry and Debate over Judge's Decision, Man Resumes His Term for Rape." *New York Times*, April 13, 1985.

———. "Sentence Is Commuted in Illinois Rape Case." *New York Times*, May 13, 1985.

Siegel, Andrew M. "Moving Down the Wedge of Injustice: A Proposal for a Third Generation of Wrongful Convictions Scholarship and Advocacy." *American Criminal Law Review* 42 (2006): 1219–1237.

Silcock, Brian. "Genes Tell Tales." *Sunday Times* (UK), November 3, 1985.

Simon, Jonathan. *Governing through Crime: How the War on Crime Transformed American Democracy and Created a Culture of Fear*. Oxford: Oxford University Press, 2007.

Simonich, Milan. "'Actual Innocence' by Barry Scheck, Peter Neufeld, and Jim Dwyer." *Pittsburgh Post-Gazette*, January 1, 2000.

Slater, Eric. "Pizza Thief Receives Sentence of 25 Years to Life in Prison." *Los Angeles Times*, March 3, 1995.

Sloan, Karen. "ABA Tackles Law School Debt." *National Law Journal*, July 29, 2015.

Slovic, Paul. "'If I Look at the Mass I Will Never Act': Psychic Numbing and Genocide." *Judgment and Decision Making* 2 (2007): 79–95.

Smith, Abbe. "In Praise of the Guilty Project: A Criminal Defense Lawyer's Growing Anxiety about Innocence Projects." *University of Pennsylvania Journal of Law and Social Change* 13 (2009–2010): 315–329.

Snow, David A., E. Burke Rochford, Jr., Steven K. Worden, and Robert D. Benford. "Frame Alignment Processes, Micromobilization, and Movement Participants." *American Sociological Review* 51 (1986): 464–481.

Snow, David A., and Danny Trom. "The Case Study and the Study of Social Movements." In *Methods of Social Movement Research*, edited by Bert Klandermans and Suzanne Staggenborg, 146–172. Minneapolis: University of Minnesota Press, 2002.

Span, Paula. "The Gene Team: Innocence Project Fights Misjustice with DNA Testing." *Washington Post*, December 14, 1994.

Steiker, Carol S., and Jordan M. Steiker. "The Seduction of Innocence: The Attraction and Limitations of the Focus on Innocence in Capital Punishment Law and Advocacy." *Journal of Criminal Law and Criminology* 95 (2005): 587–624.

Stevenson, Bryan. "We Need to Talk about Injustice." TED Talk, March 2012. www.ted.com.

Stiglitz, Jan, Justin Brooks, and Tara Shulman. "The Hurricane Meets the Paper Chase: Innocence Projects New Emerging Role in Clinical Legal Education." *California Western Law Review* 38 (2001): 413–430.

Suni, Ellen Y. "Ethical Issues for Innocence Projects: An Initial Primer." *University of Missouri–Kansas City Law Review* 70 (2002): 921–968.

Tassi, Paul. "Why 'Making a Murderer' Is Netflix's Most Significant Show Ever." *Forbes*, January 3, 2016.

Taylor, Stuart, Jr. "The Death Penalty: To Err Is Human." *National Journal*, February 12, 2000, 450–451.

Terry, Don. "After 18 Years in Prison, 3 Are Cleared of Murders." *New York Times*, July 3, 1996.

———. "Survivors Make the Case against Death Row." *New York Times*, November 16, 1998.

"This American Life—'Serial.'" iTunesCharts.net. Accessed June 22, 2016.

"Timeout on the Death Penalty, A." *New York Times*, February 1, 2000.

Tonry, Michael. *Thinking about Crime: Sense and Sensibility in American Penal Culture*. New York: Oxford University Press, 2004.

Trabasso, Tom. "The Power of the Narrative." In *Reading, Language, and Literacy: Instruction for the Twenty-First Century*, edited by Frank Lehr and Jean Osborn, 187–200. New York: Routledge, 2009.

Travis, Jeremy, and Michelle Waul. "Reflections on the Crime Decline: Lessons for the Future?" Forum Proceedings, Urban Institute, August 2000. www.urban.org.

Tuft, Carolyn. "Ex-Death Row Inmates Attack Capital Punishment, Courts." *St. Louis Post-Dispatch*, November 16, 1998.

United States v. Bonds, Verdi, and Yee, 12 F.3d 540 (6th Cir. 1994).

United States v. Garsson, 291 F. 646 (S.D.N.Y. 1923).

United States v. Leon, 468 U.S. 897 (1984).

United States v. Salerno, 481 U.S. 739 (1979).

United States v. Yee et al., 134 F.R.D. 161 (N.D. Ohio 1991).

UPI. "Rape Case Judge Calls Recantation 'Implausible.'" *New York Times*, August 22, 1985.

Valentine, Paul W. "Jailed for Murder, Freed by DNA." *Washington Post*, June 29, 1993.

———. "Man Cleared by DNA Gets Pardon." *Washington Post*, December 23, 1993.

van den Haag, Ernest. *Punishing Criminals*. New York: Basic Books, 1975.

———. "The Ultimate Punishment: A Defense." *Harvard Law Review* 99 (1986): 1662–1669.

Veitch, Andrew. "Son Rejoins Mother as Genetic Test Ends Immigration Dispute: Ghanian Boy Allowed to Join Family in Britain." *Guardian* (UK), October 31, 1985.

Vitiello, Michael. "Alternatives to Incarceration: Why Is California Lagging Behind?" *Georgia State University Law Review* 28 (2012): 1273–1312.

Walker, Samuel. *Popular Justice: A History of American Criminal Justice*. 2nd ed. New York: Oxford University Press, 1998.

Wambaugh, Joseph. *The Blooding: The Dramatic True Story of the First Murder Case Solved by Genetic "Fingerprinting."* New York: Bantam Books, 1989.

Warden, Rob. "First Wrongful Conviction." Northwestern Center on Wrongful Convictions. Accessed February 25, 2015, www.law.northwestern.edu.

———. "Four Decades and 60 Exonerations Later . . ." Interview by Karen Sloan. *National Law Journal*, September 11, 2013. www.nationallawjournal.com.

———. "Illinois Death Penalty Reform: How It Happened, What It Promises." *Journal of Criminal Law and Criminology* 95 (2005): 381–426.

———. Interview by E. Allen Campbell for Wolverton Mountain. Accessed December 10, 2014, www.wolverton-mountain.com.

———. "The Role of the Media and Public Opinion on Innocence Reform: Past and Future." In *Wrongful Conviction and Criminal Justice Reform: Making Justice*, edited by Marvin Zalman and Julia Carrano, 39–55. New York: Routledge, 2014.

———. *Wilkie Collins's The Dead Alive: The Novel, the Case, and Wrongful Convictions*. Evanston, IL: Northwestern University Press, 2005.

Watson, Bruce. *Sacco & Vanzetti: The Men, the Murders, and the Judgment of Mankind*. New York: Viking, 2007.

Weinberg, Steve. "The Exonerator." *Pacific Standard*, January 5, 2010.

———. "Miracle Worker." *American Way*, April 15, 2006.

Weiss, Robert S. *Learning from Strangers: The Art and Method of Qualitative Interview Studies*. New York: Free Press, 1994.

Wellcome Trust: The Human Genome. "DNA Fingerprinting Enters Society." December 2, 2004. http://genome.wellcome.ac.uk.

Wells, Gary L., and Elizabeth F. Loftus. *Eyewitness Testimony: Psychological Perspectives*. New York: Cambridge University Press, 1984.

Wells, Gary L., Nancy K. Steblay, and Jennifer E. Dysart. "Eyewitness Identification Reforms: Are Suggestiveness-Induced Hits and Guesses True Hits?" *Perspectives on Psychological Science* 7 (2012): 264–271.

Westervelt, Saundra D., and Kimberly J. Cook. *Life after Death Row: Exonerees' Search for Community and Identity.* New Brunswick, NJ: Rutgers University Press, 2012.

"Whitechapel Murder Victims, The." Whitechapel Jack: The Legend of Jack the Ripper. Accessed May 11, 2015, http://whitechapeljack.com.

Will, George F. "Innocent on Death Row." *Washington Post*, April 6, 2000.

Williams, Linda. "Mirrors without Memories: Truth, History, and the New Documentary." *Film Quarterly* 46 (1993): 9–21.

Wills, Christopher. "Illinois Gov. Pat Quinn Abolishes Death Penalty, Clears Death Row." *Washington Post*, March 9, 2011.

Wilson, James Q. *Thinking about Crime.* New York: Basic Books, 1975.

Wilton, David. *Word Myths: Debunking Linguistic Urban Legends.* New York: Oxford University Press, 2009.

Woodruff, Cathy. "Wesley Jailed 38 1/3 Years-Life for Woman's Rape, Murder." *Schenectady (NY) Gazette*, February 22, 1989.

Woodruff, Judy. "What 'Serial'-mania Says about the Growing Popularity of Podcasts." PBS, December 11, 2014. www.pbs.org.

Yant, Martin. "The Media's Muddled Message on Wrongful Convictions." In *Examining Wrongful Convictions: Stepping Back, Moving Forward*, edited by Allison D. Redlich, James R. Acker, Robert J. Norris, and Catherine L. Bonventre, 71–89. Durham, NC: Carolina Academic Press, 2014.

Zalman, Marvin. "Criminal Justice System Reform and Wrongful Conviction: A Research Agenda." *Criminal Justice Policy Review* 17 (2006): 468–492.

——. "Edwin Borchard and the Limits of Innocence Reform." In *Wrongful Convictions and Miscarriages of Justice: Causes and Remedies in North American and European Criminal Justice System*, edited by C. Ronald Huff and Martin Killias, 329–355. New York: Routledge, 2013.

——. "An Integrated Justice Model of Wrongful Convictions." *Albany Law Review* 74 (2011): 1465–1524.

Zimring, Franklin E. *The Great American Crime Decline.* New York: Oxford University Press, 2007.

INDEX

The West Education Network (TWEN), 92

Will, George, 82

Willingham, Cameron Todd, 210

Wilson, James Q., 118, 135–36

Wooley, James, 46–47

wrongful convictions, 4–5, 88–89, 100, 111; awareness of, 140, 156; Borchard on, 129; as civil rights movement, 165; concern with, 202–3; examination of, 221; Huff on, 129–31; identifying problems in, 129–32; journalists on, 130; Neufeld on, 159–60; Possley on, 134; prevention of, 166; racism in, 171; rate of, 134–35, 195–96, 199; reactions to, 136, 152–53; research of, 25; Scheck on, 159; shifts in, 131–32; Warden on, 101–2, 129, 132

"Wrongful Convictions: Causes and Remedies," 91

Wrongful Conviction Tax Relief Act, 4

Yee, Steven Wayne, 45–47

Zalman, Marvin, 3, 6, 68, 181–82; on Innocence Network, 165

ABOUT THE AUTHOR

Robert J. Norris is Assistant Professor in the Department of Government and Justice Studies at Appalachian State University.